REINVENTING OURSELVES

REINVENTING

Wake up and Rise into your Greatness

Erica E.C. Harpe

with

Yvette Hooites Meursing

THE CHOIR PRESS

First published in the United Kingdom in 2019
by The Choir Press

THE CHOIR PRESS

Design: Willem Hanhart
Cover photo: Stanislav Odyagailo

ISBN 978-1-78963-061-9

"We are drowning in information, while starving for wisdom.
The world henceforth will be run by synthesizers,
people able to put together the right information at the right time,
think critically about it, and make important choices wisely."

— E.O. WILSON (1929-), AMERICAN BIOLOGIST

CONTENTS

A man found an eagle's egg and put it in a nest of a barnyard hen.
The eagle hatched with the brood of chicks and grew up with them.
All his life the eagle did what the barnyard chicks did, thinking he was a barnyard
chicken. He scratched the earth for worms and insects.
He clucked and cackled. And he would thrash his wings out
and fly a few feet in the air.

Years passed by and the eagle grew very old.
One day he saw a magnificent bird above him in the cloudless sky.
It glided in graceful majesty among the powerful wind currents,
with scarcely a beat on his strong golden wings.
The old eagle looked up in awe. "Who's that?" he asked.
"That's the eagle, the king of birds",
said his neighbour. "He belongs to the sky.
We belong to the earth – we are chickens".

So the eagle lived and died a chicken,
for that's what he thought he was.

— ANTHONY B. DE MELLO

When I first came across this metaphor, it struck me to the core. You see, I grew up in such a barnyard, and witnessed certain eagles never realising who they were, or, should I say, actualising their full potential.

Later on, in my professional life, working with people in often highly demanding situations, I witnessed the same. Sometimes, in the most critical moments, when presence and full power were so needed, they would seemingly forget who they truly were. As if they did not have access to their greatness. It was unavailable to them. They were simply unavailable to themselves.

I was fascinated by this phenomenon, as I believe that we all have greatness, it's just a matter of being able to access it. To remember it. It requires taking an eagle's view, it requires rising into consciousness.

It seems the current time of transformation demands us to step into this consciousness. Never before have we had to deal with such complex global challenges. We need access to our highest capacities of imagination, intuition, creativity, flexibility, and adaptability that make us so unique as a species. To our full power, our wholeness. To transcend our ego. And to create contexts in which we enable others to rise into their greatness too! For humanity to survive, and to flourish along the way.

I experimented with this with the groups that I worked with. In line with the social architecture of Theory U – being present from an open mind, open heart, open will – experimenting with practices empowering people to reach that inner state, naturally and easily. To access their whole being.

This book is the result of this journey.

We interviewed leaders in the fields of trend watching, large scale and individual transformation, and supervisory board level. Asking them how they view the current transformation humanity is facing, wholeness and how to access it, and our responsibility within all of this. We are grateful for their views, which illustrate this journey beautifully.

Now, all roads lead to Rome. Or in this case, your greatness. Our intention is to create awareness of how magnificently we humans are built, providing you with insights into your *human design*, your *energy design*, and your *personality design*. And to provide you with practices that enable you to experience for yourself what works. Our desire is for you to find a road that works for you.

Here's to your greatness!

——————— THE BASICS ———————

What if... you are already whole?

See, you are already wired for the future. You just need to remember how to access it and align with it. How to come online.

Reinventing Ourselves offers a new perspective on *Personal Mastery* by providing you with an integral approach to your inner architecture, or into embodying your own U. It is written along the lines of Theory U's social architecture (Otto Scharmer). The meaning of this will become clear later.

This book is the result of an extensive journey with a learning lab in questioning what it is that next level leadership entails and demands. It is also a deeply personal journey. That is to say, it is grounded in practical experience and solid cross-discipline science. Our objective is to provide easy access for the well-versed and for the explorer. You may just want to read it differently according to your starting point. This book reads as follows:

- The part called Evolution provides you with the perspective of the evolution of consciousness, like a lens. If you are new to this field, it may be helpful to read this, as well as the glossary. If you are familiar with this, just move straight to the core!
- Part I explores Embodying Presence, your Human Design, how to access and align your full potential,
- Part II explores Entering Flow (or as in Theory U, Letting Come), your Energy Design, how to co-create with your own energy and that of your context, to 'go with the flow,'
- Part III explores Letting Go of your Personality Design, how to free yourself of defensive character armour installed in your body at a young age,
- Part IV provides The Reinventing Toolbox: Practices guiding to greatness!

You may be reading this book for any number of reasons. Perhaps you're a leader, wanting to move to the next level and are well acquainted with the leadership terms and theories used in this book. Perhaps you have arrived here totally fresh and eager to explore. Wherever you come from, be welcome!

We wish you a great journey!

"Every few hundred years in Western history there occurs a sharp transformation.
Within a few short decades, society re-arranges itself; its worldview (paradigm),
basic values, social and political structures, arts and key institutions.
Fifty years later there is a new world."

— PETER DRUCKER — *SOCIETAL CHANGE*

We live in times of unprecedented transformation. A pivotal age in which we have to reinvent and rearrange many of our social industries and organisations. An age in which we have to reinvent what it means to be human. But to rehumanise the future, we first need to 'reinvent ourselves'!

WHAT DOES IT MEAN TO BE HUMAN?

To be human means being able to tap into creation, intuition, and imagination: we are the only living species to have these gifts. For us to do this, we must be able to tap into our full power. This book is about how you can come home to this power. It is about getting to that place where you can resource, regulate and restore yourself, guiding you to access a deep resilience within. A place where you feel safe and free and have the space to be creative and imaginative, no matter what happens. Where you can flourish!

In this pivotal age, three cycles of time come together: cycles of climate, economic cycles, and cycles of human conflict. Science recognises it. People feel it. Stress has become epidemic, and many people find themselves fragmented, disconnected from their selves, their emotions, and their purpose. Our minds alone are no longer able to deal with the current level of complexity. We simply must step into our full potential, develop our physical, emotional, and spiritual intelligence, and knowledge of energy. We need to reboot our operating system. We need to create a foundation fit for this time. *But how do we do that?*

By *Reinventing Ourselves*!
We invite you to join us on a journey to greatness and be curious and open along the way.

To:

Grow up and become familiar with your unique *human design*. Become aware of, and experience *who you really are and how you really work*. Become aware of, and embrace your body's wisdom, your soul's guidance, the bliss of an open and pure heart, a calm and clear mind and a general feeling of wholeness. All at the same time. This is your true Essence! Become aware of, and experience, what maps are at play within you, what lenses you view the world through, of your vision and values, of your shadow and its impact. Connect with, and integrate, all of you and let go of what no longer serves you. And do all of this with intention. Every day! Realising this is your natural state, your mind just gets in the way. Connect to your whole self and from there, connect to your colleagues and organisation, your partner, children, friends and the world around you. *Connect from a conscious state*, with integrity and focus. *Expanding your inner resources will bring you more resilience and results.*

Wake up and become more conscious. *Connect to your purpose, to your soul – the part of you that is larger than your ego.* The part that holds the vision for your greatness, and knows your purpose. Where you have a helicopter view, and can easily decide from a place of what is needed for the greater good of all. The techniques to access these states have been around for thousands of years in the wisdom traditions. Now, however, neuroscience and technology have made the benefits of integrating this into our lives visible and easier to access. For the first time in history, they can be combined with the above-mentioned 'growing up' part. *Waking up to your subtle (energy) body and connecting with the collective intelligence, allows you to be all that you can be.*

Show up and *get into action with intention*, aiming to be conscious and connected, communicating and creating from that space, from centre, from the heart. Realise that it's about you and that it is up to you now to take your leadership, to take re-sponsibility for the whole. *You are needed!*

Flow by becoming aware of your *energy design*. *Optimise your inner energy*, your frequency. *Realising that your energy acts as a magnet:* you attract what you project. Realise how, through the power of your focused intention and attention, you allow your best future in. Align with and understand the energy outside of you, so that you may experience synchronicity. Realising this means that you are well on your journey. *Allowing a way of being that is like that of an alchemist: having the power to transform something ordinary into something extraordinary by accessing intuition, in-novation, creativity and collective intelligence.*

This is *Personal Mastery*; the mark of a conscious individual. Like any mastery, Personal Mastery takes focus, commitment, and practice. Know this: wherever you start, you have a source of wisdom, power and compassion inside that is abundant and always available. It is continually providing you with access to higher levels of intelligence if you open and respond to your body's wisdom, your intuition and the intelligence of the collective. It will equip you with the freedom and ability to expand rather than contract. It will enable you to recognise and overcome your reactive patterns (ego) and respond from a place of calm – your Essence, no matter what life throws at you.

This time of transformation feels like a collective metamorphosis. May this book guide you on your journey.

Welcome Home!

"We need to open up the future, to engage and interact differently with it in order to drive to greater prosperity and wellbeing in a period of such transformation. It asks us to open up our hearts and our minds towards new ways of being and new ways of doing, given that the future of our people and our planet are at risk."

— JOSEPHINE GREEN, *TOWARDS A NEW ERA OF CREATIVITY AND GROWTH*

Some of the words we use are terms that carry meaning (jargon). Below you can find our interpretation of their meaning:

- **Whole (ness)** – what is the nature of wholes and parts and their interrelatedness? In our normal thinking, a whole is made up of (static) parts much like a machine. But all living systems, like your body (or a tree), recreate themselves continuously. Unlike machines, the whole is a dynamic living being. The way we use 'whole' is to be fully aligned with all of our capacities or powers. That includes your physical (PhQ), mental (IQ), emotional (EQ) and spiritual (SQ) capacities. Knowing that we are dynamic, fully interrelated beings and that, for example, a change in your physical state or your surroundings may cause changes in your spiritual and mental states, and vice versa. A change in consciousness thus will impact your whole being.

- **Presence** – this may well be the core capacity needed to access the emerging future, to receive it, or let it come. It is to be where things happen, with your attention and energy. Fully. Present in all of your being, mind, body, soul, and emotions. Conscious and aware with an open heart, open mind & open will.

- **Consciousness** – if presence is the core capacity, consciousness may well be the key leverage point for creating positive change. It is the inner capacity allowing you to observe and make appropriate choices. The more conscious you become of your true self, your *human, energy and personality designs* (as described in Parts I, II and III of this book), the more you understand other people and the context you live in. The more you can contribute and the more you can co-create your life!

- **Awareness** – consciousness in practice. To access consciousness in all of you takes dedicated practice. If awareness never reaches beyond superficial events and current circumstances, actions will remain reactions. If you penetrate more deeply to see the larger whole and your connection to it, the source and effectiveness of your actions can change dramatically. Your response and responsibility then become natural.

Essence – in philosophy, essence is the property or set of properties that make an entity or substance what it fundamentally is, and which it has by necessity and without which it loses its identity. We see human essence as who you truly are. Not your image, your mind or your mask, but your authentic being.

Physical body – your vessel and playground this lifetime. It is what people see of you. It can hear, see, touch, taste and move. It allows you to feel emotions and to interact with a physical experience. It also allows you to create what you want in this 3D world. How you relate to your physical body is extremely important. It is vital to nourish your being on all four levels. To keep your body strong and resilient, to get the life energy flowing and help balance the mind, to nourish your body well and give it adequate rest, and to honour its role in your life: it is your foundation. It allows you to feel your true balance. *A strong foundation is key to create a whole and happy life.*

Embodied – being in your body fully. To really live in your body, consciously connect to your feelings, and be present to all senses and sensations. All day, as much as possible. That way you can learn via your body and its innate wisdom. Practice centring, grounding and flow to optimise your ability to feel.

Centre – your centre is a doorway: it allows you to experience your body fully. When you're in your physical centre, you can access the body's wisdom to address issues that are vital to you. It's the calmness, the fundamental goodness that is your true nature which lies beneath the disturbing chatter of the mind. It is naturally open, balanced, inclusive and expansive and often will come with a larger awareness of the space around you. It is a place where you can relax. Centre is key to shifting from ego to Essence. Various traditions use different centres, but Zen Buddhism and Aikido use the 'hara,' a point just below your navel, as the centre of gravitas and the place where your life energy (qi) originates. We define it accordingly.

Flow – in Mihaly Csikszentmihalyi's [1] words: 'being completely absorbed in an activity for its own sake. The ego falls away and time flies. Every action,

---

[1] Mihaly Csikszentmihalyi, a professor and former chairman of the Department of Psychology at the University of Chicago, who has devoted his life's work to the study of what makes people truly happy, satisfied and fulfilled.

movement, and thought follows inevitably from the previous one like playing jazz for instance. Your whole being is involved, and you're using your skills to the utmost.' It's a state you naturally love to be in, and you can practice to access that state at will.

The Energy or Subtle Body – the energy field surrounding your body holds all your beliefs, experiences, emotions, and feelings. It acts as your sensor and provides the lens you see the world through. It is the access point to your deepest knowing. We guide you into accessing that state. If you can connect to that state as an individual, then, for a group, you may enable access to the subtle body of the group: this is where the collective intelligence resides. Many interpret this to be the next stage in human evolution, see below.

Collective Intelligence – when individuals come together with a shared intention, in a conducive environment, something mysterious can come into being with capacities and intelligences far transcending those of the individuals. There's an access to a kind of knowing bigger than we normally experience. It is a natural phenomenon that can also be observed in animals, for example in a way that starlings are able to cross larger distances in a swarm than individually. It's an ancient innate knowing, that tribes, sport teams and rescue forces have always been aware of. *It is a field that is of huge interest, as it is believed that the answers to the global issues we face today are accessible here. It is the wisdom of the group held within the energy body of the group.*

Field of the Future – we have no roadmap for the volatile times we live in. The only thing we can do, is gain access to a deeper knowing and listening to sense and actualise new realities prior to their emerging. This is the knowing of and access to our own energy body. A number of scholars like Scharmer, Senge and Jaworski for instance, work with the future field, talking about "allowing the future to emerge." Theory U works with this process extensively on a group dynamic level. But to really access this deeper knowing with a group, you have to access the right state in yourself first, as mentioned in the energy body and the collective intelligence above. It takes practice. Our *Reinventing Rituals* are intended to enable you to enter that state more easily.

Higher Self – your Higher Self is, in simple terms, the highest aspect of you that you can attain and hold in your physical body. It is the part of you that knows, sees, and understands at the highest level possible. It has access to the energy body, while the physical part of you still continues to move around in 3D. *The process of anchoring the wisdom of the Higher Self into your physicality is currently at play in our human spiritual evolution. The higher the frequency of your body, the more easily you can connect to your soul and purpose.*

Coherence – the highest level of functioning where all your powers and systems are working together as one. Science describes coherence as a highly efficient/optimal state in which your nervous, cardiovascular, hormonal and immune systems work efficiently and harmoniously. Being coherent is a state that people can *feel*. People will feel safe in your presence and allow themselves to open up and expand. It's a state that builds implicit trust.

Resonance – the dynamic between your frequency and that of another person or persons. Does it feel good to be in this person's presence? Then you're in resonance with him/her. Does this job, or the idea about this new project excite you? Then you're in resonance with that. Like attracts like and energy always follows the easiest route.

Rituals – practices that allow you to consciously be and do in alignment with who you aspire to be, rather than react from old programming or beliefs. Research has proven that it only takes about 6 weeks to overwrite existing patterns (neuroplasticity). By practising these rituals, you can create your own blueprint for living from wholeness. These tools may take you to the next level of leadership needed for TEAL [2].

---

2 Spiral Dynamics defines TEAL as the next step in our evolutionary development (see page 40).

"A new consciousness is emerging."

— INTERVIEW WITH JOSEPHINE GREEN, SOCIO-CULTURAL FORESIGHT

"To tell the truth is revolutionary."
"The old world is dying, the new world struggles to be born.
Now is the time of monsters."

— ANTONIO GRAMSCI

We know the old word is dying. Throughout history, worldviews come and go. Humankind has journeyed through different worldviews from the Classical, to the Medieval, to the Enlightenment, to the Industrial, to the present Neoliberal Monetary worldview. Each view has represented a different way of expressing and understanding who and how we are in the world. Now, in this critical phase, once more, the present Zeitgeist is dying, and the new struggles to be born due to the vested interests. It is a delicate moment.

What seems to be incubating in this transition is the need for, and the emergence of, a new consciousness. In our material age we have not given much attention to consciousness. Such subject was seen as something religion occupied itself with, or the peripheries of society. This is now changing. There is a growing awareness that the old consciousness, the old ways of thinking and doing are no longer fit for purpose. While it may never have been, now in its more decadent phase, we find that a few have too much while the many increasingly too little. The level of behaviour underlined by a consciousness of winners and losers, competition and the survival of the fittest, is taking us into a very dangerous place. It is no longer nurturing the human race. Hence now is the time of monsters.

It is now more important than ever to start exploring: what is waiting to be born? What is the emerging consciousness? And what is the being that is fit for the future?

To survive we must take a leap in consciousness which, in turn, will influence and determine our behaviour. It is our behaviour that is creating havoc in the world right now and I can't see how this can change if we don't make space for the new consciousness to emerge. A consciousness which nurtures the ability to make the world a better place for all of us. One thing is certain: it is now time to think in terms of we and us rather than I and me! In the next emerging Socio-Ecological era our survival depends on a shift from the emphasis on stuff and the material to relationships and the immaterial. This, first and foremost, depends on and is driven by our consciousness.

The emerging consciousness is based more on the intangible than the tangible. A dimension based on immateriality in terms of connection, care, love and energy. An emerging consciousness that first of all connects us and redefines what it means to be human. It makes us realise our collective humanity, our similarities rather than our differences, and drives us to nurture and care rather than compete and destroy. Lastly it feeds our soul, heart, tummy and head in a way that allows us to be a better us.

I am intrigued by this consciousness. What is it? Is it an individual consciousness? A collective consciousness? A universal consciousness? Can this consciousness guide the roles we have as sentient beings: *what responsibility must we take?* Different models, like Spiral Dynamics, Theory U, and Barrett's Levels of Consciousness, illustrate the evolutionary journey from I to We. This is now intuited increasingly by more people as they tap into a collective consciousness, tapping into a knowledge that exceeds our personal knowledge. To experience this 'other consciousness' is to expand your universe. Through such experiences, the either/or view of the world, spiritual or material, I believe is passing.

Personally, I feel not having a spiritual consciousness makes us poorer. Perhaps it is this special capacity that enables us to be the human beings we need to be. A new era is waiting, a connection between personal, planetary and cosmic energy. This is where we need to experience and explore more. All this a long way from our present behaviour which so far centred on:

- The personal: doing & having,
- The planetary: exploitation,
- The cosmic: gods and religion behaving badly.

What I imagine future behaviour could centre on:
- The personal: being and connecting,
- The planetary: nurturing, care and custodianship,
- The cosmic: exploring and expanding individual and collective consciousness.

We must ask and explore questions here. Are the soul and cosmic energy connected? This is where science and the spiritual should cooperate. Who knows what the mystery is? I know I have a need for it. I sense that it is there, and there is purpose to it. Perhaps now we need to get closer to trying to be in tune with that purpose and that energy. Intuition, science and experiences are the pathway.

We are unique as a species as Yuval Noah Harari demonstrates in his book 'Sapiens – A Brief History of Humankind': we are the only species on our planet, that we are aware of, to have the combination of imagination, storytelling, creativity, flexibility and a unique adaptability. If we're the only ones to have this, it's not surprising that we have become dominant. But now our dominance has become dictatorship, perhaps exactly because we've lacked a sense of sacredness and spirituality. Advanced techno-market capitalism has given us much stuff, but has also made us less than we can be. Our potential has been distracted by materialism, possessions, money, technology and ego.

We've lost the soul and we've given primacy to the ego. As complex, creative and communicative primates, I feel that we really have to be thinking about how to recover and reintroduce sacredness and mystery in everyday life. So where do we go with this? One way is perhaps to emphasise doing less and being more.

The human being is a potential, a possibility. Heterarchical, human beings connect, share, care and explore. As such, being human is about freedom and about energy. It's about nurturing the human spirit, about letting go of the straitjacket of rationality, of the dominance of the ego. It's about reaching our full potential through moving more towards the non-rational, synergy and combinations between head, heart, and soul. Liberating and giving energy to our human essence frees us from the mantra of 'less is more' to 'more is more'! It offers expansion, connection, and cooperation. It's exponential, more people doing more together creates more! In essence, It's not about parts; it's about the whole.

What does all that mean? Freedom! Freedom to be, to explore, to interact, to connect. *Freedom to push the boundaries of what it means to be uniquely human.*

We have to be free to create. The future has to be about equipping us and freeing us up to explore and develop our unique capacities, and to develop consciousness of ourselves and the universe. This is where the energy must go.

I believe these uniquely human capacities will take us on our future path as increasing numbers of us explore and connect with our intuition, feelings, our body's centres of knowledge, and the energy and intelligence of the cosmos. We need to remember our wisdom. To recuperate what the ancients intuited, helped by the knowledge of science.

We must use our amazing human-ness and our humanity to take us beyond the last frontier to new territories. Spirituality and science together complimentary and complementing each other can take us where few women or men have gone before. A mantra not of either/or, but of both.

Join the Flow!

"Greatness is something all people have access to. It's a combination of several
different skills and talents. The *good news* is: almost everyone has the required
skills. The problem is: most of it is still unknown and unutilized."

— KEN WILBER

A new consciousness is emerging. More than ever we need to feel anchored in ourselves. The evolution of your consciousness starts with self-leadership. With practice
you will rise into your greatness, your highest potential: you will be able to access
all your innate forms of knowing rather than only the rational. We call this highest
potential the *'diamond of human potential'*. The most vital source of innovation is
your own consciousness!

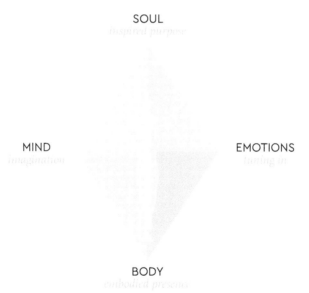

SOUL
inspired purpose

MIND   EMOTIONS
imagination   *tuning in*

BODY
embodied presence

We take you on a journey of consciousness and show you how to access your full
potential, providing easy to implement routines & rituals. We guide you to more
awareness of your operating system while focusing on the *human, energy and
personality designs*. We integrate ancient wisdom with the latest science.

Now most leadership theories involve mind (IQ), emotions (EQ) and will. But what about our body (PhQ) and our soul (SQ)? What about integrating all of them and what about the dynamics?

What we felt was needed, but missing so far, was a whole system approach to guide us towards profound alignment, while rebooting our operating system. We wrote this book as a practical guide, uniquely combining leadership theories as Theory U's social architecture, Integral Theory's alignment and Barrett's values tools with psychology, biology, neuroscience, whole system dynamics, Leadership Embodiment and (universal laws of) energy.

> *Our goal is to provide you with the insights, language and tools to facilitate awareness and a first experience of the feeling of this inner alignment. By providing a synthesis of all these fields, we aim to create a shift in perspective and a better understanding of how certain choices integrate and influence each other. Remember this: reflection is a good start, but does not sufficiently mobilise the energy for sustainable change. To embody this change, it is vital to do the practices in the Reinventing Toolbox.*

We explore what it means to be whole (or fully authentic) on an individual level. Do you know how this feels in your body (PhQ), and how to give words to this (felt sense)? How the alignment and dynamics with your mind (IQ), emotions (EQ), and soul (SQ) work? Do you know how to operate from centre rather than from personality, how to come online?

As you begin to increase your awareness and implement the rituals, you will become more conscious and begin to (re)integrate each part of you. See this as a process of self-discovery, one that will carry a rich reward! By practising these rituals, you will experience your own blueprint for how to live from wholeness.

The ideas in this book have grown out of our personal and professional experience and research. Yvette and I have dedicated ourselves to guiding people and organisations to their full potential. Over the years we have worked with thousands of people, researching and experiencing with what it is that people need, what works and what doesn't, each in our own way. In sharing this material, we have seen it have a profound effect on both individuals and groups.

I have worked i.a. through leadership journeys, coaching and learning labs. On this journey several thought leaders in the field of leadership and evolution have inspired me. I would like to especially acknowledge:

- *Otto Scharmer,* whose Theory U [3] provides a social architecture to enable the emerging future,
- *Ken Wilber,* whose Integral Theory [4] suggests synthesising human knowledge and experience,
- *Richard Barrett,* whose tools [5] make the importance of values measurable,
- *Frederic Laloux,* whose Reinventing Organizations [6] coins 'Wholeness' as a core principle for TEAL.

As well as acknowledge Phoenix Opleidingen, particularly Wibe Veenbaas and Morten Hjort, Alan Seale, Wendy Palmer and Anouk Brack, Dirk Oellibrandt, Hans Andeweg and Vedanta Aspiotti. And above all, all the people I've had the pleasure of working with. They made the material come alive!

Do you know how your human design works?

The age of individualism has resulted in the fragmentation of people and systems. We live mostly in our mind and in doing so, have lost touch with the wisdom of our body, our centre (heart), and the direction of our soul. We are yet to become fully aware of energy and its potential.

At the same time, we are subject to more input than ever before, causing our minds and central nervous systems to be over stimulated most of the time. Today, we might encounter more stimuli during a regular week in a large city, than our ancestors a few thousand years ago would have in their entire life. Our brains and nervous systems simply can't keep up the pace, and need a serious reboot.

We believe the next step in evolution urges us to be whole, to see the whole – and take responsibility for it, knowing everything is connected. We simply must update our operating system, the software of our intellectual, physical, emotional and spiritual intelligences, and our knowledge of energy. This means expanding our inner resources and integrating all of this. Consciously connecting with and nurturing our whole being is key in our ability to meet our current demands.

---

3   C. Otto Scharmer, *Theory U* – Leading from the Future as It Emerges. The Social Technology of Presencing, SOL, Cambridge, 2007.

4   Ken Wilber, *A Brief History of Everything,* Boston, Shambhala Publications, 1996.

5   Richard Barrett, *The Values-Driven Organization* – Unleashing Human Potential for Performance and Profit, Taylor & Francis, 2013.

6   Frederic Laloux, *Reinventing Organizations* – A Guide to Creating Organizations Inspired by the Next Stage of Human Consciousness, Brussels, Nelson Parker, 2014.

What is our whole being?

To understand the concept of the whole self, an iceberg provides a useful metaphor: what you show the world through your behaviour is only a small fraction of what you really feel and think. Why? The drivers behind thoughts, feelings, emotions, beliefs, values and needs of body, mind, and soul are all hidden (see page 38). A shocking 95-99% of all behaviour is based on unconscious pattern recognition, with only the remaining 1-5% to be determined by free will as we will see later (page 79). Our brain helps us create meaning by recognising patterns. Those patterns are acquired over a lifetime and depend on personal circumstances and context. Emotional patterns are the most fundamental patterns we have. So, until you become aware of what drives your behaviour, you are powerless to change.

Access and mastery of your full power, therefore, require you to dive below the surface to uncover how you operate and what is important to you. This will provide you with insights that will enable you to consciously choose behaviours, thoughts, feelings, emotions, beliefs, motivations, and attitudes that you want, and that influence your physical well-being and energy in the process. Time to create awareness, language, and rituals around being integral and embodied!

How can we Reinvent Ourselves and rise into our Greatness?

By realising who you are and what you've come here to do, and by consciously choosing your behaviour in line with that. By exploring your inner architecture and reconnecting to yourself by practising presence in mind, body, soul, and emotions. Reinventing Ourselves offers a new perspective on Personal Mastery and becoming whole. This book is written along the lines of Theory U (see next page), in fact, it is the embodied journey through your own U!

Part I Embodying Presence starts with an overview of our *human design*. *Part II Entering Flow* provides an overview of our *energy design*, and a vision of flow, our desired destination. Then, we look back and explore what we want or need to leave behind of our *personality design* in *Part III Letting Go*.

Our reinventing journey entails:

'Aligning all of you,' becoming aware of your *human design*, your authentic self. Learning to embody and integrate all of you, all of your resources or powers. It's a process of embracing your body's wisdom, your soul's guidance, a clear mind and choosing to live with an open heart no matter what. This will allow you to live from your centre, give you *a feeling of safety and wholeness*, and ultimately more resilience.

'**Entering flow**,' becoming aware of your *energy design* and the universe's rules of the game. You come to understand how, through the power of your focused intention and attention, you have the power to allow your best future to emerge. By accessing your intuition you begin to allow a way of being that enables you to tap into the collective intelligence. You come online. This allows you to *enter flow*. '**Freeing yourself**,' becoming aware of your shadow part, your *personality design* and letting go of the patterns that hold you back. Making subconscious fears conscious allows you to manage the mental, emotional and physical reactions connected with them. Freeing yourself leads to the capacity for self-observation and self-direction by connecting the mind with the heart: this is *true letting go*.

How can we Move as One?

By connecting the above three steps, 'aligning all of you,' 'freeing yourself,' and 'entering flow,' you unleash a way of being that is fully embodied and empowered, grounded in authenticity, emotional intelligence, intuition and a firm knowledge of patterns and energy. It's a conscious, integrated way of being that allows you to look at the world through the perspective of your Highest Self. It allows you to connect with anyone and anything from a place of openness: open to exploring what you know, tolerating what cannot be known, practising being at ease with uncertainty, and allowing experimentation with what 'wants to happen' or manifest itself. Your central nervous system and your mind will be forever changed for the better. You will be free!

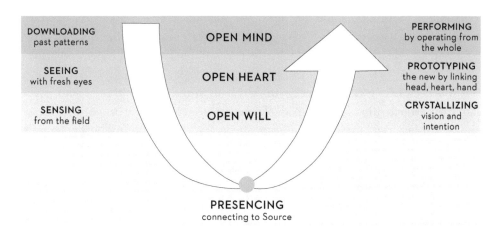

This is the inner architecture underpinning Scharmer's social architecture in Theory U, as above!

Like any mastery, Personal Mastery demands curiosity, clarity, commitment, and leadership. And all of this takes discipline and practice! But it can be done! Compare it to practice running for instance. The more you do it, the more profound its effects. Just as a professional marathon runner develops more blood vessels than a non-sporty person, and/or a highly experienced meditator's brain structure differs from that of a non-meditator [7].

> *We can all reconnect, reset and release. In doing so, you will be richly rewarded, as your life will become more aligned with your authentic self and your environment. Your work and play will mirror this: you will experience more presence, happiness, energy, synchronicity, and flow. It will create a feeling of safety in you and allow you to act freely. Your life will begin to unfold in a natural, more conscious way – in alignment with your nature, allowing you to become all you can be.*

Times like these call on us to take radical responsibility to become whole so we can take care of the whole. In other words: to rise to the next level of consciousness. We must learn to act from our heart in an intentional, conscious and collective way. To move beyond human nature and rise to our limitless selves. To build implicit trust and establish new ways of connecting and committing. Evolution is pushing us. We need to move as one, beyond ego, from our heart: from I to We.

As we awaken to the possibility of our greatness, the question arises: how can I unleash it, what is my place in the world? For each of us to make our unique contribution to humanity and the world, we must discover our greatness and our purpose first. Discovering and harnessing our greatness lies at the heart of playing a leading role in society. It brings a deep sense of belonging, loyalty, and pride.

May this book help you reconnect with your body, mind, emotions, and soul, practising and embodying presence in all of you, so you may become (more) whole and free. May it assist you to rise into your greatness and realise your highest potential!

"Look inside yourself...
You are more than what you have become. Remember who you are.
Remember... You must take your place in the Circle of Life."
— THE LION KING

---

7   Inspired by a lecture by A. Newberg, F. Travis and A. Lutz entitled *'Neural correlates of meditative experience'*, at *'Towards a Science of Consciousness'* conference at Tucson, Arizona, 2002.

Who are we and how did we get here?

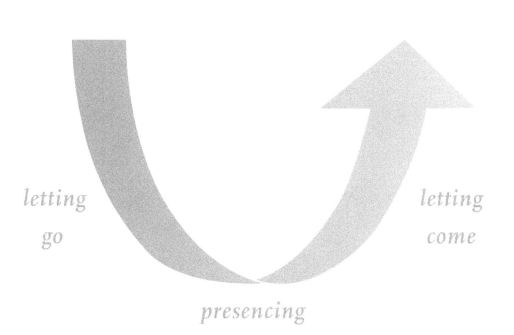

letting
go

presencing

letting
come

"Chaos should be regarded as extremely good news."

— CHÖGYAM TRUNGPA RINPOCHE

～

Since ancient times stories have helped us form a picture of how the world works to help us cope with life's challenges. We need these stories, they give us perspective, help navigate experiences, and help create a new narrative. We want to start this journey by providing you with the perspective of evolution: how did we get from Adam and Eve to Brexit and Trump?

The answers can be found through studying human history and formative psychology. The patterns of the **evolution of consciousness** have enabled us to survive and thrive since the beginning of mankind. Every stage in evolution has fuelled us to discover new ways of connecting, communicating and collaborating.

People have researched the evolution of human consciousness from various disciplines: needs (Maslow), values (Barrett, and Graves/Beck *Spiral Dynamics*) and worldviews (Wilber and Gebser), to name but a few. In this book we focus on the following theories in particular:

- *Spiral Dynamics* as a tool for the evolution of human consciousness,
- *Cultural Transformation Tools (CTT)* on measuring evolution of consciousness in people and organisations,
- *Integral Theory* on aligning interior and exterior (behaviour) in individuals and groups,
- *Theory U* provides a social architecture to enable the emerging future,
- *BodyMind integrated psychology*, various types: formative, somatic, attitudinal, Neuro Affective Personality development, character analysis and bodywork.

Mankind develops in phases, closely related to the challenges it faces at the time. Every transition leads to a new stage of consciousness that gives way to a whole new era in human history. This is visible in the way that society, economy, power, and religion take shape. Each new stage in human consciousness provides a breakthrough in our ability to connect, communicate, and collaborate.

Our current state of complex global geopolitics (chaos!) demands the ability and tools on our part to navigate our way through global complexity. This level of stimulation simply exceeds our current capacity, compelling us to move to a new level of consciousness, a new level of connecting with both ourselves and with others. *It feels like we are being challenged to connect and collaborate with collective intelligence itself.* Therefore, *integration and alignment are critical.*

We believe that we're entering a new era: a time where we are forced to return to our intuitive selves to address the complex issues facing us now. This is an era that requires more consciousness of who we really are in terms of our design and that of the universe. *Becoming whole is simply **the** next step in our evolution.*

A SYSTEMS PERSPECTIVE

Evolution today is accelerating at warp speed. But how did we develop as humans? The following outline is based on the principles of *Spiral Dynamics*: it identifies the transitioning of human psychology (in response to changes in existence) and the dynamic between the collective and individual value systems.

Spiral Dynamics describes eight levels of increasing complexity all defined by colours. Below we provide a summary of the various levels and their characteristics. Please note that *Spiral Dynamics* is closely linked to both Ken Wilber's, as well as Richard Barrett's work.

Stage 0 | Beige (the instinctual self) **key: survival**
This stage outlines the earliest developmental stage, spanning roughly 100,000 to 10,000 BC. People lived in small groups, their capacity to handle complexity was limited and there was no real hierarchy. The world-view was based on the here and now. The life theme was satisfying physical needs. Developmentally, people were comparable to newborns: there was no fully separate self yet. Today, very few people live according to his paradigm.

Stage 1 | Purple (the magical self) **key: kindred spirits**
This stage charts the shift from small family clans to larger tribes of a few hundred people, ca. 15,000 years ago. This required a big leap in terms of handling complexity and required the development of social intelligence. The worldview was one of fear, religion and magic, dominated by the unknown, making rituals an important part of life at this time. The life theme was family safety. The self began to differentiate but was still the centre of the universe. Developmentally, people at this time were comparable to toddlers of 3-24 months. Today, we still find this in tribes, be they indigenous tribes or street gangs.

Stage 2 | Red (the egoic self) **key: power gods**
This stage is the shift from tribes to chiefdoms and empires – a big step. This happened some 10,000 years ago. Thinking is shaped by polar opposites, and is still focused on the present. The worldview is: 'it's a jungle out there,' power is the name of the game; a question of control or be controlled. The life theme is egocentrism – it's all about me – impulsive, and instant satisfaction of lust. However, the emotional spectrum is still narrow. Today, we find this stage in tribal societies, underprivileged groups, aggressive or power dominated organisations (up or out style cultures).

Stage 3 | Blue (the mythical self) **key: truth force**
In this stage there is a large shift from agricultural tribe culture to civilisations, organisations, institutions, and states. The thinking moves to a Newtonian understanding of cause, effect & time. Ca. 1,000 AD. The worldview is that of an orderly world with rules and regulations, belonging, collective, them or us. The life theme is ethnocentrism. Life has meaning. Motto: keep safe and adhere to the rules. The emotional spectrum is undermined by the idea that order and predictability create safety. An individual's self-esteem depends on the opinions of others in this type of society. *Today, blue still makes up the largest group in the global population, and we find it abounds in society, stratified over social classes and genders.*

Stage 4 | Orange (the integral self) **key: strive drive**
Another major shift occurs around the Industrial Revolution in the 1700 – 1800s. The world became a place that could be shaped to accommodate your wishes: a meritocracy. Thinking refocuses on the future. Here it's about success and achievement. The new worldview is that you can create your own world – one that is centred around effectiveness, greed and individualism. The life theme is to obtain success, material wealth and individual freedom. Grab your opportunity! This is totally ego-driven, but with world-centric promise. The emotional spectrum covers innovation and prosperity, as well as individualism and greed: but ego comes out on top. *Today this is the most dominant worldview of leaders in business and politics. However, collapsing systems and the laws of nature tell us that this short-sighted overexploitation is no longer sustainable.*

Stage 5 | Green (the sensitive self) **key: human bonds**
A shift to reason, feelings, empathy and world-centric morality takes place in the late 1900s. We see a rise of the modern liberation movement: the liberation of slaves, untouchables and women. A trend towards what is fair for all humans,

regardless of race, sex, caste or creed begins. The worldview moves to 'we as people,' forming a community, and sharing the planet with nature. The life theme moves to harmony, equality and happiness. The Green stage breaks down existing structures but is less effective at building practical alternatives. *Today, this thinking is mainstream in postmodern academic thinking and non-governmental organisations.*

Stage 6 | Yellow (the integral self) **key: flex flow**
This stage is a vision of arriving in the here and now. We see things from a wider perspective and we see ourselves as instruments for the whole. We become aware of the chaos and our position within it. We look for leading principles. Change has become the norm. The worldview is that everything is connected in a self-organising ecosystem. The life theme is: effective action towards benefitting the whole. Current global problems become visible through technology, which is all-pervasive, and increasingly transparent. Spirituality returns thanks to science: quantum physics has proven the effects of meditation and the universal laws among others.

Stage 7 | Teal or Turquoise (the holistic self) **key: whole view**
This can be seen as the next step in our evolution. A step where we see the whole – and take responsibility for the whole because we know now that everything is connected, we believe in unity and we need to develop emotional and spiritual intelligence and knowledge of energy. We need to move beyond our ego in service of the whole. In other words, we need to master and transcend our ego.

AN INDIVIDUAL CONSCIOUSNESS PERSPECTIVE

Richard Barrett's *Seven Levels Model* below describes the evolutionary development of human consciousness. It enables us to form an idea of how people develop over time and gives us insight as to where we are on our journey. You may note that there is a strong correlation between Spiral Dynamics (looking at large systems and groups of people) and this model (looking at individuals, as well as groups).

Taking our earlier iceberg metaphor into account, the bottom three layers: Survival, Relationship, and Self-esteem represent our ego needs. They drive our beliefs, thoughts, feelings, and emotions. Along with our physical needs (included in survival), these three ego needs need to be fulfilled first for humans to thrive in this world. The bottom triangle of the model is based on Maslow's hierarchy of needs. *We can only live our soul purpose when we feel safe, loved, respected and self-assured.* This requires us to get beyond the transformation point, the centre of the hourglass. This is about Personal Mastery.

LEVELS OF CONSCIOUSNESS		STAGES OF DEVELOPMENT
SERVICE	7	SERVING
MAKING A DIFFERENCE	6	INTEGRATING
INTERNAL COHESION	5	SELF-ACTUALISING
TRANSFORMATION	4	INDIVIDUATING
SELF-ESTEEM		DIFFERENTIATING
RELATIONSHIP		CONFORMING
SURVIVAL		SURVIVING

One of the most important things holding us back from progress is fear. So this is about learning how to manage these fear-driven beliefs of our ego. Once we've mastered our ego needs, we can let go of personal and cultural conditioning and find our true purpose in life.

What follows is a description of the seven stages of evolution on an individual level. You will see that the beliefs underlying the three bottom layers are formed by early childhood experiences, from 0 to 7 years.

Level 1 | Survival consciousness
Do you control your world?
The first level is about the need for food, water, and safety. Basically, it's about preservation and procreation. If you had a safe childhood, you have probably developed a healthy, rational sense of survival consciousness. If not, you may have developed an unbalanced emotional perspective. You may have insecurities about survival or abandonment. You may be prone to anxiety. You may become angry easily. You may feel as if the world is a hostile place and you may often resort to using control to feel safe. *You will need to learn how to master your survival fears. Please note: safety & trust always come first, in every single situation.*

Level 2 | Relationship consciousness
Do you belong?
As children, we need to belong to survive. Do you feel like you belong in your work and your relationships? Do you always tell the truth, even if in conflict it may result in a break-up? If you were not unconditionally loved as a child, you may

demonstrate behaviour that safeguards the status quo in relationships, at work or at home. This might include conflict avoidance and excessive harmony seeking. *You will need to master your relationship fears.*

Level 3 | Self-esteem consciousness
Winning is the name of the game
Do you feel good about who you are and take pride in your performance? Are you praised for who you are instead of what you do? If not, you may always feel the need to be successful and focus on your image so that you may receive the recognition you didn't get when you were young. You may be highly competitive and focused on winning. Your self-esteem may be built on your image and achievements. *You will need to master your self-esteem fears.*

Level 4 | Transformation consciousness
Personal Mastery, individuation, and authentication
This poses the question: who are you? It's time to understand and unleash your true self. To break the emotional chains of the past that have kept you tied to the first three ego levels of consciousness to make choices and express yourself truly, no matter what. This generates freedom and authenticity which in turn bring integrity and honesty. *You may need to return here again and again to uncover deeper levels of fear. It's a continuous journey!*

Level 5 | Internal Cohesion Consciousness
The discovery is a journey
What is your work? What is the gift you have come to give to the world? Open up to your soul and find your purpose. What are you passionate about? What makes your heart beat? What is your special talent? You will know you have found it when your life is in flow and synchronicity works along with you. *Uncovering your soul purpose will provide you with meaning as well as great joy.*

Level 6 | Making a Difference consciousness
Collaboration is key
Everything you have done so far has led you up to this point. Who shares your purpose and values? You will search for people with similar purpose and values. *You realise that your impact in the world depends on your ability to collaborate with the right people.*

Level 7 | Service consciousness
Making a difference is your way of life
Aligning with your soul and realising its purpose in the world is what you live for. The flow arising here can feel fantastic. Balance is the key word: surrendering to your soul and taking care of the needs of your body and mind will provide you with the sustainability that you need.

SUMMARY — HUMAN EVOLUTION

We started this journey by sharing perspectives around human evolutionary development. These patterns of *consciousness* have enabled us to survive since the beginning of mankind. They enabled us to deal with the growing complexity the world brought us.

Collectively we have evolved from:
- Hunting and gathering (beige and purple),
- Horticultural (magenta),
- Agrarian (red),
- Industrial (blue and orange),
- Informational (orange and green).

Individually we are evolving from the ego needs of:
- Survival,
- Relationship,
- Self-esteem,
- Transformation, *to reach our soul desires of:*
- Internal cohesion,
- Making a difference,
- Service.

According to Ken Wilber, we're at this point in evolution transforming *Tier* [8], the first of its kind, encompassing all values of all preceding phases. He too, states integration and updating our 'software' is necessary. This enables us to co-create the future. NOW is the time to create the conditions for all to thrive!

---

8   "Conventionally, a tier is just an arbitrary grouping of stages. Integral Theory often high-lights three tiers: First Tier, which consists of the levels up to and including Green altitude; Second Tier, which consists of Teal and Turquoise altitude; and Third Tier, which includes all post-Turquoise levels of development" – source: www.integrallife.com.

"We already have all the answers!"

— INTERVIEW WITH WENDY VAN TOL, CONSULTING LEADER, PWC NL

Reinventing Ourselves is a book on 'being whole.' What does this mean to you?

I think there is an extraordinary added value to be found in harnessing the full extent of people's potential – not just their minds, but also their intuition, feelings, and energy. Society has developed an undue focus on the rational mind over the past 30 years, and this has made us smaller and more limited. It has narrowed the idea of what it means to be human.

The question is: Why do we create a shadow paradigm in which we appreciate only part of ourselves? Why don't we, for example, use new technological developments to conduct rational tasks so humans can free up time and space to unlock other human capacities, such as our imagination? We could envisage a different future, just as a child looking at an empty cardboard box says: it's a castle, don't you see?

> *If you ask me what the human value is in the digital age, I believe that this age creates an opportunity for humans to be more human. And leaders need to be even better than that: they need to create space which will enable technology to be productive and people to be creative.*

I see this daily in my role as consulting leader with our consultants and clients. We retain this paradigm of the mind because it gives us an illusion of security. Anything rational, we can discuss it, we can hold onto it. We have not yet developed language for many of the other human values that is appropriate to quantify or appreciate them fully.

We have mostly lost our trust in intuition and emotional connection. When someone says "I have an idea," but can't back it up with data, the idea is often not even considered. Yet most revolutionary innovations have started with imagination, daring to go where needs exist that have not yet been defined.

To come up with solutions for today's problems, it is crucial that we start using the full extent of people's potential and power sources. If, for example, a system is built on traditionally masculine values, it will put a premium on masculine energy. Different sources of potential, such as intuition, may therefore not be valued, making them difficult to defend, and easy to dismiss. Without appreciation, an idea or an approach cannot flourish, just like a plant that is not watered or exposed to sunlight. How can we organise organisations and society so that different ways of thinking and types of values receive more sunlight?

What does it mean to be human and how do you do this?

Personally, I try to stick to my values. Every decision I make is guided by the following:
- Am I making a difference?
- Is this independent thinking (is this my opinion or am I following the group)?
- Is this coming from my ego or my true self?

It is, of course, important to realise that the ego needs space too: I like my actions to be visible. It's not always easy to strike the right balance, and an element of give and take is involved. When I make decisions that are not aligned with my values, I try to be aware of this, discuss it and possibly revisit the issue with others while being open to challenge. Self-reflection and being humble are crucial for everyone who is taking decisions that may impact others.

All of us have a more or less well-developed ego, and that may affect our choices. However, it is often in moments of reflection that you can feel where your decisions really came from. Do you dare to take the time to listen to yourself and revisit a decision when necessary? Or do you decide that it's good enough for now?

I make sure I take the time to reflect. I've noticed that deliberately clearing my mind in meditation, but also when exercising (doing sports), or in situations such as long-haul flights leads to richer ideas and better decisions.

We already have all the answers, but they are in places we cannot yet reach or don't listen to.

What does this mean for organisations and leadership?

Our system demands us to be available 24/7, and that can make things complicated. Let me give you an example. One of PwC's core values is 'Care.' One of the ways in which this manifests in day-to-day business, is answering phone calls, emails and meeting requests, as we like to be there for people all the time. When you're a leader, people expect you to be present, responsive and available. They feel that you care when you respond to their requests. That expectation feeds the action mode, responding to these requests as fast as you can. But doesn't taking time out for reflection also add value? We do need to get to the point where we think about this, and appreciate that value too. We need to change our thinking here, and that is not easy because we like replication. It is how the brain works. As long as our minds stay within a beta wave frequency, see page 146, all we can do is replicate. But creativity requires space and silence. And that, in turn, demands a different design and a different layer.

But I see hope on the horizon, which I often refer to as early signals of Spring arriving. I joined PwC as the first sociologist they hired, 19 years ago. I had never thought I would become partner, let alone have a leadership position, or become consulting lead. The fact that PwC would give a person with a very different way of thinking an important position, makes me hopeful about the possibilities for other novel responses to enter the mainstream.

What is your view on energetic leadership?

For me, this is like radiating truth. It causes a shift in energy. Let me give an example. Have you experienced teamwork where you felt the team operated in a flow? All of a sudden the team has answers for issues they did not think they were capable of finding. These things can happen in a group without you fully realising what you have done. You operate within a zone where people are interconnected in a kind of collective intelligence.

One thing I consider a challenge and a pity is that I'm not in that zone all the time. So, I wonder: How could I get there more often? How could I create a situation in which I feel that connection with others and myself every day? I consider it coming into my own wholeness – coming home, as it were.

We have trained our cerebral cortex every day for years. We don't often enough explicitly train or practise to be whole. So how do we return from being unaligned to being whole? How do we become fully human again?

Coming back to my earlier example on our action mode: our need to respond to requests as fast as we can, we all appreciate as hard work. But, actually, a day of reflection is harder work than answering emails, especially if you're aiming to be self-reflective, self-critical and vulnerable. Deep meditation takes effort because it requires you to let go before allowing the new to come in. Our Western appreciation systems are not geared for this yet.

So, how do we move from replication to creation? It will only happen when people can also use the full range of their imagination, creativity, and empathic skills – all true human values. It will happen when people use their sensing mechanism and feel what needs to happen, be it within their organisation or in society.

Human flourishing delivers value to all. At the end of the day, that's what everybody wants.

Aligning Body, Mind, and Soul

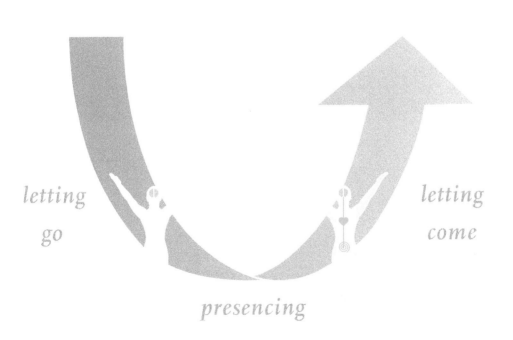

letting go

letting come

presencing

moving from available to aligned

Embodying Presence

Embodying Presence entails moving to an aligned position. Aligned with all your powers, that is. Moving from purpose, with your focus and intention crystal clear, your emotions free, your energy present (flow), and your heart open, you have a solid foundation, you are fully present. This enables you to sense reality and respond to it, from Essence, rather than ego.

*Awareness of your **human design**, and practising conscious connection with your mind, body, emotions, and soul will guide you to your greatness.*

*In harmonious resonance, totally coherent, **you will move as one**.*

"When we are embodied, we become learners.
We learn from situations, from our experiences, from life.
If we do not live in our body, the seat of our experience,
we are only capable of reacting in mechanical ways.
Identifying with the body gives us the ability to genuinely respond to life."

— RICHARD STROZZI-HECKLER

"Attention or conscious concentration on almost any part of the body
produces a direct physical effect on it."

— CHARLES DARWIN

What if...

- We are living a mind dominated existence, a contracted version of ourselves,
- We have everything we need to realise our full potential (but fail to use it),
- We *just* need to reinvent ourselves?

Reinventing Ourselves then explores our inner architecture, our human design. It explores how to access and align mind, body, soul, and emotions and how to become truly present and embodied. How to access your greatness.

So how can you embody presence?
It all starts with being open and curious! Become aware of how your *human design* works through engaging with the material and the practices we provide. Make it a (daily) practice. Wake up to who you really are, and to what you want to be and do in life. Be aware of who and what gives you energy. Fully inhabit your body, and show up through choosing to be open to the present moment and commit to working and living as such by using intention. Choose to step into the flow of alignment by entering into practice. Build in routines and rituals that serve you and let go of old patterns that don't. In short: *become conscious of you and of life!*

Do you really know how your human design works?
In our experience, most people do not! By human design, we refer to the function of and dynamics between body, mind, soul, and emotions. Presence is often still a somewhat mental concept, not an embodied experience for many people.

This part of the book looks into **how you embody yourself**, your passion and your triggers. It takes you into your human operating system. From page 59 onwards we provide *practices* to experience presence in mind, body, heart, and soul and discover the whole you. We aim to give you as close to a felt sense [9] of this as we can with words. What is the difference between a felt sense and having someone explain something to you? Compare it to us telling you how a strawberry tastes, versus you tasting a strawberry yourself, so juicy, sweet and fragrant – nothing beats experience!

What is Embodied Presence?

> *Embodied presence is a coherent presence: all your powers are 'on' and aligned, your posture shows visible alignment of mind, emotions, and soul. Your energy is focused, and your action is a synergetic flow.*

Embodied Presence is the presence that radiates from you naturally. It is what people see and feel when they look at you. To make it tangible: Barack Obama is said to embody the American Dream and the European values of dignity and human freedom. Creating a consciously embodied presence, like Obama's, means being conscious of who you are, and aligning with that, and taking full responsibility for that. It means owning yourself!

So how do you achieve this? It's really about *attention and energy* and where you direct these. See, energy and attention are the bodymind dynamics defining who you are – physically, emotionally, spiritually and psychologically.

Attention is the *intentional focus of your mind*. By consciously focusing your attention in daily life, you create a quality of *awakening*: enabling you to experience life through your body, anchoring you in the present and giving you direction. This expands you beyond merely surviving. Direction is key in embodying yourself. Work with intention! Cultivating this enables you to find out who and how you are.

---

9 An experience difficult to capture in words, maybe: a physical experience that tells you something about your life.

Attention energises. Try this, to give you an idea: sit comfortably with your eyes open. Look around you in the room. Bring your attention to the chair you're sitting on. Now shift it to a person near to you. Now to the sensations of your feet on the floor, the sun on your face, the smell in the room, the birds chirping outside and to your heart. As you shift your attention, it illuminates and energises each object in turn. It's all there at the same time, yet attention brings it into the foreground.

> *When you consciously place your attention in your body, you begin to feel, and your feelings connect you to your energy. Your energy informs you of your direction and meaning in life. Of your Essence! It can tell you whether you love what you do, how you feel about a person and whether they give you energy or take it from you. Your body will tell you and – it never lies!*

Attention magnetises energy, *where attention goes, energy flows!* We can direct our attention to both our inside and our outside world. Consciously paying attention to what you do provides the space that allows awareness or self-inquiry. This is a doorway to evolution.

Energy is your life force, your qi, your aliveness, *the experience of your living body.* You can feel this energy as sensations, like warmth, vibrations, tingling or a rush of excitement. For instance, try clapping your hands, rubbing them and then holding them apart. Do you feel the energy build in your palms? Focusing on the senses and sensations in your body brings you into the moment.

You want your energy to be available and unblocked because when it is, it allows you to feel alive, strong and radiant. From time to time it can be blocked by difficult situations or emotions like stress, grief or pain. Focus on keeping your energy flowing!

> *The energy pulsing around your body is your energy field or energy body. Your energetic footprint. At this point in our evolution, we are all becoming more sensitive to this energy field. Part II of this book is all about energy and how you can open up to this. The reason why this is so important is that our energy plays a key role in manifesting our desires: it has the power to animate life!*

What if we were to ask you: *Who Are You?* And *What Do You Want?* Would you be able to answer those big life questions?

Think of a time when you really felt alive and you completely lost track of time. Maybe you were looking in the eyes of someone you love deeply and you felt the love well up inside of you. Or you had just climbed a mountain, something you had always wanted to do and you looked around taking in the stunning scenery with the sun sparkling on the snow-capped peaks. How did you feel? Chances are you felt totally open and alive, fully expansive, and energised!

Moments like these are termed 'flow' by Mihaly Csikszentmihalyi [10], and are full of passion and vitality. In flow, you are, in his words: "completely absorbed in an activity for its own sake. The ego falls away. Time flies. Every action, movement, and thought follows inevitably from the previous one, like playing jazz. Your whole being is involved, and you're using your skills to the utmost."

Now how would it be to be able to deliberately tap into flow even when things get rough? What would it take to feel in a state of flow, free yet focused, and move from a strong foundation? To feel energised and expansive, able to access possibilities and act rather than re-act? What would it take to be open, accessible and transparent and to drop the mask?

This book aims to provide you with a first 'felt awareness' of our *human design,* through a synthesis of insights and practices that enable you to experience, maybe for the first time, to feel whole. Or, as we say, practice presence in the whole You (or U, analog to the U of Theory U).

Now, this is, of course, a vast topic on which we could write a series of books. For now, we hope to cultivate in you a desire for more. Many great books have been written on the mind, the body, the soul, and the emotions separately. Should you wish to explore further, check out the selected reading list at the back of the book.

In this part of the book, we will explore:

The Body – our sense-maker and vessel; what people see of you. It is the vessel with which you experience the world, and it has its own wisdom with its two brains: in the heart and the gut. *How do you step into the highest potential of your body?*

How do you create an unshakeable foundation and use your perceptual intelligence (awareness of what you sense & feel) to the max? We will provide insights into how you can access this potential and be more consciously embodied and present.

---

10 Mihaly Csikszentmihalyi, a professor and former chairman of the Department of Psychology at the University of Chicago who has devoted his life's work to the study of what makes people truly happy, satisfied and fulfilled.

Within our body, we pay special attention to the heart and gut:

- *The Heart* – our real centre. Where you feel what is real. It communicates these feelings to the brain. It synchronises all (all!) [11] physical processes. This means that when you open your heart, you allow your life energy to flow through you much more freely. You feel expansive. When you close your heart, however, you block this life energy. You feel contracted. Practicing presence in your heart means committing to feeling, to be open to the new, to let go of control. To experience life as it is. To flourish!
- *The Gut* – our seat of power. It houses our intuition, and is our body's frontline defense in letting you know what is good or not good for you. It communicates its findings directly to the brain. Our gut plays a major role in the health and well-being of our body. When we feel anxious or stressed, we will often feel it in that area. Hence the sayings of 'butterflies in your stomach' or 'something is hard to digest,' for instance. We should pay more heed to our 'gut feelings.'

The Mind – our decision maker and occasional saboteur. *How do you step into the highest potential of your mind where you imagine, create and collaborate with magic?*

How do you create embodied presence? We will provide insights into the workings, as well as share practices to access more clarity and focus. To integrate best of both worlds, we will provide recent Western scientific insights, as well as ancient practices of the East. Furthermore we will demonstrate that we can practice presence by creating space and choosing to step into new pathways that serve us.

---

11 Institute of HearthMath Research.

The BodyMind connection – a dynamic of great potential. It is only just being picked up by science. What if your brain could become the pathway to the future by neurological rewiring?

The Soul – our guide or Essence. Pure consciousness. *How do you align with the highest potential of your soul?* How do you find inspired purpose, tap into limitless passion and enter the collective field? Aligning with your soul gives you a life of meaning and fulfilment, guided by consciousness. It allows you to express yourself.

Emotions – the importance of freeing yourself from negative emotions and patterns stored in your body, is a huge topic, discussed separately in Part III.

How do you step into the highest potential of your emotions? How do you sense into the essence of yourself and others, and connect at that level? How do you develop the ability to self reflect? How do you access your full guidance system?

Stress – what it does and how it works. We will show you how certain techniques enable you to arrive at a position where you can choose a more measured and conscious response, instead of reacting by falling into old patterns. How you can come from a place of calm.

We offer this new perspective on our human design to enable you to choose and commit to fully embody who you are, and rise into your greatness.

> *We see a Conscious Leader as one who is fully embodied (**foundation**), living a life guided by purpose (**flow**), steering clear of negative emotional patterns (**free**), and having a clear mind (**focus**). We call this Personal Mastery.*

Of course, like any mastery, Personal Mastery demands leadership, clarity, and commitment. It also demands dedication and deliberate (daily) practice [12]! It demands that you move beyond theoretical knowledge into a felt experience of your potential.

Below you find an overview of our human design to increase your awareness, followed by practices to implement from page 59 onwards.

---

12 Professor Anders Ericsson, eminent researcher on genius researching among others expert musicians, talks about the merit of deliberate practice. This is when you actually pick a target – something that you want to improve – and you find a training activity that would allow you to improve that aspect. He also talks about the 10,000 hours rule as the magic number for true expertise. Malcolm Gladwell popularly cited this in his book 'Outliers.'

"Mr. Duffy lived a short way away from his Body." – JAMES JOYCE

"Our body is our temple. We should therefore respect it, understanding its importance and always return to it; it is our refuge." – THICH NHAT HANH

Our sense-maker and vessel
Your body is what others see of you. It is the book of your life; it tells the story of
who you are. Whatever goes on in your body shows up, and is what people read
and see first. Your posture in and of itself tells a story. Your body makes sense of
everything that you experience. It is a reflection of your thoughts, values, beliefs,
and behaviour. It also has its own wisdom. Paying close attention to your body lets
you experience who you are. It also enables you to manifest your desires in tangible form. It's the vessel for your soul to exist in 3D and, as Thich Nhat Hanh says,
your temple.

Have you ever been in a place where you could feel a person's presence? Maybe
she was very passionate about her presentation, and you could feel her upbeat
energy. Or maybe you felt someone's frustration at not being able to deliver the
answer the CEO wanted. Or you felt the CEO's power. Could you feel their energy?

Now imagine you're in the presence of a great leader, someone who inspires
you to be your best you. Make your imagination vivid and think of their movements,
their body language, their energy. See the effect of all of this on their environment.
Feel their expansive and inclusive presence. Feel how truly embodied they are.
Feel how good, strong and natural this feels.

Dualism?
Here in the West, we have lost touch with our body. Since the scientific revolution,
some 500 years ago, we have put the mind above all else. As Descartes [13] put it:
"Cogito ergo sum," or "I think therefore I am." This has brought us many good
things, like structure, science, technology, and wealth.

Now though, it seems we have really lost balance. We've become identified with
the mind, we have put it in charge, and act as if body and mind are separate. We
are not in tune with ourselves. The stress that this has put on our bodies is creating
major physical issues from burn-outs to chronic heart and back illnesses, as well

---

13 Descartes, a 17th century French philosopher, was considered the father of the modern phi-
    losophy on rationalism.

as mental ones, like depression. **Stress** is now the second most frequently reported health problem in Europe [14], and the number of people suffering is likely to increase. It is also the biggest causal factor of other health problems!

We talk of vitality and life-work balance, yet we simultaneously run our bodies in ways they're not built for. Not only that: by failing to align with our body, we miss out on the wisdom of the brains in our heart and guts. We are, like Mr. Duffy "living a short way away from our body."

It doesn't have to be this way! What if we could tap into ways that would allow us to come from our centre core and remain open and expansive? Some twenty years ago it was discovered that humans have three brains: one in our *head*, one in our *heart* and one in our *gut*. This coincided with the rise of the internet and a new worldview; forcing the contemplation of distributed intelligence instead of topdown hierarchy. With this view in mind, we are maybe able to consider the idea of more than one brain, and of cooperation in shared intelligence [15].

You see, your mind may say 'go for it,' but your body will let you know if you really like someone or something, if situations are safe or not, and if you need to sort yourselves out and act differently. It will tell you it's time to change. Through the brains in the gut and the heart, it will talk to you through feelings and sensations and tell you what is truly in alignment. You only need to open yourself to it! Of course, you may refuse to listen, but then your body will talk louder, and you may get sick, numb, burned-out or chronically injured. It is through your body that your feelings make sure they can't be denied.

No whole!
Somatics defines the body as a functional, living whole. It is a change theory, taking an integral approach and viewing body and mind as a unified expression of all that we think, feel, perceive and express. It looks upon humans as a combination of biological, psychological, emotional, and evolutionary aspects, shaped by social norms [16].

---

14 According to the findings by the European Agency for Safety and Health at Work (EU-OSHA) among European workers, it comes after musculoskeletal disorders. The study noted that over a nine-year period, almost 28% of workers in Europe reported exposure to psychosocial risks that affected their mental well-being.

15 Frederic Laloux, *Reinventing Organizations*, Nelson Parker, Brussels, 2014.

16 Somatics is the field which studies the soma: the body as perceived from within by first-person perception. When a human being is observed from a third-person viewpoint, the phenomenon of a human body is perceived. But, when this same human being is observed

Our first survival needs are physical (food, drink, safety and love), and these are of course the first needs we need to attend to, as Maslow [17] and Barrett [18] point out. A well cared for body is our foundation, the basis upon which we build the rest of our expansion!

> *Through our body, we experience life in the present moment*, *through felt sense: feelings, sensations and interactions. If we open up to the innate wisdom of our body, we open up to the unknown, to new alternatives. This is, however, not predictable and may not give us what we necessarily want.*
> *Through our mind, we experience life in the future or the past*, *through fantasy or memory. The mind craves predictability and uniformity, and this is how it creates that. We do what we always do, or what we think we want. The sense of control we may feel by doing this, however, is a big illusion!*

So, if you want to live your life in freedom and authenticity, mind, body, soul, and emotions need to be integrated.

What then enables you to feel whole?
Where to begin? How does being free, whole and aligned feel? Can you practice it? Yes, you can! In my work with learning labs, I often work with Aikido as a way into the body. People love it as it is practical, simple and fun. Richard Strozzi-Heckler and Wendy Palmer [19] are my teachers who combine Aikido with Leadership. The theory and exercises described below originate from them.

Four things are essential here: *centring, grounding, expanding and blending*. It all starts with centring. A centring practice can bring you, as it suggests, (back) to your physical centre instantly.

---

from first-person viewpoint, a very different phenomenon is perceived: the human soma.

17 Maslow's Hierarchy of Needs is a motivational theory in psychology comprising a five-tier model of human needs, often depicted as hierarchical levels within a pyramid. Maslow stated that people are motivated to achieve certain needs. These needs motivate our behaviour. It goes from physical survival via safety, love/belonging, esteem to self-actualization. Once a level is fulfilled the next level up is what motivates us, and so on.

18 Barrett's Seven Levels Model is based on Maslow's Hierarchy of Needs. With minor changes, this has been transposed into a framework of consciousness. By doubling the pyramid into an hourglass, actualisation was differentiated. Transformation was added, next to the soul's desires for Internal Cohesion, Making a Difference and Service.

19 Richard Strozzi-Heckler: *The Anatomy of Change*, North Atlantic Books California 1984, and Wendy Palmer, *Leadership Embodiment*, with Janet Crawford, CreateSpace, 2013.

Centring is consciously connecting with your physical centre. Your centre is defined by the dimensions of your body: length, width and depth. It is the starting point: it establishes a focus and place of departure in your body. It is a place that you can come home to, where you can trust what you feel and sense. It is a place that is safe, where you can relax.

Traditional Eastern disciplines define different centres in the body. Here we follow Zen Buddhism and Japanese martial arts, and work with the 'hara' a point just below the navel where your *qi* or lifeforce originates.

The state of your centre is a doorway: it allows you to experience your body totally. Your hara is the centre of your feelings. It's the calmness, the fundamental goodness that is your true nature and lies beneath the disturbing chatter of the mind. When you're in your physical centre, you can access your body's wisdom to address issues vital to you. You will find it is naturally open, balanced, inclusive and expansive, and often will come with a larger awareness of the space beyond you: the room, the people, sounds, etc. A centred state is key to shifting from ego to Essence. Centring can be developed through practice. It can be done anytime, including during important meetings or crises. It makes for a great start of the day and is a valuable practice to return to during the day!

> **Centring** *is a simple and quick embodied experience that you can use as a way to focus, learn and transition.* **Being in your Centre** *is an attitude you practice toward yourself to feel present in yourself and your situation, and acts as a metaphor that you can bring to daily life. It brings both rootedness and flexibility. It is the experience of being fully here and open to the now.* **Moving from Centre** *creates a present, aligned relationship with the body.*

The sensations you notice in your body are your connection to your aliveness. The exercises teach you how to build energy and settle, again and again. As you build and settle your energy, notice how alive your body feels. Building this capacity to notice sensation will enable you to bring more of yourself to life and the task at hand. Developing the capacity to work with energy will help you bring more presence into work and life, even when you're stressed.

The centring practice below is a great way to start the day, and can also act as an SOS instrument when you feel yourself contracting or closing down.

Centring Practice [20]

1 Focus on *breath* – inhale up and out of the top of your head, lengthening your spine as you straighten and uplift your posture. Slowly take twice as long to exhale down your front all the way into the earth, softening your jaw and shoulders as you go.

2 Relate to *gravity* – gravity offers a natural venue for relaxation. Feel the width of your body and the weight of your arms pulling your shoulders away from your ears and relax the tension in your jaw. Allow gravity to settle you into your personal space and onto the earth.

3 Balance *personal space* – ask yourself: is the back of my personal space, balanced and even with the front? Is the left equal to the right? And is above equal to below? Expand your personal space out to fill the room.

4 Evoke a *quality* – your quality represents something you want to cultivate in yourself. Working with quality is a practice of inquiry [21]. Ask: if there were a little more… (ease, confidence, compassion, et cetera) in my body, what would that feel like? Where do I notice that quality?

Ground

If centre is the application of your personal energy source, ground is your connection to the qualities and capacities of that energy. Grounding connects us to the earth and to gravity, and enables us to let go and relax. Grounding yourself through your legs gives you a sense of being "carried," a sense of security.

A simple yet powerful grounding exercise is the ancient Taoist Zhan Zhuang, or Standing Like a Tree practice. It is a standing practice in an upright posture, as if standing like a tree. The tree metaphor is apt: your legs and torso form the trunk of the tree, your head and limbs the branches. Your feet, sinking and extending down beneath the ground, emulate the roots.

---

20 From *Leadership Embodiment* – How the Way we Sit and Stand Can Change the Way we Think and Speak, by Wendy Palmer and Janet Crawford, CreateSpace, 2013.

21 Self-Inquiry is a method for self-observation. It has many meanings in spiritual traditions: it's the quest for your true self, like Percival's quest for the Holy Grail.

Standing Like a Tree

1 Stand with your feet parallel and firmly on the ground at shoulder width. Grasp the ground with your feet while keeping the tip of the toes extended.
2 Imagine a golden string extending from the crown of your head into the sky. You want your head to feel like it's floating above your neck, effortlessly suspended above your spine.
3 Roll your hips slightly forward as if you were sitting at the edge of a high barstool. This will straighten the spine in your lower back.
4 Keep your knees slightly bent.
5 Relax your shoulders round your upper back.
6 Let your arms rest comfortably at your side.
7 Let the palms of your hands face your hips.
8 Tuck your chin in and keep your eyes slightly open with a soft gaze ahead. Sink all of your body's weight and tension into your feet (without collapsing your posture), allowing it to be absorbed into the ground. To support this grounding process, imagine roots growing out the bottom of your feet, extending deep into the ground beneath you.

The goal of this practice is to hold your body in as much of a relaxed, extended, and open position (thereby reducing the curvature of the spine) as possible to open the flow of energy. Your mind will be empty, active, and alert. You want to use minimal effort when maintaining this posture. NB: this relaxation comes more easily after you've learned how to maintain the correct alignment.

Leaders with a strong personal presence generate a feeling of inclusion. People feel like they are part of something bigger than themselves. Developing and expanding this personal space is a wonderful tool that is described as being easily observed in elite athletes in 'The Body has a Mind of its Own' [22]: "When athletes are on the court or field, they are mapping the space around them and people in that space in ways that most of us cannot match. Their personal space and body maps, along with a newly discovered mapping system called grid cells, seem to be exquisitely developed, which may be one reason they score so many baskets and goals."

---

22 Matthew & Sandra Blakeslee, *The Body has a Mind of its Own* – How Body Maps in Your Brain Help You Do (Almost) Everything Better, Random House USA, 2008.

The following technique helps you create a space that influences you and your surroundings in such a way. In expanding your space, all people and objects in it, are naturally included. In giving it a certain feeling or colour, you give a 'flavour' to your space that people will feel. See, for instance, the Inner Smile Meditation on page 71 for a radiant effect on your expanded space.

Expanding your Personal Space

1 Focus your attention on the heat radiating from your body.
2 Imagine that the felt-sense of body heat represents your personal space.
3 Ask: *'What is the size of my personal space?'*
4 Think about your personal space forming a bubble around you
5 Add a colour to the space inside this bubble.
6 Expand your personal space to twice its size.
7 Expand your personal space even more. Ask: *'How far can I expand it? Can I fill the room?'*

Blending entails working with a situation, rather than resisting it, and seeing the world from someone else's point of view. While at the same time remaining both centred and grounded. You will find a Blending practice on page 94.

The Heart

"Your heart does not answer to your mind; your heart reveals the deepest wishes of your soul. No amount of clever justifications or smart excuses alters your heart's wish; it just delays the richly fulfilling life you truly seek."
— ROBERT BENO

"If the 20th century has been the Century of the Brain...
the 21st century should be the Century of the Heart"
— GARY E.R. SCHWARTZ, PH.D., AND LINDA G.S. RUSSEK, PH.D.

In our body, the heart plays a very special role. You see the heart is our most refined instrument. It may well be that we do not yet know all the wonders of this masterpiece. It is an energy centre, has its own brain and affects every aspect of our life.

When our heart is allowed to guide the body and mind, great things can be achieved!

The heart produces the largest electromagnetic field in the body which acts as a carrier wave for all other information, and provides an overall synchronising signal for the whole body. It functions as the coordinator of the frequencies of our brains, consciousness, perception and energy field (aura). This ability of our heart to sync all of our body's systems can be defined as *heart intelligence.*

Developing heart intelligence can bring a higher state of awareness that helps you perceive the world differently, giving more clarity, focus, harmony and happiness!

The HeartMath Institute [23] has been researching heart-brain communication and how this affects consciousness since 1991. They help people bridge the connection between their heart and mind, and have made electromagnetic fields between people scientifically measurable and visible.

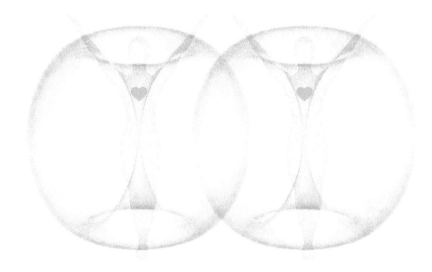

---

23 The HeartMath Institute empowers individuals, families, groups and organisations to enhance their life experiences using tools that enable them to better recognise and access their intuitive insight and heart intelligence.

One of the things that they have identified is *Heart Coherence*. Positive emotions create coherent frequencies, and negative emotions create incoherent frequencies. By learning to shift negative emotions, we change the information in our heart field to a coherent one. This enables a major impact on ourselves and our environment: we become more sensitive to information coming towards us.

Love is known to harmonise all bodily functions. It makes us feel safe, reduces our stress levels and opens us up. It also provides us with an endless source of energy, happiness, creativity, stamina, resourcefulness and a willingness to step into the unknown. As you will see in part II, the state of love is a state of high energy and frequency. It's a state you love to be in!

You can access this state at will anytime. Just close your eyes and think of someone you love, someone who puts a smile on your face, or your favourite spot in nature. Can you feel it? A beautiful piece of music can get you there too. When working with (large) groups, we usually start with music. It is amazing how classical cello or violin music, for instance, Bach's Air on a G string (played live), instantly connects people to their heart. Even in a large group at the end of a long day in the middle of a major reorganisation. The shift is instantaneous.

Heart-brain harmonisation is also the hotline to our subconscious. Just like the brain, the heart has its own brain cells, called sensory neurites, or the little brain in the heart. The heart's brain learns, thinks, remembers and communicates independently from the brain in our head. There is continuous communication between both brains, with the communication from the heart to the brain exceeding that from the brain to the heart by far. The brain then responds by sending a physical, hormonal response.

> *The quality of emotional signals from our heart determines what chemicals, such as cortisol or serotonin, the brain releases.*

We may, however, not (yet) recognise this language, as we are so conditioned to see the world through our brain. When we harmonise heart and brain it gives us access to our extended neural network. *This extended neural network is precisely what sets us apart from all other forms of life.* It gives access to really fast information recall, extraordinary intuition and empathy, as well as provides access to our deepest knowing.

Heart-brain Coherence [24]

This simple 3 minute exercise allows us to access our extended neural network. This ancient act is the key to personal resilience. Its benefits last up to 6 hours.

1 *Shift your awareness from your mind to your heart.* Place your hand on your heart centre. Your awareness will follow this touch. This signals your body that you are turning your attention inwards.

2 *Slow down your breathing.* As a guideline, think 5 seconds on the inhale and 5 on the exhale. This sends a signal to your body that you are safe, and it allows your body to let go of stress. It awakens the healing chemistry.

3 *Focus on feeling.* Feel one or a combination of the following: care, appreciation, gratitude or compassion. These four keywords will trigger the experience between your heart and brain that creates coherence.

It is said by indigenous people that for us as humans to come full centre, we must travel from our brain (polarity) to our heart (unity). It is our heart that is designed to connect us with our everyday world and beyond. Thus far, however, we have been used to viewing and relating to the world via our brain.

As a metaphor, we offer you the Sufis' view of how heart, soul, and mind cooperate. The Sufis view the soul as the queen or king of your heart. In their view, your soul is meant to take the decisions in your life. Your heart is the throne room of your soul; it's your ability to feel. The mind is the servant, whose job it is to guard the door to the heart.

In most of our lives, painful things have happened that instilled fear within us. Trying to protect us, our mind then locks the door to our heart bit by bit. Sadly, however, when your heart is closed, it's as if your spirit is asleep. What we need to learn, is to give our mind permission to open the door to the heart, to feel again. In that way you can reawaken your soul and regain that deeper intimate connection. This leads to freedom from fears, and avoidance of the negative patterns of childhood that no longer serve you.

---

24 The HeartMath Institute and Greg Braden.

How do you know if your heart is open? To experience presence and a deep connection in your heart, you have to let go of control and allow yourself to be released from fear and into being open to experience everything that surrounds you.

The next visualisation may help you experience that living in connection and love, instead of trapped in fear, is the way to be open to receive what is. This practice creates neuroplasticity. In other words, letting in the new creates new neural pathways, replacing the old pattern of fear with pleasure.

Heart Meditation

1 Make yourself comfortable. Close your eyes. Put your hands on your heart. Take a deep breath. On the inhale: feel you're opening that door to your heart, tell your mind it's OK, it's safe. On the exhale: let go of expectations or fears.

2 Take another deep breath. Inhale and receive the present moment and the feeling of being connected with everything around you. Feel the beauty of it. Exhale and let go of expectations or fears.

3 One more time, take a deep inhale and see if your heart can open a little more to this present connection and intimacy. And exhale: let go.

Practice this for as long as feels good and sit with it for a while. Take a moment and feel how much more open your heart has become. Feel how good it is and allow yourself to relax into the feeling of being vulnerable, to let go even though you can't control everything. Feel what it's like to be more creative and expansive. To be in touch with the right side of the brain and open to new experiences. To truly connect to yourself.

To experience presence and deep connection in your heart, you have to let go of control and allow yourself to be released from fear into the experience of the love and beauty that surround you.

Take a moment and ask yourself: is there a place or a relationship (in your private or professional life) where there is a blockage, a blockage preventing you from opening your heart? Where did it come from? Was there a moment that you shut down your heart and your mind locked the door to your heart to protect you?

Perhaps you feel that you're now ready to wake up because your soul wants more. That awakening process means waking up to your heart, senses and the now. It's about starting to live life in technicolor where you now might still be living in black and white, in fear, afraid of experiencing openness and of your power as human being.

You can do this visualisation every day to build up your intimacy muscle. You see, your heart is a muscle; it can be trained. When you find yourself angry, irritable or reactive, take a moment and apply this practice. Notice its effect on you. Reconnecting to your heart moves you out of a frozen place. Reconnecting to your heart means rebalancing and rejuvenating by reducing stress and learning to self-regulate emotions.

Living a heart-centred life provides you also with the qualities of connection and compassion. The essence of heart-centred consciousness. When consciousness drops down to the heart, it becomes apparent that emotions are the language of our soul.

The Gut

Think of a situation where you had facts, reason, and logic on your side, and you believed there was absolutely no way the other person could say no to your proposal. Nonetheless, she dug in her heels and refused. She wasn't convinced by the logic. She had a gut feeling. See, decision-making isn't logical, it's emotional, according to the latest findings in neuroscience [25].

This voice of the gut is called by different names. Some call it instinct, while others prefer intuition. What your gut really is, is the voice of your subconscious. Often the reason why your gut feeling is so strong, is because it's your subconscious tuning in to the right answer before your conscious brain kicks in.

This intuition can be seen as a turbo assessment of:
- *The past*: your experiences and knowledge, and also your fears,
- *Personal needs* and *preferences*: your beliefs, and how you want to feel,
- *The present*: feelings, choice of words, surroundings, and other people's signs.

---

25 Neuroscientist Damasio's groundbreaking discovery studied people with damage in the part of the brain where emotions are generated. He found they all couldn't make decisions. They could describe what they should be doing in logical terms, yet found it very difficult to make even simple decisions. The very point of choice is arguably always based on emotion.

The combination of these factors leads to a calculation of a likely best way forward. It's a knowing that is based on more elements than the rational mind can deal with at any one given moment.

In a simplified situation, take an elementary school level question like what equals 1 + 1. The answer flashes into your brain: 2. You don't need to think about this. At that moment, your subconscious brain arrived at the answer to the problem instantly.

However, since the gut is related to the subconscious, you may imagine that it may also give you reactions based on outdated information. Think of fears or beliefs you picked up about the world when you were very young, that do not reflect the current reality or who you want to be. For example, you meet a new colleague at work. His behaviour reminds you somewhat of the scapegoat in your family. Although you are not conscious of this at all, you will meet this new colleague from a place of distrust. As Anaïs Nin said: *"We don't see the world as it is, we see it as we are."*

The more you realise who you are, shadows and all, the clearer the lens through which you view the world, the more free you are. This is why we place so much emphasis on this, making more of the subconscious conscious on the journey to Personal Mastery: we have addressed this separately in Part III: Letting Go.

The gut houses not only the aspects of you that are below the waterline, like fears and beliefs (think of the iceberg metaphor), it is also the birthplace of creation. Can you imagine that the more familiar you are with your subconscious, the more free you are, the more creative? It allows you to be more open to the emerging future!

What is this gut feeling about, is there any proof behind it? Yes, there is! Physiologically, the enteric nervous system is the reason why you can sense danger. It is a "Spidey sense" governed by your stomach, gut instincts and the like. The stomach sends the signals of this intuitive sense to the brain in your head. According to Dr. Michael Gershon [26], this intuition has no consciousness, it just is.

So how does it come about? Developmentally, the neurites in your stomach, heart, and brain originate from the same material. Starting from the same tissue at the moment that the embryo starts developing, the brain and neurites in the heart and stomach take separate roads of development. They split to govern separate areas of

---

26 Dr. Michael Gershon is the author of 'The Second Brain' and Chairman of the Department of Anatomy and Cell Biology at Columbia University.

the body. This is where the material changes to form the brain, the central nervous system, the heart's brain, or sensory neurites and the gut's brain; the enteric nervous system. Both the brain in our heart and our gut remember, think, and process independently from the brain in our head.

This means that the neurites in the gut are also part of the extended neural network we discussed earlier under The Heart on page 63. The interesting aspect of this split revolves around the *vagus nerve*. The vagus nerve connects the three nervous systems. Through this connection, the brain, heart and gut share neurotransmitters and hormones.

As the discovery of the brains in the heart and the gut is relatively recent (some twenty years ago), science is still relatively young on this subject. What is known, is that the gut contains a system made up of some 100 million neurons. This is more than in the spinal cord or the peripheral nervous system. The nascent field of neurogastroenterology is still discovering why we have this complex neurological system in our linings. However, with all this in place, it is no wonder that our gut is one of our primary stress containers.

So what to do about the situation with the colleague that we just touched upon? If you catch yourself and notice your behaviour (ah yes, it takes awareness!), it may help to do a so called 'inquiry' [27]. This could go along the following lines:

Inquiry

Sit down, take a couple of deep breaths and bring your attention to your body. Ask yourself: What is going on here?

A potential answer may be: *'I feel anxious and unsafe in his company.'*
What makes you feel that way? *'The way he looks at me.'*
How does that feel? *'I feel a pit in my stomach.'*
Do you recognise this feeling? *'He reminds me of my volatile nephew.'*

Can I accept this feeling?

---

27 Inspired by the Inquiry method (see footnote 21).

With that, you might be able to look at the new colleague afresh and open, without the undue emotional load. Inquiry is a wonderful tool for deepening your knowledge of yourself, and cultivating your growth.

"All things found in the world and beyond are illusions created by one's own concepts. Grasping at them further distorts perception. Give up grasping and see things as they are."
— DALAI LAMA

Before we explore the mind, we need to be clear about what it is, as there is no one singular definition. Sometimes it's referred to as the seat of human consciousness as if it were separate from the body, but it is more than that.

In some traditions it's viewed as the totality of information that is processed by the brain and the nervous system. It is the 'I' that experiences sensations, thoughts and feelings, and holds beliefs. It is, therefore, using the earlier iceberg metaphor, all that is present below the waterline.

Our current time of chaos, unprecedented change and aggression, is creating tremendous fear and fragmentation. Fear puts us straight into survival-based reactions. Particularly when we're stressed, our mind 'flips' to busy mind or 'monkey mind.' Meaning, our thinking and opinions take over, and we contract. As we've seen before however, the ideal situation is to remain expanded. It's the route to feeling space, clarity, ease, and freedom from patterns, beliefs and negative emotions.

Through our work and our own journeys, we have experienced the benefits of both Eastern philosophy and practices, as well as Western scientific developments in neuroscience. By synthesising East and West we aim to provide you with an awareness of the workings of the mind and a choice of rituals and practices you can try.

Practices to calm and centre the mind
Well-known practices are meditation, mindfulness, and reflection. The benefits of these are:

- The ability to hold many things in your awareness,
- The ability to detect subtleties,
- The ability to detect constructive themes.

Meditation implies becoming familiar with and guiding your mind. It enables you to take the position of the 'observer,' freeing you of the drama of the mind. It de-excites the nervous system. We meditate to relax, rest and get better at life!

Below, and in our Reinventing Toolbox from page 193 you'll find several practices.

Throughout history, meditation has played a role in various religious and spiritual practices. The most well-known among them are the increasingly popular Buddhist Practices.

One such Buddhist based movement is the Tibetan Shambhala tradition [28], taking its name from a legendary kingdom famous for being an enlightened society. This tradition was brought to the West by Chögyam Trungpa Rinpoche. He fled Tibet in the early 1960s to help reduce the current aggression in the West, and aid the transition to a more enlightened society by awakening our potential.

Shambhala is about practising fundamental goodness, seeing it in others and in yourself. According to Shambhala, you accomplish this by achieving mastery of your mind [29], realising it's your mind that creates your heaven or your hell.

It implies *you need a mental discipline*, through regular (daily) mediation, where you allow yourself simply space to be. This space enables you to start to see the passing nature of thoughts and emotions, to let go of drama and train yourself to embody your fundamental goodness: the ocean of calm beneath the chaos.

The following practice is a meditation meant to expand your personal space. The Inner Smile Meditation helps balance and integrate your sympathetic and para-sympathetic nervous systems, promoting health, resilience, and vitality. It can be used as a pick-me-up anytime and makes for a great start of the day. It takes you to that place inside where it is calm and clear and where it simply feels great!

---

28 Today, the global Shambhala network (200 centers in over 50 countries) brings together people of all ages and walks of life who are interested in exploring their own minds, transforming their experience, and *awakening their potential as humans.*

29 Sakyong Mipham, son of Chögyam Trungpa and current Shambhala leader, wrote *'Ruling your World'* about this.

Inner Smile Meditation [30]

1 Sit or lie down in a quiet place. Relax, close your eyes, and let your breath come to its natural rhythm. If you doze off during meditation that's OK!

2 Connect with something beautiful in nature: the sun, a tree or the sea... go to your favourite spot. This may bring you a deep sense of unity with all there is. You can use the memory of this experience to evoke your core values. Make sure you are alone there. Feel the beauty and abundance of this spot around you, but also in your body. Feel, see, hear, smell and taste the quality of this spot. Very often a sense of space and rest will appear, as well as a colour sometimes. Often people see a golden yellow, but any other or no colour is just fine as well.

3 Let the light of this spot come together in a cloud or spiral in front of your face, and let it enter your skin. You can hold your hands there, and use these to let the light flow through your body. Hold your hands in front of the spot where the smile is directed. Focus particularly at a point between and above your eyebrows (third eye [31]).

4 Feel how the light enters your skin and permeates deeper into your tissues. Let it flow from your face through your throat to your heart. Feel how your heart reacts when the light, together with your loving smile, enters there. Take your time and let your entire chest area fill itself with this light. Enjoy the space and the abundance of energy. Then, let the accumulated energy, together with your smile, flow to your stomach area, down through your belly and finally to your entire pelvis. Make sure you remain in connection with the abundance of nature that you connected with earlier.

5 At the end of this meditation, let the light and energy come together in one spot deep in your belly, behind your belly button, in a concentrated ball of energy. The energy you have gathered can be used later for things you value, such as work, leadership, health or loved ones.

---

30 In the Taoist tradition, each person assumes responsibility for their emotions, regardless of what triggered them. It transforms emotions by transforming the associated physiological systems.

31 The third eye is your ability to see what might be, to see potential. Everyone has access to this. For example, when you have a hunch and act on it, you've used your third eye. It is a sense you can develop to be more refined and accurate than just a hunch.

Mindfulness is a specialised meditation introduced by Dr. Jon Kabat-Zinn [32] to his terminally ill patients. It brings the focus of attention to the present. It creates an awareness of the bodymind cooperation. In essence, it's a way of bringing total awareness to what you do in the moment. For example: when practising mindful eating, you truly see, smell, and taste the food. Try, and enjoy the difference!

The following *Mountain Meditation* [33] is a mindfulness practice to remind you of your stability and strength. If you find you resonate in some way with the strength and stability of the mountain in your sitting, it may be helpful to use it from time to time as a reminder of the unwavering core stability inside you.

Tip:
Record yourself reading below instructions so you can replay, and relax into the experience.

Mountain Meditation

1 Sit comfortably, with your whole body relaxed, and let your breath come to its natural rhythm.
2 Imagine yourself sitting in a field or on a hill across from a beautiful mountain. In your mind, allow the image to form the most magnificent mountain you have ever seen or can imagine, letting it gradually come into greater focus... and even if it doesn't come as a visual image, allowing the sense of this mountain and feeling; its overall shape, lofty peak(s) high in the sky, the large base rooted in the earth, it's steep or gently sloping sides... Notice how massive it is, how solid, how unmoving, how beautiful, whether from afar or up close. Perhaps your mountain has a snow blanket on its top and trees reaching down to the base, or rugged granite sides... there may be streams and waterfalls cascading down the slopes... there may be one peak or a series of peaks. There might be meadows and high lakes.
3 Now, imagine that your body becomes one with the energy of the mountain; like it's taking that on. Your hips and legs become the solid, grounded foundation; the base of the mountain, deeply rooted in the floor or your seat. Your torso the slopes and the body of the mountain, being lifted through the spine

---

32 The American Dr. Jon Kabat-Zinn is the man who brought mindfulness to the West. He was the first to translate lessons from the Buddha and other wise lessons from the East in an accessible way, he also did scientific research around them.
33 Slight adaptation of Jon Kabat-Zinn's Mountain Meditation.

so that your head and neck become like tall peaks, supported by the rest of the body. With every breath, become a little more like a mountain; steady and stable, grounded yet tall, still and beautiful.

4   When you think of this mountain, you will notice that as the days, months and years go by, 'life' happens around the mountain. Seasons change: in spring, it might be covered with trees and flowers; in summer, with sunshine and grass, and in winter it might be completely covered in snow. There may be violent storms on the mountain, blizzards, glaring sunshine, people and animals coming to visit it... but see how the mountain itself, its core and foundation, do not change. None of the outside occurrences matter to the mountain, which always remains its essential self. All of the outside changes come, and go. They are not permanent. The only thing that is permanent is the mountain itself.

5   In the same way, in our lives and meditations, we can learn to experience these principles in our self. We can connect to the part of us that is grounded and does not change, regardless of whatever life throws at us. We can connect to the stillness that is always inside, through both stormy days and sunshine.

6   As you sit here, take a moment to feel your sense of grounding and stability, keeping this feeling as your anchor.

7   Then gently bring your attention back to your breath and your surroundings. Move your fingers and toes a little bit... maybe stretch out your arms over-head and take a big stretch... and when you're ready, open your eyes...

By attuning to the mountain in our meditation practice, we can link up with its strength and stability and adopt them for our own. It can help us to see that our thoughts, feelings, and worries are a bit like the weather on the mountain. They too come and go while the essence of who we are stays the same.

Reflection is learned silence: the more quiet you become, the more you can hear! It's a core activity of consciousness: a perspective flowing back and forth between the heart and the mind. *Through reflection, we give meaning to our feelings and may discover the truth.* It's like the silence in between the notes in music. Reflection helps us realise our purpose.

We also want to provide you with awareness of the workings of the brain and the nervous system, our physical aspects processing our daily information and inter-actions. To be free, it's important to be conscious of how these systems work as they have a huge impact on us!

So, how does the brain work?

"To understand ourselves, we have to understand our animal nature first.
It's important to remember that the game we play is a shared one.
It's called survival: 'I want it all, and I want it now' is the brain speaking.
The psychological instincts of the predator, parasite or scavenger
are present in our history and blood.
They will not go away, which means there is no point in turning a blind eye to them.
We are all, in our own subtle ways, manipulators and con men, and we
all own a little bit of the beggar too. We too are territorially and materially acquisitive.
We are pathetic, but also wonderful.
And when we know this, when we recognise our inflation, or the scavenger, the con men
and the road-rage creature within us, then we can learn how to say yes or no to them."

— IAN MCCALLUM [34] — *ECOLOGICAL INTELLIGENCE*

The evolution of the brain physically reflects the different stages of our human evolution and modes of decision-making. Evolutionary development has resulted in three smaller brains in our head; the *Triune Brain* [35]. This is made up of the Reptilian Brain, the Limbic Brain, and the Neocortex.

- The *Reptilian* region, is oriented towards base level survival,
- The *Limbic* system is the emotional centre of the brain,
- The *Neocortex* is responsible for higher-level and future forward thinking, reasoning, and free will.

The reptilian brain and the limbic brain are ready and formed before the age of 7. The neocortex comes into play later. Thus, all experiences happening before the age of 7 will be categorised by either the reptilian or the limbic brain, meaning the beliefs we have built up in that period are governed by instincts and emotions rather than ratio. Hence, they may interpret certain situations completely different than realistically would be appropriate (see Part III).

---

34 Ian McCallum is a psychiatrist, author and wilderness guide. 'The Earth doesn't need healing. We do. It is our task to rediscover ourselves in Nature. It is an individual choice. We either continue to believe that someone or something else will rescue us, show us the easy way, or even take the hard path on our behalf, or we choose the opposite – we take it upon ourselves.'

35 The theory of the *triune brain* is proposed by neuroscientist Paul MacLean, who correlated human behavioural manifestations – actions, emotions, and thoughts – with the physiological structures inherent in the brain.

1   *Reptilian brain: sensory brain*
The first brain to develop is found in all living creatures. It's located in the deepest section of the brain, underneath the larger brain mass.

It looks after our survival, regulates autonomous body functions, and makes decisions based on survival instincts: survival of the creature and the species. *Protect* is its motto: so, fight – flight – or freeze response. It's *linked to the sympathetic nervous system* which, when in danger, shuts down many functions simply to prepare us to fight or flee. In the meantime, we are flooded with stress hormones as a consequence of direct stimulus-response, resulting in competition, aggression, domination, procreation, and the desire to hoard resources. Actions instigated by instincts precede thoughts. *Get out of danger now* is the message!

2   *Limbic brain: the emotional brain*
The second brain to develop is found in all mammals. It sits on top of the reptilian brain, just above the brain stem. Comprised of the hippocampus, hypothalamus, and the amygdala, its function is to generate and regulate the flow of chemicals and their interactions that create our emotions.

This area *is about resonance, regulation, and rewiring*, meaning that: we emotionally attune to those around us (resonance), we have the ability to affect the mood of our context (regulation), and our emotional patterns may be altered either by being around people with healthy emotional patterns, or by consciously retraining them through neuroplasticity (rewiring), see below.

The decisions that the limbic brain makes about survival are based on subconscious beliefs, generated by emotions linked to personal memories. Functions include security and safety in a social context.

The limbic system acts as a buffer between our thoughts and actions: our emotions generate feelings within our physiology that make us aware of the impact of our actions on others. As with the reptilian brain, emotionally driven decisions precede thought.

When the amygdala is triggered, it activates our sympathetic nerve system. We act as if we were one of our ancestors chased by a lion, and are flooded with stress hormones. These days we're rarely subject to life-threatening moments, rather we are confronted with daily stressors such as not being able to answer a boss's unexpected request (freeze reaction), or mentally checking out of a meeting (flight reaction).

In the West, we are so identified with the mind that we are emotionally quite illiterate and immature. Children and animals have a much bigger somatic awareness of their emotional states and that of others. However, we too can regain this skill and learn to integrate this and refine our body's ability.

> *Part of this transformation is growing up emotionally so that we become much more attuned to this resonance, be it inner (relating to ourselves) or outer (relating to our context). This often still happens unconsciously. Developing this area has huge potential as positive resonance creates implicit trust.*

Imagine being fully able to be who you are and bringing that into relationships and life, effortlessly attracting that which you want! See Part II, the Law of Radiance and Attraction.

3 Neocortex: the mentalising brain

The third and most significant section to develop is the most advanced and ramified (memory-containing) area of the brain of humans and higher-order mammals. Physiologically, it sits above the limbic, and reptilian brain and it accounts for the largest area and mass of the whole brain.

It makes decisions based on the conscious beliefs of the society and culture you grew up in. Its main function is to process information using logic and reasoning. But it also encompasses reason, art, music, science, creativity, language, and a host of other skills and traits that define us as humans. The neocortex gets involved in decision-making after the actions generated by instincts (reptilian brain), and emotions (limbic) have been triggered, and the fear associated with them has gone.

The neocortex is designed to function as *the executive control centre* of the brain, and its proper functioning serves to regulate the activities taking place in both the reptilian and limbic brains.

How do these command-and-control functions work?

The neocortex is structurally divided into two halves, the left and right brain hemispheres. Dr. Jill Bolte Taylor, a neuro-anatomist gave us major insight into the workings of the two brain halves after she experienced a stroke. She describes her findings as follows:

"We are the life-force power of the universe, with manual dexterity and two cognitive minds. *Our right hemisphere is about now. It learns kinaesthetically through the movement of our bodies, and thinks in pictures.* Information, in the form of energy, streams in simultaneously through all of our sensory systems, and then it explodes into this enormous collage of what this present moment looks, smells, tastes, feels, and sounds like. I and we are energy-beings connected to one another through the consciousness of our right hemispheres as one human family.

Our left hemisphere thinks linearly and methodically and is about the past and future. It is designed to take that enormous collage of the present moment, and start picking out details, and more details about those details. Our left hemisphere organises all information and associates it with all we've ever learned, and projects options into the future. It thinks in language. It's that on-going brain chatter that connects me and my internal world to my external world. It says *I am.* With that, I become separate, a single individual, separate from the energy flow and you."

So, you need balance between the two hemispheres to ensure you can tap into both your rational brain and your creative brain. Particularly in case of stress. A good way to activate/connect to the creative part of the brain at the start of the day is to take in a thing of beauty, music, poetry or art. Any form of art that touches you.

Communication patterns

Did you know that the various layers of your brain do not communicate with each other due to different dialogue patterns? It's important to understand that:

- The *reptilian* brain asks for safety and attunement,
- The *limbic* brain asks for resonance and relationship,
- The *neocortex* asks for framework and understanding.

Although we have all three brain parts, often the circuits in two brain parts are dominant. *These preferences underlie all our choices of communication and relating.*

It helps to know your preferred brain position, just as it helps to know your MBTI type [36]. For example: 'reptilian and limbic brain' people are very good at resonating and feeling, but excel less at language, which is the field of the cortex. When they work with a 'cortex' person they might misunderstand each other.

So what then drives our behaviour?

To successfully lead yourself and others, in-depth knowledge of human behaviour is a must. Recent social neuroscience research has turned general Western beliefs about our human design upside down. It shows that the vast majority of our behaviour and decision-making is determined even before thought hits our

---

36 The Myers–Briggs Type Indicator (MBTI) is an introspective self-report questionnaire.

conscious mind. Great news: it enables you to break free of belief systems that no longer serve you and instead use intention to direct your life (and organisations).

You really can reset yourself!
But how is our behaviour generated? Our behaviour is generated in three ways: instinct, patterns, and free will. These ways are linked to our different brain parts: the reptilian brain (instinct), our limbic brain (patterns), and our cortex (free will).

1 Instinct: having to do with survival and safety
As discussed in Evolution, the way humans live has undergone epic shifts, but is essentially shaped by our past on the African savannah. Safety, ease and a better future have driven our prefrontal cortex to continuously imagine ways to make life easier, causing us to evolve from tribal nomads to the global networkers we are today. It has made life a lot easier, however, has taken us far away from our human design: innovation has outpaced our adaptation capabilities. Time for an upgrade!

Neuroscience shows that instinct drives us much more than we are consciously aware of. Our instinctual behaviour is driven by the reptilian brain, which precedes thoughts. We are designed as social beings. Way back when this was critical for our survival: being cast out of the tribe meant that we were easy prey. *Thus, the brain's default position is sensing the emotional state of our context and those around us.* Mirror neurons pick up this mostly non-verbal information. We are also very sensitive to social cohesion. We are built to detect incongruence. *Our body is the biggest influencer of congruence.* Most people are not yet all that aware of their body language. However, *once we sense incongruence, we don't feel safe* and will act upon that.

So how does all this play out in the office? When people are stressed, instinctive reactions may result in powerplay like excluding relevant information, lowering other people's status (creating social threat) or name-dropping, or shrinking and withdrawing in case of someone more powerful. *These practices all erode trust.*

2 Learned patterns
The brain functions practically 99% on auto-response via patterns or instinct. Humans can learn and adapt to present circumstances. The neural resource we have with which to process all information on the spot is, however, very limited. Hence our brain is wired to recognise patterns to auto-respond wherever possible. Learned patterns, just like instinct, operate unconsciously. They are acquired over a lifetime and relate to our history. This functioning is governed by our limbic system.

Emotional patterns are the most pervasive patterns we have. Part III deals with these patterns: they shape our personality. They involve encoding of sensitive neural patterns developed in response to relational interactions and observations. They can lead us totally astray if dysfunctional. If we become aware of them, however, and release them, they provide a huge step to higher consciousness!

3   Free will
To put it very bluntly, despite our belief to the contrary, only roughly 1-5% of our daily decisions are made by free will; the rest is based on patterns or instinct. These patterned decisions are usually driven by survival, fear or ego. They lead to a contracted response.

So, you could reflect on your behaviour and ask yourself: how free am I? *Personal Mastery is being free to choose behaviour that serves you.*

The BodyMind connection

There is a new normal. The bodymind connection is one of great potential, and more is being discovered on a daily basis. Science is only beginning to grasp the complexity of our human and energy designs and their dynamics. We will see in part III that *our personality creates our reality.* Our thoughts, the language of our brain, and our feelings, that of our body, together determine our personality.

What if you could consciously create a new self, and leave behind the old self?

Science now helps to demystify what Eastern mystics have known for thousands of years, and enables us to apply it to our lives. So let's get right to the juice.

> *How can you apply this to your life? It demands a lifestyle choice. When you have memorised an internal state independent of your external environment, that's when you begin to master your life and your environment.*

As we saw, the brain is an artifact of the past: past events and external environments drive most people's biology. *What if your brain could become the pathway to the future?* See, the privilege of humans is that we have a frontal lobe. It is our creative centre, our workshop. When we consciously imagine our future, this part of the brain comes on line. This enables you to change your internal state independent of the outside world.

When we begin to wire new neurons, we literally change our mind (= the brain in action). Focusing on intention causes you to mentally rehearse a new future, it installs new hardware through neuroplasticity. You need to combine this with an elated emotion. This is because we may think something, but we can only accept, and remember the thoughts that are aligned with our emotional state. So when you can feel how wonderful this new self would be, you're teaching your body to reproduce it – creating the software. And when you rehearse both, your body knows it as well as your mind. Now it becomes subconscious programming.

All of this is underpinned by science. Various branches of science like quantum physics, neuroscience, neuro-immunology, neuro-endocrinology, and epigenetics, are all researching the bodymind connection. The most obvious physical representation of the bodymind connection is the vagus nerve, a sort of super highway connecting your body and your brain.

In the last 20 years, a number of important findings have been done, as we already saw: from neuroplasticity for rewiring the brain, to heart-brain coherence for tapping into our extended neural network, to the body housing two brains that communicate with the heart. To name but a few.

Some of the pioneers working at the intersection of these sciences and synthesising this knowledge are Ken Wilber (philosopher and mythic), Dr. Bruce Lipton (biologist and former professor of anatomy), Dr. Joe Dispenza (physician, neuro science) and Gregg Braden (scientist). All of them look into how to become the master of your life and destiny. The techniques we're describing in this part are taught by Dr. Joe Dispenza (and confirmed by the other scientists above).

Now all of this sounds great, but what if you're burdened by stress? Stress causes the brain and the heart to be incoherent (all of this is measurable). Stress causes people to contract and become energetically denser. It requires you to bring back balance to your life, for example by:

- *Physically* – bringing in yoga, aerobics and any kind of exercise or massage,
- *Chemically* – choosing a clean diet, easy to digest food and eliminating toxins,
- *Emotionally* – practising meditation and taking care of your energy and psyche.

When you meditate, you become more fluid, and the field around your body expands. All energy is frequency, and all frequency carries information. If you set an intention, you carry that with you in your field.

In short: commit to the discipline to choose the thoughts and emotions you want. Then install the neurological wiring in the brain. Create the right environment through proper instruction, and surrender to the present. Get your behaviour to match your intentions. Now you will experience a new emotion. This teaches your body chemically what your mind already understands. If you repeat it, you begin to neuro-chemically condition mind and body to work as one. When you repeat this often enough, it becomes a state of being.

The above follows some of the main principles of the universal laws (see Part II):

- We live in a field of energy, the quantum field. This field is pure consciousness.
- The quantum field responds not to what we want, but to who we are.
- Our consciousness notices everything. It observes, and is aware of our thoughts, dreams, behaviours, and desires. It 'observes' everything into physical form.
- Change requires coherence: aligning thoughts and feelings with action.

C. THE SOUL

"We are not human beings having a spiritual experience.
We are spiritual beings having a human experience."
— PIERRE TEILHARD DE CHARDIN

I Our soul is our Essence

Our soul is the aspect of us that resides both in the physical and in the spiritual world. Its main interest is fulfilling its purpose and growth in service of the evolution of consciousness. Its deepest desire is to know and experience our greatest potential. It's at ease with uncertainty, and it thrives on change. If you would follow your passion without (ego) fears, it's all you could be.

Our soul connects us to the quantum field. At the quantum level, everything is part of one universal energy field. It's the gateway for source or consciousness to enter. *Our soul is about meaning.*

Our ego is the part of us that wants to keep us safe. Connected to our body, it's driven by survival, relying on our senses and mind. It understands rules and regulations but cannot look beyond this lifetime. Scared of the unknown, it believes in limited time and scarcity. *Our ego is about control.*

As we've seen in Part I in the *Seven Levels of Consciousness*, these two aspects within us, soul and ego, both have their own needs, or as we call it in the case of the soul: desires. Note that we will only be able to fulfil our soul's desires if we have dealt with our ego's needs. Or as Bertolt Brecht [37] puts it: "Don't talk to me of my soul until you've filled my stomach."

We need Presence now!
At the deepest level, a true leader is the symbolic soul of a group [38]. Never before in history have we needed soulful leadership as much as we do now. Whereas our minds just notice the blinding chaos, our soul is awakening and sees the underlying order.

A lot has been written about the soul. Some of our world class teachers in that field are Deepak Chopra, Joseph Jaworski, Richard Barrett, and Alan Seale. Below their wisdom is synthesized.

As we saw earlier, the complexity of this time far exceeds the capacity of our mind. It's time to integrate our body and soul and embody soulful presence. It's up to us to create the future!

Soulful presence is your inner radiance, how you show up, the energy your 'being' creates, the amount of magnetising energy you exude that makes others join in your quest, the passion you display in following your dreams. It's your soul that enables magnetising presence.

Think about Nelson Mandela or the Dalai Lama. They live(d) from their purpose and were/are devoted to creating good for the whole. Everyone can feel that, and it's infectious: people want to join! When you are connected to your soul, your inner light and passion shine through you.

For developing true presence, therefore, you also need to connect with your soul. How do you begin to do this? You can do this by finding and living your purpose. When you find your purpose, commit to it by living your values and moving to a more transformational presence. Below we offer practices to help you get a feel for this.

So again, if you would just ask yourself: *Who am I?* And *What is my work?* What would you say? We could also pose the questions: what do you really want? What is your passion, what do you stand for and what are your values?

---

37 Bertolt Brecht (1898 - 1956), was a German poet, playwright, and theatre practitioner.
38 Deepak Chopra, *The Soul of Leadership*, Random House, 2011.

II Purpose – your real calling

"Your time is limited, so don't waste it living somebody else's life.
Don't be trapped by dogma – which is living with the results of others' thinking.
Don't let the voice of others drown out your own inner voice.
And most important, have the courage to follow your heart and intuition.
They somehow already know what you truly want to become."
– STEVE JOBS, STANFORD, 2005

What is your passion, your dream? What is your calling in life? What are your special talents? When you become silent and get into a conversation with yourself, you will find your purpose. Look at what you're good at, what makes you tick. Look at the people you love to surround yourself with. Listen to your body and notice what you respond to with enthusiasm and what makes you content.

Should this be relatively new to you, a good start could be to begin with creating your *Soul Profile*. Answer the following, be candid and intuitive and let first responses guide you.

Soul Knowledge [39]

1   What is my contribution in life?
2   What's the purpose in what I do?
3   How do I feel when I have a peak experience?
4   Who are my heroes and heroines?
5   What are the qualities I look for in a best friend?
6   What are my unique skills and talents?
7   What are the best qualities I express in a relationship?

Using keywords, write a brief profile of your soul as if you were describing another person. Keeping your Soul Profile at hand, move on the next step: defining your vision. Answer the following questions according to your own truth.

1   I want to live in a world in which...
2   I would be inspired to work in an organisation that...
3   I would be proud to lead a team that...
4   A transformed world would be...

To match your present work with your vision, answer the following:

1   How does your work in the world reflect the vision you outlined above?
2   What do you need (from your team or organisation) to get closer to your ideals?
3   What can you offer (to your team and organisation) to move it closer to your ideals?

Define your vision as specifically as possible to start bridging the gap. Clarify the world you envision and how you see yourself in it.

Lastly, create your mission statement. Merge your values and your vision into a statement of your overall life mission using the following template:
My mission behind everything I do is...

Keep it simple and concise, a child should be able to understand it.

---

39 Deepak Chopra, *The Soul of Leadership*, Random House, 2011.

III Values: who you aspire to be

"Everything can be taken from a man but one thing: the last of the human freedoms –
to choose one's attitude in any given set of circumstances, to choose one's own way."
— VIKTOR FRANKL FRANK

Your core values connect you to your soul. They enable you to create the future in the way *you* want to create. Deeply held values define who you *aspire* to be. They provide an inner compass that helps you to make the right choices and navigate both calm and stormy waters. They enable you to remain true to your Essence, no matter what. If you value love, let love inspire your actions and decisions. If you value integrity, let integrity inspire your actions and decisions.

Values are a method for classifying beliefs and behaviours that an individual or a group consider important. Richard Barrett [40] has provided a method to make values measurable, on a personal level, and a group level with teams or organisations.

What if you could fully create your own story to navigate life from a blank canvas, rather than from the beliefs instilled in you by your parents or culture? Who then do you want to be? What is meaningful to you? How do you want to contribute? How do you want to show up?

Values

How do you find your values? To give you an idea, possible values could be: accountability, balance, commitment, compassion, courage, discipline, enthusiasm, efficiency, ethics, excellence, fairness, friendship, honesty, humour, integrity, intuition, love, openness, respect, responsibility, trust, wisdom and health.

To connect to your values, think of your role model(s), who might be anyone from Mandela to Gandhi to your grandma, and think of why they seem like a role model to you. Pick three to five core values. What are the beliefs behind these values? And what behaviour do you show because of this? Then go out and connect with everyone and everything you come across, with those values in mind. If you find yourself in a difficult situation and one of your values is trust, for instance, remind yourself of that value, and ask: what would trust do here?

---

40 Richard Barrett's tools are one of the most detailed and comprehensive cultural diagnostics and values assessment instruments commercially available, to leaders, consultants, and coaches. They are designed to support building high-performance, value driven cultures.

IV Transformational Presence – coming online

"As for the future your task is not to foresee it, but to enable it."
— ANTOINE DE SAINT-EXUPÉRY

Transformational presence is described as *a state of being in which someone lives from a deep connection with their soul, their mission or purpose and their higher Consciousness.* This presence, defined by Alan Seale [41] creates an energetic space into which transformation is invited. It opens up to the greater potential that awaits at any moment. It implies holding a clear intention and creating the optimal circumstances for revealing the greatness of the other. It also means reserving space for exploring, opening wide to the continuous growth of knowledge and wisdom.

To develop a transformational presence, you need to have:

- Deep self-knowledge at soul level,
- Commitment to living by your purpose and values,
- Intuitive thinking,
- Insight in the laws of energy (see hereafter Part II, from page 107 onwards),
- Commitment and practice.

Now let's put it to work! Look back at the seven basic human needs we saw in Evolution, page 39.

Tune in with yourself and decide where you think you are at this point. Now that you are (more) aligned with your soul, purpose and values, how can you align soul and ego? You can also do this with a group, in which case the subtlety of carefully tuning in with all group members is of utmost importance. Address people where they are, remembering, basic needs come first.

Soul and ego: a partnership

Closing the gap...
All leading evolution theories agree that, at this point in history, we have arrived at

---

41 Alan Seale, *Create a World That Works* – Tools for Personal and Global Transformation, Weisser Books, 2011.

a crossroads involving the alignment of ego and soul, and the search for authentic and wholesome ways of being. Failure to do so threatens our survival as a species. Creating this alignment means that we are concerned with being true to ourself, and, at the same time with being of service to the world. This marks the next stage of human consciousness we're moving towards. As we saw in Evolution: we need to move from I to We.

To do so, you need to be concerned with questions of meaning and inner truth:

- Does this decision seem right, am I being true to myself?
- Is this in line with who I sense I'm called upon to become?
- Am I being of service to the world?

Popular recent business literature subscribes to this notion too. We learn this from the twelve organisations that Laloux points to in his book *Reinventing Organizations*. We see this in Jim Collins' great companies in *Good to Great* and the *Firms of Endearment* identified by Sisodia, Wolfe, and Seth. **All of these organisations are superior performers because they have soul.**

We have given the ego tremendous responsibilities, yet it's the soul that has the helicopter view, the bigger consciousness. It's the soul that should provide safety for the ego to take the next step in evolution.

The balance between soul and ego, however, can be delicate. Given the fact that your ego is the manifestor for your soul in the world, of course, the ego's survival needs come first. Once these conditions are met, however, we arrive at the desires of our soul. Do you recognise the thrill of taking a very big step – only to find yourself held back by your ego? The ego's total risk averseness and limited consciousness can cause it to freak out. How do you deal with this?

Aligning Body and Soul

In the West, we have mainly been focused on *doing* rather than *being* in almost all things, including education. Talking about soul and about energy isn't mainstream just yet. However, times are changing. In this transition period, there is a growing belief that it is the soul that will save mankind. Hence there is more openness and interest for the soul and its potential.

You could think of the axes of a cross to depict *the soul – the being* – as the vertical axis and *the ego – the doing* – as the horizontal axis. The vertical axis connects you to all of your being, meaning: you are grounded and inspired, and you are aligned with body, mind, emotions, heart, and soul. You could think of this axis as a column of light.

You can imagine that any action taken from such place of being online is authentic, totally reflects who you are and therefore highly magnetic.

The following practice will help you get a feel for this.

Aligning Body and Soul: coming online

To align yourself with your being, bring your attention to your breath. Feel your central column by making contact with the earth (grounding your body) and connecting with the crown of your head (making contact with your soul). Now imagine a column of energy (or light) spiralling from your crown to your feet. Stay in this visualisation until you feel a solid column of vibrating energy from top to toe.

This vertical alignment brings you in contact with your innate powers. It aligns your inspiration with your head, heart, and intuition (gut). It brings all aspects of your being, your thoughts, beliefs, intentions, and perspectives, in alignment with your Essence. It also puts you in contact with your soul's mission. When you are aligned vertically, you will feel centred and grounded, full of trust, full of energy and full of inspiration. You have come online!

When you have found your vertical connection, move from there into the horizontal for action, the doing. Taking your innate powers and aligning all aspects of your being into the action that needs to be taken, being totally present. This vertical axis and horizontal axis overlap at the heart, there soul and ego come together and align.

Remember: the deeper your consciousness on the vertical, the more alignment with all aspects of yourself, the emerging potential, consciousness and energy, the bigger your impact and influence on the horizontal plain.

So what does embodying presence feel and look like?
Embodied presence requires awareness and alignment of your total being. Below we have addressed in Ken Wilber's Integral Quadrant what this means. The quadrant depicts the individual and the group on the horizontal axis and the interior and the exterior on the vertical axis. When people are aligned on an individual level, there is personal and mission alignment. When there is alignment within the group and with the person as well, we speak of structural and value alignment.

'I' is your interior as an individual, 'It' is your exterior, or your behaviour. 'We' is the interior of a group or team you're part of, and 'Its' the group behaviour:

I

Embodied Self-Awareness

- Overall body and posture awareness
- Embodied state awareness
- Health awareness

- Breath awareness

- Mood and emotion awareness

- Activity / rest cycle
- Awareness of personal and transpersonal intuition

- Awareness of purpose
- Awareness of values

It

Embodied Self-Management

- Body and postural adjustment (right posture)
- Embodied state management
- Movement itself (flexibility, strength, speed, grace)
- Breath adjustment (e.g., deep 'belly' breathing)
- Mood (embodied disposition) management
- Activity / rest cycle management
- Accessing and managing personal and transpersonal intuition through felt sense (e.g., focusing)
- Purpose
- Value management

We

Embodied Social Awareness

- Social body awareness (aware-ness of others, individuals and group moods)
- Social attentional awareness

- Somatic assessment (evaluating alignment)
- Group mood awareness (used by performers)
- Empathy (via mirror neurons)

- Felt intuitive sense of others (via unconscious mirroring)

- Awareness of group purpose
- Awareness of group values

Its

Embodied Social Connection and Influence

- Non-verbal mimicking, leading and rapport building

- Resonance and connection somatic counts transference
- Direct somatic intervention, e.g., postural alignment
- Interruption of unconscious mirroring (closing conflict cycles)
- Establishing an empathic and emotional connection
- Leadership and emotional impact (charisma, presence, gravitas)
- Protective use of force
- Trust building (especially sincerity)
- Living group purpose
- Living group values

"It's not the load that breaks you down; it's the way you carry it."
— LOU HOLTZ

In our time, stress is virtually a daily given. We are bombarded with information and requests since technology opened up the world to us. The pressure is on 24/7. How do our bodies respond?

Brain hijack

In case of stress, the amygdala is triggered; it activates our fight-flight system or sympathetic nerve system. Control is diverted from our cortex to our reptilian brain. We are flooded with stress hormones that are released to prepare us for gross muscular movement. *Our neocortex can think but it cannot produce behaviour.* Our brain hijacks us. We feel as if there is no choice!

We simply are not equipped for the arousal we face to date! Our stress neuro response was designed to save us from episodic, rapid physical danger, by flooding us with adrenalin and cortisol so we could either fight, flight or run. These days, however, with social threats virtually a daily presence, our bodies physiologically still react as if we could be eaten at any given moment. Thus, as we live with a continuous sensory overload, we're also continuously flooded with hormones, which we're not able to release from our bodies easily. *We have to find ways to consciously deal with this and enable ourselves and our bodies to relax!*

So how can we act from our core, a place of calm, regardless of the circumstances? The main options are: connecting to our body, connecting to our breath or connecting to our mind. Below we provide practices to help you unwind, and relax via the body, the breath, and the mind.

1 Connecting to the body

The key to managing your state of mind and stress level lies in your ability to activate the calming parasympathetic pathways of your nervous system on command. Typically, this cannot be controlled at will, but it can be regulated via the body: via centre, breath, and grounding or gravity.

You know now that your body enables you to make decisions from a deeper knowing, and that you can learn to trust your feelings about the present. But how do you tap into this inner knowing when you feel overwhelmed?

> We need an environment where the principles of grounding, centring, and contact, are learned through the body. This provides us with a solid foundation from which to operate. We also need experiences to get familiar with our inner knowing. It will enable us to show up in a way that is true to ourselves and true to our purpose, and will provide us with a solid foundation to deal with stress and transition in everyday life. In short: we need new rituals to replace the patterns no longer serving us.

On page 58 discussing the body, we've described centring as a basic practice. Below, we suggest how you can relate to others from your centre. Remember: your centred self or Essence has access to energy reserves and resources unavailable to your ego. This is because Essence is open and vulnerable, whereas ego needs a lot of contraction and energy to keep certain parts hidden. Ego also has an element of control with regard to other people's reactions, which takes up lots of energy. Being open and going with the flow, Essence is connected to the whole, collective intelligence, and creativity.

So how do you keep confidence in the midst of upheaval? Fully connecting with others, professionally or personally, fully entering into a relationship, often without knowing where it might go? What happens when you get pushed, literally or metaphorically so? How do you come back to centre?

Each of us has a unique combination of control, safety and approval postures, and behaviour patterns: a postural stress signature if you will. Knowing this helps to be able to shift back to centre easily. The practice described here may give you some valuable somatic information as to how you react when pushed:

Stress posture (discover your personal pattern) [42]

1 Stand so that you and your partner are facing each other.
2 Extend your arms forward.
3 Ask your partner to take hold of your fore arms slightly above your wrists.
4 Ask your partner to quickly apply light pressure (push you) and sustain it.
5 Notice where and how your body constricts, or puts up a boundary in an attempt to keep the pressure from entering into your personal space.
6 Survey three areas of your body:
   - Head and neck,
   - Chest and arms,
   - Abdomen, hips and legs.
7 Notice and reflect on the position of your head, heart, and centre opposite a partner. Try to discover what moved forward, backward and what you withdrew. Many variations are possible. You may step aside (flight), you may focus on the head to try and control things with the mind. You may also push back (fight), or you may freeze. Or...

When we work with this exercise, people are amazed at how accurately the body shows your stress tendency! Knowing your natural stress signature enables you to make a change should you desire so. You may choose for more space for instance, or choose to stay in your centre or connection. It's an insightful and fun exercise you can use in any situation, at work, but also with your family!

A fundamental Aikido practice that empowers us during a crisis is *blending*. In case of an attack, blending ensures that the attacked works with the motion and force of the aggressor's attack, thus redirecting the energy. We ensure we see the viewpoint from the attacker's point of view. We've included a blending exercise here:

---

42 Wendy Palmer and Janet Crawford, *Leadership Embodiment* – How the Way we Sit and Stand Can Change the Way we Think and Speak, CreateSpace, 2013.

Blending [43]

1 Stand about ten metres away from your partner, and have him begin walking directly toward you.
2 When he is about one metre away, step to the side, allowing him to continue his walk.
3 As he passes, begin walking next to him.
4 As you walk next to your partner, see if you can enter into, and blend with his rhythm, speed, and length of stride.
5 Blend as deeply as possible with your partner; breathe the same way, swing your arms the same way, take on the attitude of the walk. Is it aggressive, timid, relaxed?
6 Try to blend with your partner so thoroughly that you begin to feel what it is to be this person. So deeply, that you can feel yourself in their skin.

Grounding
Grounding connects us to the earth and gravity and enables us to let go. Grounding ourselves through our legs gives us a sense of being 'carried,' of security. The *Standing like a Tree* practice that teaches this can be found on page 60.

2 Connecting to the breath
Another very powerful tool is connecting to the breath [44]. The breath is, of course, a vital conduit of life force. The breathing process is governed by the autonomic nervous system.

> *Stress causes our breath to become higher up in the body. It also becomes more shallow, shorter and less complete. Meaning, we don't inhale to full capacity, and, very importantly, we don't exhale to full capacity either. The issue with incomplete exhales is that this causes a chemical imbalance within our bloodstream which is akin to a slightly diluted version of hyperventilation. This in and of itself causes the body to feel as if there is a stressful situation going on, creating a vicious cycle of increased stress. In the long run, it can lead to a frazzled nervous system and potentially burn-out.*

43 Richard Strozzi-Heckler, *The Anatomy of Change* – A Way to Move through Life's Transitions, North Atlantic Books, 1997.
44 By Anne Rose van Ooijen, psychologist, yoga teacher, and holistic coach.

In essence, the feedback system of the breath is a two-way stream. Automatic signals from the body can cause the breath to change, influencing the way we feel, and creating a positive or negative spiral.

It's possible to consciously influence our nervous system by managing our breath and making deep relaxed breathing a regular practice. In this case, the nervous system takes cues from our deliberate actions and we can begin to reverse any negative spiral or damage that stress has created.

One of the most important factors in using the breath to relax is **deep belly breathing**. When we are in a calm state, our breath fills the whole lungs and expands the belly on the inhale. When we exhale, the belly softens back down. Often people experience the exact opposite, due to being so accustomed to stress and maintaining a posture where the abdomen is constantly being pulled in. They experience the belly going in and the chest puffing up on the inhale, and the belly expanding on the exhale.

Breathing Practices

A very easy way to begin to *deliberately deepen and slow down your breath* is by trying to expand the belly on the inhale, then feel it relax naturally on the exhale. Continue with this for a few full breath cycles, or, if you have the time, take 5 or 10 minutes to breath this way. Preferably, this would be made into daily practice. Doing this a couple of times a day will create a shift in making this way the new norm for your body and mind, and counterbalance the effects of stress and shallow breathing.

Another powerful way to relax is by *expanding the exhale to last longer than the inhale*. A simple exercise is to breathe in for 5 seconds and then exhale for 7. The point is to have the exhale last at least 2 seconds longer than the inhale. While exhaling, focus on completely and fully emptying the lungs.

What this does, is send a signal to the nervous system that you are safe, and that it is time to relax. For this reason it's a perfect exercise to do in the evening, after work or even right before bed while already lying down. Follow this way of breathing for 5 to 10 cycles, or set a timer for 5 to 10 minutes. As with the first exercise, it can be done for a very short period at any point during the day, when you feel the need for instant calming down.

Keeping some awareness on the breath during everyday life, and aiming to breathe full belly breaths as much as possible, is a great way to incorporate more relaxation and to begin to counterbalance any stress you might experience. The two techniques described above are only a fraction of what there is on offer [45] although these are some of the simplest exercises geared towards calming the mind and the nervous system.

3 Connecting to the mind

Neuroplasticity was discovered some twenty years ago. It's the brain's capacity to continuously create new neural pathways. The brain acts like a muscle. That means that we now can literally leave our old stories and beliefs behind, and shift straight into a more resourceful mode.

The brain's capacity for arousal, regulation, and organisation of your life and work depends on how much energy is released from the more primitive parts of the brain (reptilian brain and limbic brain) and how much balancing energy is regulated from the more developed parts of the brain. The structure of the nervous system, stemming from the reptilian brain, determines which interactions are possible. It has no inside or outside but is influenced by how it is stimulated. This means that if you shed (emotional) issues, and dysfunctional setting(s), you will find yourself with much more (brain) capacity and energy! This is what Part III addresses.

Physically, the cortex (higher brain) is no match for our unconscious emotional patterns. In case of an amygdala hijack as mentioned above, enhancing our awareness may help us to redirect our behaviour before the brain needs to kick in.

However, be aware that the window of change is very small: in less than a fifth of a second, the brain produces a sign of discomfort. So you need to act fast if you want to make a significant change and override an established pattern.

The way in which we make use of this window of change has been described by Wendy Palmer who calls this the window of choice [46]. We need to do two things: instantly recognise unhelpful patterns, and buy time through centring.

---

45 For a further exploration of the breath, one might try a pranayama class or look up some pranayama techniques to practice. Pranayama is an important part of yoga focusing on the conscious control of the breath in order to let the flow of life force energy (prana) through the body. It is used in various ways, from creating more heat and energy, to detoxifying the body, to calming and soothing body and mind.

46 From *Leadership Embodiment* by Wendy Palmer and Janet Crawford, CreateSpace, 2013.

In essence, it's about being aware and creating space. When we can insert a pause, our limbic system can activate the para-sympathetic or rest-digest system needed for our basic living functions, to bring us out of the frozen sympathetic nerve system back to our normal life nerve functions. In essence, it has the same effect as the Heart Meditation mentioned earlier on page 64.

If a person's neocortex becomes significantly imbalanced towards one brain hemisphere, it will cease to function as the executive control centre of the brain as a whole. Instead, the control functions will be downgraded and turned over to the reptilian or limbic brain, depending on the imbalance.

Once we start to become aware of this we can begin to work toward the healing of the brain and in doing so, address these aspects of our consciousness. Only by achieving a balance between the two hemispheres can we develop a state of higher consciousness.

In stress situations, the reptilian brain comes into play. This part of the brain needs to calm down first. It has no language, so as a result, cannot respond quickly. You need to take time to snap out of it, only then are you able to address someone from the position of your strength and ability to find a solution.

It's important to integrate the various layers of the brain. As we saw earlier, different dialogue patterns mean the various layers of the brain do not communicate with each other. The reptilian brain without language, asks for attunement and resonance. The limbic brain asks for interaction and relationship. The neocortex asks for framework and understanding. By practising in the different layers of the brain, the brain becomes more fluid and more opportunities are created to deal appropriately with experiences. Many problems have a deeper cause, often going back to the pre-language phase. That is precisely why it's critical to practice tuning and being mirrored properly. It ensures that you can think more clearly. This is also referred to as *mentalising* or connecting your cognition with your heart. You are essentially connecting your cortex (thinking) to your limbic system (feeling) and your reptilian brain (sensing) [47].

Neuroplasticity

Only over the last two decades, brain research has popped up proving that the adult brain, like muscular tissue, develops when being used and reduces when it's not.

---

47 Marianne Bentzen and Susan Hart, *Through windows of opportunity*, Taylor & Francis, 2015.

You could think of the brain as a dynamic, connected power grid. There are billions of pathways lighting up when you use them. Well traveled pathways represent our habits or patterns. When we do things differently, we carve out new roads – essentially rewiring our brain. We all have this ability to rewire!

Without going into detail, we do want to address this, as it's so relevant to Personal Mastery. In neuroplasticity there are three main mechanisms:

- The creation of new neurons.
- The development of *myelin* or neurons which speed up signal transmission when engaged in deliberate practice. When disengaged, myelin breaks down.
- The reorganisation of the neural circuitry, meaning our brain structures can change in line with our experiences as adults through the creation of new synaptic connections.

According to Neuroscience [48]:

Experience coupled with attention leads to physical changes in the structure and future functioning of the nervous system. Moment by moment we choose and sculpt how our ever-changing minds will work. We choose who we will be in the next moment in a very real sense, and the choices are left embodied in a physical form.

Expanding your mind
A wonderful tool to rescript your neural pathways and reset your emotional state is a visualisation. It is extremely powerful and expands your mind. Deliberate practice is key to getting better, physically this may change our nervous system!

As Rabindranath Tagore said: "One's mind, once stretched by a new idea, never regains its original dimensions."

---

48 Merzenich and deCharms.

Visualisation [49]

1   Sit comfortably, with your whole body relaxed, close your eyes, and let your breath come to its natural rhythm.
2   Imagine you're on holiday, you don't have a care in the world.
3   You're in a mountain meadow, surrounded by snow-capped peaks, taking in the magnificent sight.
4   You're barefoot; feel the wet grass, the sun on your face, and the crisp mountain air.
5   You feel powerful, peaceful and so relaxed.
6   You walk along a little stream and enter a forest. You smell the pine trees.
7   At the end of the forest you hear the sound of water. You follow the sound and see a very special little waterfall.
8   You know that this waterfall can clean you of all your negative beliefs, fears, doubts, insecurities and anything else that has been holding you back from being at your best.
9   You step under the waterfall and feel the water take away all the negativity.
10 When you're done, you step away to a spot in the grass and let yourself dry up in the sun.
11 You feel so great – you feel like all you can be!
12 You start to walk back to the forest, on a winding path.
13 At the end of the path, you see a golden door.
14 As you approach it, you start running faster and faster; you are so excited to open the door!
15 When you open the door, you see the life you've always wanted.
16 Take a very good look and notice what your life looks like in terms of:
    a You: how do you look and feel, inside and out?
    b Your relationships: who is around you, how is your interaction?
    c Your work: what do you do? Does it fulfil you?
    d Your impact: what are you bringing to the world?
17 Take some time to revel in this state and take it all in.
18 Then go out and create what you just saw!

---

49 Inspired by Robin Sharma.

E THE DIAMOND OF HUMAN POTENTIAL

SOUL
inspired purpose

MIND   EMOTIONS
imagination   *tuning in*

BODY
embodied presence

We can learn to live and work at a higher order of consciousness. This higher order of thinking, learning and creating is necessary if we are to transcend our limitations, embrace our whole selves and contribute to the myriad of systems we are part of.

Just like you have to practice to be able to run a marathon, operating from your greatness demands continuous (daily) practice as well.

So, what does the diamond of our (human) potential look like?

In our experience, this shows up as:

Body *– embodied presence*
Physical practices unlock the wisdom of the body: calmness, intuition, perceptual intelligence. It enables you to be totally in the moment with all that you have. Presence creates intimacy & openness. It is a pre-requisite for generative space between people. For stepping into collective intelligence. Think of the strength and stability of a mountain. Life happens around the mountain, its essence stays the same (see the mindfulness meditation on page 72).

Mind – *imagination*
Mental practices unlock the wisdom of the mind: creativity, connection, and innovation. It gives you space, and allows you to access both your linear and your creative brain parts. Think of a clear sky, with space for new things to show up.

Soul – *inspired purpose*
Spiritual practices enable you to see the whole and your part in it, to connect with source (your limitless energy), and to enter the field of collective intelligence. Think of the eagle, having a clear view and focus from high up. It's your North Star, your Inner Leader.

Emotions – *tuning in*
Emotional awareness and practices unlock self-awareness and the trust & optimism to venture in the unknown. It helps the rational and emotional to come into unity. It is your GPS. Think of the ocean, waves coming and going, always moving with the flow.

Embodied presence, imagination, inspired purpose, tuning in, and the integration off all those, are the highest expression of our human potential. They are the attributes of a highly conscious, free individual. A master of her – or himself, who has learned, through continuous practice, to not only connect with all these four powers, and integrate them, but to also to free her – or himself from limiting patterns, views, emotions, etc, to reach a state of oneness within.

SUMMARY: EMBODYING PRESENCE

Remember who you are! Reconnect with your body's wisdom, resonate with your soul's purpose, live your values, release negative emotions and rescript your mind. Rise into your greatness.

Practicing presence in mind, body, and soul and thereby consciously connecting with all of you, enables you to experience what is real, and enables you to expand. Updating your bodymind software in that way is what is needed now to flourish! Three things pop out: **attention, energy, and space.** Attention and energy together form the bodymind dynamic that determines who you are, physically, emotionally, mentally and spiritually. Space is the element that enables you to build awareness. It connects everyone and everything. **Space to just** *be,* **is possibly the biggest gift we can give ourselves** in this time with ever growing demands.

1 We have a body

Your body is your vessel and sense maker, it's what other people see of you, and to you, a vital source of information. Through your senses and feelings, it will interpret the present moment, and inform you how you feel. It is your very foundation. Here in the West where we have so far neglected our body, there is a world to win.

Re-connecting with your body or practising presence in your body, enables you to be here and now. It allows you to come from a place of calm, no matter what. To act rather than react. Practicing presence in your body starts with being centred. Centring makes you feel your true nature and makes you feel safe. It unlocks the wisdom of your body, and it provides you with a sense of space and unity.

Practices: Centring, page 59, Grounding, page 60, Expanding your Personal Space, page 61.

In our bodies, we should pay close attention to:

I **The Heart**: our magnificent coordinating instrument that we are only just starting to grasp. It carries the biggest electromagnetic field in the body and coordinates all bodily processes. Practicing presence in the heart by practising positive emotions, gets us into heart coherence on a high frequency, where we feel connected, creative and energetic. This is great for us and our environment!

Practices: Heart-brain Coherence, page 64, Heart Meditation, page 65.

II **The Gut**: the house of our intuition that we also are just starting to grasp. Developing the connection to your subconscious, and allowing yourself to inquire what really is going on (also see Part III) helps you to become free and unleashes your creativity.

Practice: Inquiry, page 68.

2 We have a mind

Our mind is our decision maker and survival tool. However, it has not evolved much since our days on the Savannah. This means you are not geared for the continuous over-arousal of this day and age, and might find yourself frequently in fight-flight behaviour that isn't necessarily warranted by the circumstances. You might just get an unexpected demand from the CEO, for instance. Nothing lethal, but your body reacts as if it were. Practicing presence in your mind will enable you to come from a place of calm where you have a clear focus, freed from patterns no longer serving you. It will enable you to use your imagination and visualisation, particular human traits so needed now!

Practicing presence in your mind requires discipline and adopting new practices, like a regular meditation practice for example. This will enable you to come back to your breath (body), and will create feelings of clarity and expansion, as well as create new neural pathways! A second great practice would be to, when you are over-aroused or triggered, become aware of the situation and give yourself space to deliberately create a window of choice before you make a move.

Practices: Inner Smile Meditation, page 71, Mountain Meditation, page 72.

Special attention should be paid to:
The BodyMind connection. A field of such potential! It's key to learn how this connection works and how to overcome blockages. Continuous over-arousal of your brain and central nervous system takes a lot of energy. Practicing presence in your bodymind connection also means shedding (emotional) issues, and/or dysfunctional settings and finding more (brain) capacity and energy! More information about this topic in Part III.

3 We are a Soul

Your soul is your Essence. It's that part of you that is connected to the physical and the spiritual realm. The part of you that has the helicopter view of your life. The part that knows what it wants to achieve in this world, and that wants to serve in this world. It can direct your mind and body to materialise your desires if you allow it to. If you choose to overcome the ego's fear, it's all you can be.

Practices: Soul Knowledge, page 84, Values, page 85, Coming Online, page 89.

4 We are vibrational beings

We discuss this in Part II. We want to mention it here, as it is an essential element of our human design.

5 Stress

Stress has become a constant given for many people. When you are stressed, you live in contraction, you cannot access your whole being. You are unavailable. To yourself, and others. But there are ways to remain cool and open in the face of it all. Working with the body, breath, and mind, allows you to come out of contraction, and remain expansive.

Practices: Stress Posture, page 93, Blending, page 94, Breathing Practices, page 95, Visualisation, page 99.

6 The Diamond of our Human Potential

Personal mastery provides access to the highest potential of all four of our innate forms of knowing (PhQ, IQ, SQ, EQ). Integrating and embodying all of these, enable us to live and work at a higher order of consciousness.

> *Practicing presence in your unique human aspects and fully integrating this, allows you to grow up, wake up, and live your greatness. It enables you to become and feel whole! It may also just be the only way to alleviate stress and burn-out.*

"Awareness at the still point of life."

— INTERVIEW WITH DR. KARIN JIRONET, GUIDE IN TRANSITION

I am led to believe that people know quite well what is needed in any given situation and respond accordingly. I encounter this on a daily basis; individuals who follow traffic rules, sense when someone needs encouragement, pick up a child at the right moment, correct misunderstandings – the fabric of life and its movements is quite a miracle.

Until the minute when you ask: so, what are you doing, and how do you manage this issue or how could it be better managed? At that moment it's like self-confidence and trust in the process, as well as the belief in being guided or other factors related to being grounded, trust and relationship, go out of the window.

At that point, it's very difficult to remind the group, or the individuals in the group, that just 5 minutes ago you were doing quite well. In fact, the way you were working together, was exemplary of flow. So, by problematising, we rationalise intuitive processes, and experiential knowledge and inner wisdom are easily replaced with self-consciousness, which is contrary to self-awareness. It is a kind of paradox that while seeking control one often abolishes it, and becomes alienated from the actual activity of the relationship.

Awareness of who you are dramatically increases the chances of understanding the other, and how to interact in any given situation in a natural way. Of course, it's not simply about 'being myself,' it's about consciously, truthfully acknowledging and accepting one's character and inclination to make the best of it. Wholeness doesn't necessarily mean 'complete,' in the sense of harmonious perfection. I think it can also mean affinity with multiple, contradictory parts of the personality. What's 'good conduct' in one instance – say trust, loyalty, compassion, might be inappropriate in a different situation when one is called to a very different approach. Knowing how to tune in with the present-now truly requires self-awareness, as in, being at ease with idiosyncrasies.

One idea that I believe is very relevant at this point, is to see and understand the benefits that may be harvested from silence. *"Silence is the language of God. All else is poor translation,"* said 13th century theologian and Sufi mystic Jalal ad Din Muhammad Rumi, often referred to simply as Rumi. I am reminded of the profound truth in this saying whenever I do my morning practice. Then the day happens, the knowing residing in silence reveals itself. And, on the days I get to work with a business leader, one on one, him or her expressing great urgency, frustration, or complications, then I consider it my job to lean into that silence and hold the space for silence. I go back to my morning practice because that's where my client or friend will find clarity, peace, and awareness of context and soul. Having discovered how much silence has to reveal, the leaders I work with today unanimously seek conscious access to that inner still point intermittently during the day. Silence is a kind of beacon, directing you back home to yourself when you need it the most.

You ask how we get there, to that kind of rich, full and peaceful silence?

My guess is that the journey is different for each and every one. It's interesting, by the way, that it takes movement, a journey, to get to the personal still point. What does that mean? It's in me, yet, I must develop to reach it – something like that.

Then, how does development happen, individuation, becoming, who I am in essence? How do I know it, manifest it, and am free to live it in all dimensions physical, emotional, mental, spiritual – at the same time? This notion of *"I am"* is strictly personal, even incomprehensible. But the journey to that realisation might not be individually tailored. In fact, I've come to believe it follows certain commonly shared characteristics.

Two of the stations on the path, that I simply cannot see obliterated, are suffering and love. *Suffering* I feel is underrated, but plays a major role in development, and is a very useful tool for transition. Consciousness thrives on suffering and is an effect of it. Most people with a bearable level of suffering will tell you that it's good, that something good will come out of it, that it changed them for the better and has induced their personal development.

Love has a similar impact. It eludes all definition, rationality – most often it's not even seen by onlookers as appropriate or healthy. When truly in love, you do everything for it – whether in a relationship, with a mission, with creativity, or with life itself. People in love sometimes feel doomed and believe nothing good will come out of it. Love might just be the most powerful influence on life. It stretches beyond the notion of development into mystery, passion, surrender and the simplicity, essence, of living life.

Arts like great opera and literature have captured the essence of this tension between love and suffering.

I am personally touched by the willingness and effort of those I may work with to venture into the depths of silence and find guidance to lead.

I'm happy to live to see it.

or Letting Come

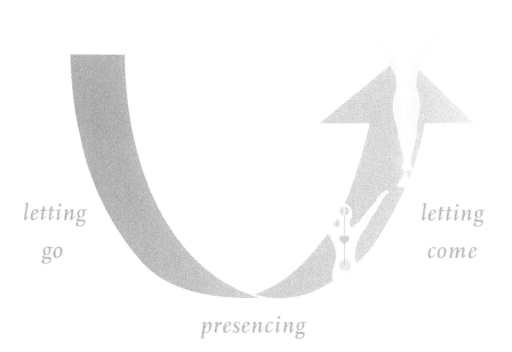

letting
go

letting
come

presencing

moving from aligned to online

Entering Flow

Entering flow is the intention to open up to the field of pure potential we live in, to Source. Opening up to Source means tapping into your highest wisdom. The wisdom that is held in the subtle or energy body. Trusting that, if you can open up to that state in yourself, and create a conducive environment, working from a shared intention, you may take your team with you. Realising that we're all connected, and together you may access the field of collective wisdom and find answers that you could not have imagined by yourselves. Opening up to the emerging future, as Scharmer says in Theory U.

*Awareness of your **energy design** and that of the universe, and working with these principles will enable you to move to that state of flow.*

Life will become magic.

"Everything is energy, and that's all there is to it.
Match the frequency of the reality you want,
and you cannot help but get that reality.
It can be no other way. This is not philosophy. This is physics."

— ALBERT EINSTEIN

Now that you have an idea of your *human design* how can you truly flow and create a life in harmony with your desires and context? Do you know:

- What energy is and how it works?
- What your *energy design* is?
- How you receive and transport energy in your body?
- How raising your vibration enables raising your consciousness, experience synchronicity, effortlessly manifesting and tapping into collective intelligence?
- Which rituals or practices enable a sense of flow within?
- The *universal energy design?*

We live in a time of awakening where people are becoming more attuned to the subtle and to energy. However, we often do not yet have the tools or language to play with it or to deliberately tap into the energy and go with the flow. From page 124 onwards we give you some insights and practices to enter flow.

So, let's talk energy
What is energy to you? Oil, electricity, fossil fuels? Wikipedia defines energy as "a quality (action) creating an effect (reaction)." This materialistic view forms the basis of earlier mentioned science. There are other views now, backed up over the last twenty years by quantum physics.

Science now accepts that the universe, including us, is made up of energy, not matter. Actually, this is not new. It was already posited in Europe by Socrates and in India by gurus thousands of years ago. Socrates said that energy or soul, is separate from matter and that the universe is made of energy; pure energy which was there before man and other material things like the earth came along. At the end of the 17th century, however, Newtonian physics became the cornerstone of science. This was based on the theory that there is only matter and nothing else. The whole universe was viewed as a machine made of matter. Science has now largely moved on to quantum physics, but medical science is still stuck in the Newtonian concept.

Quantum physics [50] says that as you go deeper and deeper into the workings of the atom, you see that there is nothing there – just energy waves. An atom is an invisible force field, a kind of miniature tornado, which emits waves of electrical energy. Those energy waves can be measured and their effects seen, but they are not material, they have no substance because they are, well, just electricity. Science now embraces the idea that the universe is made of energy.

When you think about it, everything starts as energy; as an idea, inspiration or thought. The more we are fully embodied or present in the physical world, the easier it becomes to transfer non-physical energy (like ideas) into the physical world (manifestation).

Just to be clear: again, we aim to provide you with an overview and first glimpse and taste of how this works. For years people have been fascinated by this and have been searching for these keys. In the selected reading list you will find a few of them. It is our intention here to give you 'aha' moments enabling you to get you on your way to becoming a conscious creator.

How can you practice flow?
In this time of transformation, systems are falling apart, but people are starting to wake up! One of the things people are starting to wake up to is their sense of energy and the impact of their energy on the whole and vice versa.

Organisations such as The HeartMath Institute [51], are currently doing research into how our personal energy shapes social relationships and ultimately affects global consciousness.

---

50 Quantum theory is the theoretical basis of modern physics that explains the nature and behaviour of matter and energy on the atomic and subatomic level. The nature and behaviour of matter and energy at that level is sometimes referred to as quantum physics.

51 The HeartMath Institute empowers individuals, families, groups and organisations to enhance their life experiences using tools that enable them to better recognise and access their intuitive insight and heart intelligence.

> *Quantum physics considers the possibility that it's the energy of consciousness (or spirit) that is at the basis of how things materialize. Or to put it differently: in quantum physics it's found that the researcher is the person shaping the "objective" reality, hence demonstrating the absence of objective reality. In layman's terms:* **"you get what you focus on."**

Energy is information, it's the motivating force driving everything. It's around us everywhere we go, visible and invisible like in the case of magnetic waves enabling internet, telephone, radio, television, etc. Everything in our universe is made up of energy, from the book or screen you are looking at now, to the trees I see outside my window, to your body, thoughts, and your consciousness.

More on energy in general, can be found in the section on the universal laws. First, we'll explore our own energy design. More to the point, how you can learn to consciously work with it. Once again, the answers are all in the body.

"When a human grows, he opens his abilities to accept higher levels of vibrations,
of energy and consciousness that come in....
As we grow, we fall more in tune with our Essence.
The more in tune, the more expansive our consciousness,
the better we're able to use the Universal Laws."

— BARBARA BRENNAN

What is our Inner Energy?

What if you already have the most powerful guidance system imaginable, isn't it time you learned to use it? You have a phenomenal source of infinite energy inside you, always available for you to tap into and fill you up. It does not depend on food, sleep or meditation. It's just there! You should know about this energy because it's your birthright!

This inner energy source is called by many names, the most familiar being qi, chi, prana or kundalini (in various Eastern disciplines). When you fall in love for instance, and you feel as if you could achieve anything, you experience this inner energy source. When you're highly inspired, you experience it. Or when you are blown away by the marvel of a beautiful spot in nature. This life energy can restore, replenish and recharge you anytime. When it's flowing strongly, you feel as if you could take on the world!

How would it feel to know what makes you tick energetically? Well, let's put it this way: if you have a body built for sprinting it will be very hard to run a marathon instead. You may really want to, may train very hard, but in the end, you probably will not succeed. Can you imagine that the same goes for your energy body? That you need to know what your design is, and take ownership of it, to unleash your full potential?

In the West, we've become focused on caring for our *physical body* and refuelling it through food, rest, yoga, etc. Most of us are, however, totally unaware of, or ignore, our *energy body*, our inner energy. Inner energy and consciousness are complete mysteries to us. We study energy outside of us and do not realise that we have our internal energy system that is alive and intelligent. It acts as the connection between the physical world and the metaphysical world. Looking after your energy system means looking after your most profound needs: physical, emotional, intellectual and spiritual. So how does it work?

Why is this energy easily accessible sometimes, and difficult to find at other times? How can you be conscious of it and cultivate it? Our physical bodies are what we can see and touch. They are tangible. We now know, however, that each piece of our physical body is made up of energy. Collectively they have an energy field.

So what about the energy connected to our thoughts, feelings, and emotions, life experiences, perspectives, and moral compasses? There is no physical location for these elements of us. They may not be tangible, but they carry just as much energy (vibration). They are part of our spiritual body: that which transcends the physical world.

Our physical body and our spiritual body both have and generate energy and an energy field. This energy that makes up all of us is called *the energy body (or subtle or light body)*.

> *Our **energy body** is completely integrated and dynamic. So, for instance, when a shift is made in the physical body, there is a shift in the whole energy field. Meaning there may be a resulting shift in the spiritual body as your emotional state changes. Likewise, when there's a change in the spiritual body, for instance, your soul experiences growth, again, there is a shift in overall energy results, which may be accompanied by physical sensations for instance. Energy connects all: all things arise from energy!*

What does our energy design look like?
Our body is controlled by a network of intelligence. You could say there is a physical and an energetic you. Most of us in the West are much more familiar with the physical body. But the energy body is very real too! It can even be captured through methods like Kirlian photography. So what is it made up of?

1 Aura
Your aura is an energy field that surrounds, penetrates and extends beyond your physical body. It's made up of varying types of vibrations or frequencies, and it's electro-magnetic. An aura surrounds every living thing (humans, animals and plants), and every inanimate thing (rocks, earth, sun, moon, all planets).

> *The aura has layers of physical, emotional, mental and spiritual elements, and consists of a constant flow of energy. It is the frequency of this energy that makes you what and who you are: it reflects your health, character, mental activity, and emotional state.*

It is believed that our energy field emits out from the body approximately 60-90 centimetres on all sides, extending above your head and below your feet. You can contract and expand it at will. Your energy level greatly influences the size of your aura. It has to do with the frequency you emit. Happy and loving thoughts, for instance, hold a high frequency and expand your aura, while sad or angry thoughts, low frequency, contract it.

Your aura can set a shield of protection around you, and assist your body to retain its life force energy. It is affected by your surroundings. Therefore, just like it's important to have good personal hygiene by showering and brushing your teeth, it's also good to have a healthy energy hygiene and protect and balance your energy system by clearing out negativity, thought patterns and emotional blocks for instance (see the Cleaning the Temple exercise on page 132 for instance). What is also very useful, is cultivating a very clear awareness of what makes you feel great (what raises your energy) as well what saps you (what drains your energy). Having a clear understanding of the workings of your aura will give you more insight into your life and your well-being in body, mind, and spirit.

> *Auras are made up of many colours and shades that constantly change, reflecting the constant change in your mind, body, and soul. In a way, **your aura is your energy signature**. It's sometimes said that more than any other single human trait, your aura manifests the sum and substance of you.*

2 Chakras

'Chakra' is Sanskrit for wheel. The chakras are the seven powerful base energy centres (magnetic fields) in our bodies. Every chakra is connected to the central nervous system running through our spine. They also are connected to levels of consciousness and growth phases in life, body functions and more.

Through your chakras, you exchange energy and information with your environment. Chakras govern the endocrine system that in its turn regulates all of the body's functions. Energy flows from the universal energy field through the chakras into the energy systems within our bodies, including the meridian system. As most people in the West are not so aware yet of their energy body, the energy flowing through their body may be just minimally there. Their chakras have become blocked by emotional baggage, fears and limiting beliefs for instance. This constricts the energy flow between the chakras, hence in the whole being, and may manifest as physical disease. The chakras are connected through energy channels. Together they make up for what's known as the energy body (or subtle body). So how do they work?

Traditionally, there are said to be seven main chakras. They are located along your spine and provide gateways to understanding aspects of your soul and ego. There is one at the very base of your spine *(root chakra)*, one a little below your navel *(sacral chakra)*, one a little above your navel *(solar plexus)*, one in the centre of your chest *(heart chakra)*, one in your throat *(throat chakra)*, one in your forehead *(third eye chakra)* and one at the very top of your head *(crown chakra)*. The bottom three chakras work with the denser physical energies, while the top three chakras relate more to spiritual issues. In the fourth chakra, the heart, they all come together in union.

Each chakra reflects an aspect of consciousness that is essential to our lives. Through the chakras, we gain a deeper understanding of how we experience life and how we relate to ourselves, others and society. *Chakras are powerful tools for self-discovery.* They hold the keys to deeply held feelings and our deepest sense of who we are and how we fit into all there is. You may notice that the seven chakras correspond with the Seven Levels of Consciousness model as well as Spiral Dynamics.

Yoga considers chakras as the keys for transforming universal life force into the body's energy system.

Chakra 1 – Root Chakra
At the base of the body • connected with the colour red • tactile • earth element
Your first chakra is *your physical connection to the life-force energy*. The root chakra is all about you. It has to do with your grounding. The more you are grounded, the more life energy (or qi) can move through you, the more confident you'll feel. Other people can easily feel that: a well-opened root chakra feels like a strong charisma. A sort of animal magnetism, very earthy, like its associated element. If you are not well grounded, you could be easily overwhelmed by what you feel and look for numbing, or control in other ways. Through addictions, for instance. Addictions seal off the root chakra. The more closed off the root chakra is, the more we are taken over by illusion instead of living in/facing reality.

You could say that the root chakra contains our potential in the manifest, physical world. It's the seat of masculine energy in the body and the place from where the *kundalini* [52] enters it. Indigenous people believe the root and the earthly energies are essential to completing the full human and spiritual experience.

Chakra 2 – Sacral Chakra
Just below your navel • connected with the colour orange • emotional • water element
The second chakra is about passion, creativity, sexuality, desire and belonging. When your sexuality is open and able to flow freely – creativity flows. When your creativity flows, your relationships flow. When you shut down your sexuality, you shut down your life force or vitality. When you flow freely, life starts to happen. You feel a sense of freedom: you are at ease with your primal essence. You go with the flow – in line with the element of water. The second chakra is the root of the feminine. It symbolises your creative impulse, your ability to identify your feelings and fully experience them.

Chakra 3 – Solar Plexus
Above the navel • connected with the colour yellow • personal power • fire element
The solar plexus is a complex energy centre. It is here you realise what you are about and start to live your life according to your purpose and values. Here you speak your truth. But it's also here that you have to deal with, transcend and include rejection, fear, anger, attachment, control, and pain. It deals with self-esteem, confidence, humility, power, and need. Power is, of course, a big issue for many people. Humility is necessary to not believe ourselves to be the rulers of the

---

52 Kundalini is really the fuel for all energy in the body, and of all consciousness.

world, but understand we are merely its safe keepers.

The solar plexus is *the centre of your bodymind* , it's your nervous centre, physically your most vulnerable place. If people attack you verbally, you'll feel it here! It's the home of your integrity (conscience). It's where you integrate emotions and intellect, where you exchange energy with the world around you.

The solar plexus is a challenging place as, if you want to self-actualise, you must face the unknown. You need to summon all your courage and strength (fire in the belly) to face your shadow, surrender, and let go of control. You need to realise that every person and thing around you acts like a mirror, for you to know yourself. You need to become (more) aware of your inner battles and stop projecting them outside. You need to begin to see that everything is happening to you as a gift on your journey.

Essentially, the solar plexus is the place where you heal yourself: healing the split between mind and body, between ego and soul. To continue to your heart chakra, you need to balance ego and soul. This healing is the growth each person seeks! *A healthy third chakra allows us to become whole.*

Chakra 4 – Heart chakra
At the centre of the chest • connected with the colour green • love and soul • air element
The heart chakra is about expansion. It's about your capacity to unconditionally love and see the whole person and situation. It helps you to move beyond the mere physical, emotional, and intellectual parts of your being to a larger, more spiritual perspective. It's a melting pot in a sense: opening up the flow of love transforms all issues to a level of understanding, a broader perspective, and, ultimately, peace. This chakra is about integrating and being fully present, letting go of any expectations or attachments.

The heart is the physical residence of the soul. It's where you find balance, between love and will, feminine and masculine. The soul wants to grow. Allowing love to freely pour through you is the way. It will lead to your Essence. Your Essence is love. Unconditional love is the love of the soul.

When you reach unconditional love, you allow people and events to be, come and go freely. *It's from this place that you will find your home and your peace.* On page 126 and in the Reinventing Toolbox we have attached a very special, long meditation called the *Love Bomb* guiding you to experience the bliss of this feeling.

Chakra 5 – Throat chakra
In the middle of your neck • connected with the colour blue • finding your voice • ether
The fifth chakra is all about living and speaking your truth. It's about giving voice to your true power as felt in your solar plexus. The throat chakra feeds life-force energy to the spiritual aspect of your being, as the root chakra does to all chakras. It's about reflection, looking down at the lower chakras, and your experiences in life so far. It may also involve having to let go of that which no longer works. Inner shifts that may feel like inner deaths. Use your emotions as fuel; it will help the healing process. Through this process, there is space for the new to emerge. In this time of huge transformation, feeling your power will help you ride the waves.

Chakra 6 and 7. Not many people live in the top two chakras yet. Therefore, there is less experiential information. You find the basic theory below.

Chakra 6 – Third-eye chakra
In between the eyes • connected with the colour indigo • clarity • light & dark
This chakra has to do with clear vision. It allows you to access your future. When it is open, you have ideas and see opportunities. When it is closed, you cannot see beyond the present, which may lead to anxiety. In terms of manifestation, the third-eye chakra enables you to visualise an idea coming in and then projecting that out into the world. It's here you realise you can build the mental and spiritual discipline to visualise the reality you want, as *your thoughts create your reality*. Set up a discipline of meditation and reflection. When you take time, regularly, to listen to your soul, it will set you free.

Chakra 7 – Crown chakra
Top of the head • connected with the colour violet • spiritual connection • time & space
When you have activated the crown chakra, you experience one-ness with spirit. You are in a place beyond time. You have the helicopter view and are at peace with all there is. From here you may connect to your higher self or your spirit guides.

So now that you have an idea of the aspects the various chakras deal with, what to do when one or more are blocked? For example, the throat chakra may be blocked by things like not expressing yourself, or letting people walk all over you. Past fears and childhood trauma may have caused you to be afraid to truly express yourself. These things need to be addressed and healed to have clear communication, and a healthy and full functioning throat chakra. It's a similar healing process for the other chakras, bearing in mind each chakra deals with different aspects.

We want to give you a feel of the energies your seven chakras represent and the role they play in your overall system.

Tip:
Record yourself reading below instructions so you can replay, and relax into the experience.

Chakra Meditation [53]

Make yourself comfortable and take a deep breath, allowing yourself to settle into a deep meditative state. Imagine yourself in a beautiful green meadow surrounded by trees. In the middle of the meadow is an ancient stone pool fed with clear sparkling water from an underground spring. Feel yourself diving into the water, and starting to swim. This may be the most refreshing experience you have ever had! You feel awake, alive, and invigorated. And as you swim in gentle, easy strokes through the cool sparkling water, allow any heaviness in your life to simply wash away. Step up onto the stone wall surrounding this beautiful pool. Feel the warmth of the sun as it quickly dries your body and bathes you in light. The warmth of the sun reminds you that spirit is indeed inside of you and is connecting the light of your soul to the light of the universe.

1   As you take in the majesty of your surroundings, the beautiful trees, meadow, and flowers, and hear the birds singing, feel the strength of mother earth pouring into your body. Feel it come up your legs, through your hips, into your torso and out of the top of your head. Feel this *bright red earth energy*, this great life-force energy, surge though your body and know that you are a part of the earth.
2   Feel the bright orange light of the sun, the brilliance of this colour. Feel it pulse through your body, as your creativity is opened and inspired, truly connected to Source. Feel your primal passions for life open.
3   The warm and embracing *yellow light of the sun* now penetrates your skin, so you know you are safe, secure, happy and loved. This warm yellow colour emanates through all of your body and shines out for others to feel. You know you can claim your place in the world with confidence. You can acknowledge the light and dark parts of yourself, and let them coexist peacefully. Feel your ambition and desire, and realise that these are healthy

---

53   Alan Seale, *Intuitive Living: a Sacred Path*, San Francisco, Red Wheel/Weiser, 2001.

feelings when ego and soul are balanced.

4 Look once again at the *beautiful green rolling meadow,* the lush green of the trees, and feel yourself being healed in this brilliant green washing through all of your senses. Feel yourself enveloped. You may even want to lie down in the grass, feeling the cool earth and grass embracing you. Know you are loved.

5 While lying on this rich, thick grass look at the *beautiful bright blue sky.* Float up into the heavens and know you are free to be, to say and sing; no longer are feelings and emotions trapped inside. Feel your throat open as never before and feel spirit pouring through and out of you through your glorious sound.

6 Now float gently back to earth, having felt and claimed as your own the freedom that comes through opening to the heavenly realms. Peer into the *indigo blue waters of the pool,* allowing yourself to be lost in it. See reflections, connections to ancient times, pictures – anything that comes to you through the water. See it, bless it, and know that God comes to you as you open up to seeing, hearing and feeling.

7 Look once more toward heaven and see the *violet rays* of the sun coming through scattered clouds. Jump onto one of these rays and let it carry you back up into heaven. Feel the top of your head open and spirit enter. Hear spirit's voice. It may sound like your voice or the voice of someone familiar to you, or it may be a completely new voice. Open to spirit and just listen. You may hear specific sounds or words, or you may simply experience through transference. Just open and let be whatever is. Allow spirit to speak to and through you – to live through you. Remain here for a few moments and commune with spirit.

In a moment you will come back to this space. But before you open your eyes, take a moment to remember the sun in the pool. Remember the red life-force from mother earth; the bright orange light from the sun, the yellow embrace of the sun, the deep healing in the green grass and trees. Remember the blue sky; the indigo blue water and the violet sunrays. Feel all these energies intermingling in you and know that you are love.

I hope this gave you a tangible experience of the chakras. If you would like to learn more you may check out *Intuitive Living* by Alan Seale or Rosemary Buyer's *Wheels of Light.*

3 Qi – or your infinite source of energy

Now that we have covered the aura and the chakras, we want to address, and give you a felt experience of, your infinite source of energy, your life-force, called by different names, including qi, chi or kundalini. We mentioned it before in our example of flow on page 52.

Where your heart chakra is the coordinator of all energy, kundalini is the fuel for and energetic axis of all of the energy in the body, and of all consciousness.
The basic release of this life-force energy into the body lies within the root chakra. From there it travels up the spine, awakening and connecting all other chakras. Its chief purpose is conscious awareness of ourself, the universe and our connection with it. The kundalini shoots up the spine towards the crown, but at the same time has an opposite movement into the earth or ground. A fully open kundalini channel allows you to experience several levels of awareness at the same time.

We humans have two systems within us: the physical/emotional system and the mental/ intellectual system. Kundalini allows us to be aware of our emotions and feelings and carries this through the physical/emotional system to the mental/intellectual system when it flows freely.

Wherever kundalini is blocked, consciousness stops. Therefore, kundalini is essential to our spiritual journey! This visualisation may help you feel how kundalini can travel up the spine and fill you with its radiant vibrancy and lust for life, waking up all other chakras on its way.

Tip:
Record yourself reading below instructions so you can replay, and relax into the experience.

Kundalini Practice – for the brave ones!

One thing that is causing us so much suffering, is getting into rigid brain patterns. This happens when you get mentally stuck on things and repeat them over and over again. The physical shaking in this practice liberates your vagus nerve and brain. It enables you to get rid of stuck emotional baggage from the past. The first part of this exercise is about shaking yourself loose. This could be done by literally shaking, or dancing or bouncing on a trampoline for instance.

As you shake, allow every bit of your body to move. And let yourself make sounds. This is an important release. Any kind of sound, whatever feels real to you, just express it and let go of any thoughts.

The second part is a meditative visualisation where you activate your kundalini energy in the root centre and bring awareness to your pelvis, the seat of your power. Try to visualise a ball of light and imagine kundalini energy inside that ball. Your aliveness as a human being. Acknowledge it, and start from a place of total self-love and acceptance. As soon as you feel grounded in love, bring the ball up your spine to take the energy and vibrancy to all other parts of your body. After this practice, you'll feel a change in your aliveness and awareness, and in how you go about your day.

Phase 1 – shaking (if you prefer, replace this with dancing or bouncing)
Start with your feet a little bit wider than hip distance apart and let a shake come through your entire body like a rumbling. Maybe put on some dance music that you like to help this along. The shaking will relax your muscles and release pent up energy. You may start to yawn! As you continue to shake, inhale deep, full and slow. Make a sound on every exhale. Continue like this for a minute.

Phase 2 – awakening kundalini energy and letting it feed the chakras
Visualise a ball of light at the height of your root chakra and make contact with your kundalini energy. Feel this radiance that is part of your being.

Phase 3 – circulating the kundalini through all your chakras
1   Come to a seated position and visualise a pearly ball of light at your pelvis. Allow this ball of light to grow and expand until it's as big as your hips. Feel this pearly ball of light as your primordial kundalini energy. The beauty, innocence, and pleasure you came here with. Then shrink it back down in your pelvis.
2   *Sacral Chakra* – inhale and move the ball from your pelvis to your tailbone. Feeling a luscious, watery energy awakening your whole sacral area. Exhaling bring that pearly ball back down via the front of your body to your pelvis. Inhale the pearly ball up to your tailbone, feeling this luscious energy again, and exhaling bringing it back down to the pelvis.
3   *Solar Plexus* – now inhale from the pelvis up to the back of the spine to the level of the solar plexus. Feeling power, fire, and will increase. Exhaling, bring the ball back down via the front of your body, feeling it melt down back into the pelvis. Inhale that pearly ball up along the back of your spine all the way up to

the level of the solar plexus, feeling heat, fire, willpower again. And exhaling, bringing it all the way back down to the pelvis.

4 *Heart Chakra* – now inhale all the way up the spine to the back of the heart. Feel the ball of light enhance love, air and compassion through your entire chest area. And exhale letting the ball drop all the way back down via the front of your body to your pelvis. Inhale all the way up the back of the spine to the heart, feeling love, compassion, and exhaling, bringing it back down to the pelvis.

5 *Throat Chakra* – inhale all the way up the spine to the back of the neck, feeling the ball increase the amount of space, a connection to the meta-physical, openness, the highest genius. Let it expand the power of your voice. Exhale and bring it all the way back down via the front, to the pelvis. Inhale all the way up, to the back of the throat at the level of the spine, feeling genius, high creativity and the spaciousness of the universe. Let it melt all the way back down into the pelvis.

6 *Third Eye Chakra* – inhale all the way up the spine to the centre of the brain. Visualise an increase in meditative awareness, expansion, and ability to move beyond duality into a deeper truth. Exhale, bringing it back down via the front of your body to the pelvis. Inhale all the way up the spine to the centre of the brain again and feel this deep meditation and peace. Exhale, feeling the ball of energy come back down to the pelvis.

7 *Crown Chakra* – inhale and now bring the ball all the way up to the very top of the head. Feel an increase in spirituality and heightened awareness, and the activation of your deepest and truest self. Exhaling, bring it all the way back down via the front of your body to the pelvis. Inhale again all the way up to the crown of your head. Feel the expansion, your deepest truth, and your true nature. Exhale and bring it all the way back down to the pelvis.

Once more, inhale all the way up to the top of your head. This time touch the roof of your mouth with your tongue to facilitate movement of this energy up and down your body, and exhale that energy down, bringing it down with your hands. Step by step, melting that pearly ball of energy down from your crown to the centre of your brain, down your throat, your heart, through your solar plexus, your belly, your sacral chakra and all the way back down to your pelvis. Feel it solidify at the base of your body. And exhale growing roots from the pelvis all the way deep, deep, deep into in the centre of the earth. Feel those roots going all the way down, as deep as they can go, rooting you, grounding you.

Feel your body alive with kundalini, radiant, while deeply grounded and centred.

A ENTERING FLOW — RAISING YOUR VIBRATION

So, now you know about your energy design, how to raise your vibration? Where to start?

1 Become more open

Our main energy centre is the heart. Our state of openness defines how much love we can feel. However, we usually don't consciously control how open we are. Our state of openness is governed by our psychological experiences. It's made up of the parts of the iceberg below the waterline: thoughts, impressions, beliefs, etc.. We are programmed based upon past impressions in such a way that all kinds of things can cause us to open and close. During a single day, this opening and closing happens multiple times, without us having conscious control over it. All things unresolved like pain and trauma get stored in our energy body, and radiate out. But we can learn to take control by letting go as described in Part III, and set ourselves free!

You see, when the heart is open, it produces a coherent pattern. Harmonic resonance creates psycho-physiological coherence, meaning greater harmony and efficiency in the activities and interactions of all bodily systems, as well as a decrease of stress and internal mental dialogue, and an increase of emotional balance and mental clarity, intuition, and cognitive action. It also synchronises left and right brain halves, all of which The HeartMath Institute has proven (see page 62).

OK, so maybe this sounds easier than it is. How do you stay open when you're under stress, when things go wrong or when you suffer a great loss? You may choose to:

- Connect to your inner guidance and co-create your life (inner control), or,
- Remain reactive, based on emotional patterns (outer control).

Your life is the effect of this: if you don't change the input – you'll keep getting the same output! It doesn't have to be this way: you can connect to your true self, and use your purpose and values as your inner compass. Your vibration will rise, emotions will calm down, and your life will become more in flow.

2 Become more present

You need to learn to optimise your inner energy by becoming more present, as we explained in Part I. If you want to make an impact in the world, you have to increase your coherence or frequency. As you become more present and conscious, you will feel more clear and focused, calm and relaxed, with plenty of time and energy to manifest your ideas into reality. You can do less, with more tangible results. This is the fastest way to be more powerful and effective! If you're not present enough in your body, your impact is weak, even if your mind and ideas are strong.

3 Raise your vibration

The next most important thing you can do for yourself is raising your vibration! Your consciousness is the aware part of you connected to the highest vibration you can be in your body. When you raise your vibration, you become connected to the place where you feel free. Not only will your life run more smoothly, you will automatically affect those around you! When you're happy and in high energy, you're truly the magnet that you want to be, and you will thrive in the world. *You just have to know how to access that.*

First, awareness. How will it feel like to consciously raise your vibration?

- You'll be able to tap into energy, harmony and inner balance continuously.
- You'll learn to expand your intuition to experience a life of synchronicity.
- You'll take charge and be able to enjoy a life of love, abundance, joy, and fun.
- You'll be able to manifest what your heart desires, and, above all:
- You'll feel your true *Essence*.

> *When you get the frequency of your physical body higher, more of your spirit can come in. Your spirit is your highest frequency and your connection with Universal Wisdom. This is true integration.*

In his book *Power vs. Force*, Dr. David Hawkins, Psychiatrist and Consciousness Researcher describes the levels of consciousness as determinants of our human behaviour. Our thoughts, feelings, behaviours, emotional states, and attitudes determine from where we are operating. These levels of consciousness also determine our perspective of life, and direct or dictate the way in which we will react and relate to life.

He calibrated emotions, and formulated a hierarchical model of personal development with a score of 0 - 1000 describing human levels of consciousness (0 being the lowest and 1000 being the highest level of consciousness). We can move up and down the scale or fluctuate, but in principle we have a predominant state from which we view our life.

For example, say you live your life based upon a feeling of *fear*, you live from scarcity, you have a low frequency, calibrated by Hawkins as 100 on the scale of consciousness. If this is your predominant level of consciousness, your worldview will be fear-based, and, since we are magnets, you will unconsciously and unwillingly spread lower vibrations and magnetise more fear-based experiences.

On the other hand, when you consciously adopt *unconditional love* as a lifestyle, calibrated at 500, you live from the heart. You take care of your energetic footprint, you know everything is connected and united; a greater force guides you, your intuition is strongly present. You live from abundance, have a high frequency and will project and attract more and more love into your life!

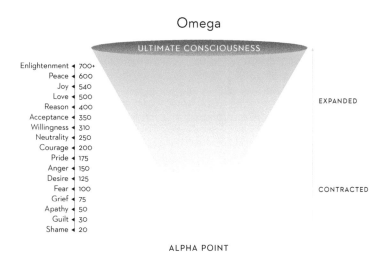

We are all capable of consciously reaching higher states and higher awareness of self. Hawkins mentions two important turning points for personal development:

- Level 200, *initial empowerment*, where we stop blaming others and accept responsibility for our own thoughts, feelings, actions, and beliefs, and,
- Level 500, *love* and non-judgmental forgiveness, is where we begin exercising unconditional kindness to all persons, things and events.

A person who is powerful engages from a high frequency. Their lives are filled with synchronicity and joy, their success is continuous and constantly growing. Maintaining these higher frequencies progresses a person on both levels of individual awareness and external success. *As a person moves into higher states of consciousness, they embrace power over force as the means to accomplish their goals.*

According to Hawkins, societal development is possible when increasingly large groups of individuals embrace higher frequencies and support each other in moving into higher states. The consequence is development of consciousness. The world will become a more coherent place when more people join in these practices. In fact, the shift has already started: there's a global shift to TEAL or more wholeness happening right now, amidst old systems collapsing. It all starts with you, as Gandhi said with the phrase: "Be the change you want to see."

So how do you access higher vibrations?
By consciously connecting with high-level emotions, such as love, gratitude, and joy, through practices that give you a felt sense of these. The crux is the felt sense. To feel being supercharged with love, the *Love Bomb* below is great.

Tip:
Record yourself reading below instructions so you can replay, and relax into the experience.

The Love Bomb [54]

Make yourself comfortable and close your eyes. Imagine someone you love sitting about two feet in front of you. Really see their face, their hair and what they're wearing. Are they happy? Ideally, this is someone you love very much. Alternatively, imagine something that inspires the feeling of love inside of you.

On your next inhale breathe that sensation of love into your body and supercharge every single cell of your body with it. As you exhale, imagine that you're sending this out to the person you love. Almost blasting them with love, so that you're supercharging every cell in their body with this feeling of love.

On your next breath, breathe into the sensation of love, charging every cell of your body with it. And as you exhale, imagine sending that out to the entire room. Just filling the room you're in with this beautiful current of love.

---

54 Inspired by Emily Fletcher.

Some people like to imagine this as white or golden light. Whatever feels good to you is perfect.

On your next inhale, breathe in the sensation, supercharging your body with love, and as you exhale imagine sending this out to the entire city. To every person, place, and thing in the city where you live. To all your friends, colleagues and your boss. Just blasting them with love.

If you feel like you're losing that sensation, simply come back to the person you love and just see them across from you, notice how that changes you, notice how that softens your face, and changes your heart.

Let your next breath be a delicious inhale, supercharging every single cell in your body, and as you exhale, imagine sending this love out to the entire universe. Blast the whole universe with as much love as you can possibly create. And know that as you're sending this sensation out, it's absolutely coming back to you.

Imagine sending this love out as far as your mind can conceive. Beyond the solar system, beyond the galaxy, the clusters of galaxies, and out in the entire universe, to the entirety of All That Is.

Just for a moment, as you send this love out to the whole universe, remind yourself that you are part of a greater whole. Remind yourself that you are part of the universe and that the universe is part of you. Allow yourself to surrender into this sense of connectedness, and support. Almost imagining that you are one wave in a giant ocean of consciousness. You are one wave in this giant ocean of energy. And allow yourself to receive all of the love that's coming back to you from the universe. Let that fill you up from the source. Let it supercharge your body. You can take that with you into your life. Into your job, into your family.

Translating it from practice into real life
From this place of connectedness and having supercharged your body with the sensation of love, imagine that you're going into a situation that's important to you. Imagine that you're just about to give an important presentation to your board for instance. You really want to show up at the top of your game. See yourself right there, about to open the door.

Here's a little pep talk.

Notice what feelings come up for you. Maybe it's a little nervousness, or anxiety, or what-if, or... Simply come back to the sensation of love or the breath, and allow yourself to feel the following as true:

You are meant for greatness. This situation is important to you, and you might be feeling some nervousness or anxiety, because you care a lot about what you do. You want to show up as the most amazing version of you. Give yourself full permission to feel everything that you're feeling. If you're nervous, be nervous. If your heart is racing, let it race. Don't push against the feelings; they'll only push back harder. So take a moment to accept what is. Let it talk to you. Usually if you simply listen to the body, it will say whatever it needs to say and the sensation will dissipate.

Now this opportunity you care about wouldn't even show up if you hadn't been through a lifetime of work and dedication and creativity. So take a moment here to acknowledge all of your successes and celebrate them. Celebrate every win that brought you here. You can't build on top of success that you don't acknowledge. Celebrate the success that has led to this big opportunity.

Imagine that you could have a magic wand and this situation could go any way that you would want. The board says yes. You're confident, you're easy, you're funny, and you're charming. Play this movie in your mind best-case scenario. You get the deal! Let whatever comes up in your imagination come up. There is no right or wrong way to do this. Just play with it. Imagine you're leaving the room, and just notice the feeling inside you. Proud and excited about what you brought to the table.

Now from that place, step through the door. Deliver what you just imagined. And when you feel that you've done your best, you've done everything you can, let it go and give yourself a big high five.

Take a big inhale, breathe some life into your hands, into your feet, and exhale, let go of what isn't serving you. One more big inhale, breathe some life into your body, bring your awareness back into the room. And in your own time, whenever you're ready, you can start to slowly, gently open your eyes.

E RITUALS ENABLING FLOW

What helps to become more present and raise your vibration, is to build in new practices, or as we call them, *rituals*. Rituals enable you to consciously connect with all of you, your heart, body, soul, emotions, and mind. In this book we've brought together our favourite practices, old and new, so you may experience feeling tapped in, tuned in, turned on! They allow you, from that conscious presence, to step into the energy, intuition and purpose you choose. In doing so, you have the opportunity to clear energy and patterns no longer serving you.

It is wonderful to start your day with a ritual, as it sets the tone. Likewise, it's also a great idea to end your day with one.

Below you can find a morning and an evening ritual. Some of these practices have been around for thousands of years like the Inner Smile and the Metta. They may help to connect you with your body, decrease stress, increase positive energy/life force while helping you off-load dysfunctional energy. The movement practice is also built on old techniques using Aikido.

Morning Ritual – reconnecting to yourself: a 15-30-minute ritual to kick off your day

- Metta – connecting to your heart and tuning in,
- Movement – connecting to your body by grounding and centring,
- Meta – connecting to your intuition and setting your intention,
- Meditation – connecting to your mind and emptying and focusing it.

1 Metta – *opening your heart, raising your frequency*
   Step into this short but beautiful Buddhist Loving-Kindness practice. Being kind to yourself may prepare you to relax your mind and open your heart. Get settled in a comfortable position to meditate. Close your eyes. Say the mantra: "May I be in my heart, may I be happy, may I be healthy, may I be safe." Really feel this. It all starts with self-love! Then repeat this for your loved ones, really see their faces, feel their presence, insert their name. Then for your circle of friends, again, making it a felt experience. Then practise the same for strangers, finally the world. This practice should leave you with the charge of love built in your heart.

2   *Movement* – *grounding and centring*

These practices develop centre and help to align with your body. They work with the breath, gravity, space, and quality as natural ways of support/relaxation to bring you back into your body. Sensations noticed in the body are your connection to your aliveness. As you build and settle your energy in these exercises, notice the aliveness in your body. Building the capacity to both work with energy and to notice the sensations, will help you bring more (leader) presence into your work, even when you're stressed.

Centring [55]

1   Focus on *breath* – inhale up and out of the top of your head, lengthening your spine as you straighten and uplift your posture. Slowly take twice as long to exhale down your front all the way into the earth, softening your jaw and shoulders as you go.

2   Relate to *gravity* – gravity is your natural way to relax. Feel the width of your body and the weight of your arms pulling your shoulders away from your ears and relax the tension in your jaw. Allow gravity to settle you into your personal space and onto the earth.

3   Balance *personal space* – ask yourself: is the back of my personal space, balanced and even with the front? Is the left equal to the right? And is above equal to below? Expand your personal space to fill the room.

4   Evoke a *quality* – your quality represents something you want to cultivate in yourself. Working with a quality is a practice of inquiry. Ask: if there were a little more... (ease, confidence, compassion, et cetera) in my body, what would that feel like? Where do I notice that quality? Choose the quality that feels best to you.

3   *Meta* – *raise intuition and tune into energy* [56]

Ask yourself the following questions:

- What are three things I know to be true right now?
- Which of these holds power?
- What wants to shift here?
- Who is that shift asking me to be?
- What is one step I can take today?

---

55 From *Leadership Embodiment*, by Wendy Palmer and Janet Crawford, CreateSpace, 2013.
56 *The Deep Simple*, inspired by Alan Seale.

4 *Meditation* – *Inner Smile*

1 Sit comfortably, with your whole body relaxed, close your eyes, and let your breath come to its natural rhythm.

2 Connect with something of great beauty in nature: the sun, a tree, the sea... go to your favourite spot. This may bring you a deep sense of unity with all there is. You can use the memory of this experience to evoke your core values. Make sure you are alone there. Feel the beauty and abundance of this spot around you, and also in your body. Feel, see, hear, smell and taste the quality of this spot. Often a sense of space and rest arises. The colour people often see is a golden yellow, but any other or none are just fine as well.

3 Let the light of this spot come together in a cloud or spiral in front of your face and let it enter your skin. You can hold your hands there, and use these to let the light flow through your body. Hold your hands in front of or at the spot where the smile is directed. Focus particularly at a point between and above your eyebrows (third eye).

4 Feel how the light enters your skin and deeper into your tissues. Let it flow from your face through your throat to your heart. Feel how your heart reacts when the light, together with your loving smile, enters there. Take your time and let your entire chest area fill itself with this light. Enjoy the space and the abundance of energy. Let then the energy, together with your smile, flow to your stomach area. From there let it flow into your belly area and finally your entire pelvis. Make sure you remain in connection with the abundance of nature.

5 At the end of this meditation let the light and energy come together, in one spot deep in your belly, behind your belly button, in a concentrated ball of energy. Because you bring this energy together you can use it later for things you value. Your health, loved ones, work, or your leadership.

Evening Rituals

To close off the day, you want to move into a calm, peaceful energy where you are grateful for the things that were good and leave behind the things that were not. You could simply keep a gratitude practice, where you journal on the five things you were grateful for that day for instance. You could imagine standing under a shower, cleaning you from all that you want to leave behind. Or, actually take one! For a more in depth ritual, if you've had a heavier day, or feel some energetic residual, try this practice. It's designed to clear the body's energy field and calm you down.

Cleaning the Temple [57]

1 Sit with your legs lightly bent before you.
2 Circle with your hands around your belly button, with a soft touch. Take care to melt your attention and your eyes with the places of your touch. Spiral until you feel yourself sinking from your head deeper into your belly.
3 Then bring both hands to your lower back and move them via the sides and back of your legs to your feet. Stroke the soles of your feet in circles and follow the insides of your legs back up to your belly. Repeat this 3-10 times until you feel that you are calmer and the reactions subside.
4 Then spiral again with your hand palms around your belly button, and move up via your stomach to your chest area. Stay spiralling until you can make contact with your heart. Then, using one hand, follow the inside of your arm to your palm. Stroke via the back of your hand and the outside of your arm over your shoulder and via heart and stomach back again to your belly. Repeat with both arms, again until calm.
5 Finally start, by using one hand, to spiral via your navel, stomach, heart, your shoulder, over your neck and skull, face, to the inside and outside of your arms, and back again to your navel.

Your body may react in different ways to the cleansing of your three energy centres. The reactions will tell you what kind of tension you hold in your body. For a summary of various reactions possible, see page 220.

---

57 A Taoist practice by Dirk Oellibrandt to clean our three energy centres: head, heart and belly.

Living from and connecting to your Soul/Higher Self

Combining physical presence with energetic presence is very powerful. Integrating this awareness into your day-to-day life implies expanding your physical identity with your energy identity. When you have this internal strength, you do not sway with life's motions. You respond instead of react. But how can you embody this?

You do this by aligning with your purpose or soul. That brings you to a state where you can see the bigger picture. Your soul or higher self is the part of you that is aligned with the quantum field of energy. In Part I we elaborate on page 84 and 86 on how to connect to your soul/Higher Self and how to join your Higher Self with your ego in an equal partnership on page 89.

C UNIVERSAL ENERGY DESIGN

Now that you are aware of your internal energy system, we move to the bigger picture to explore the universal energy design.

People have always tried to make sense of the universe. To gain insight into the nature, the meaning and the rules of the universe, insight into the true nature of reality and ourselves as part of it. Over the last twenty years, science, through quantum physics, has proven the wisdom traditions' knowing that the universe operates in accordance with ancient laws. It has proven that everything in the universe is part of one interconnected whole that works according to these universal principles.

These principles, or Universal Laws [58], help us to understand the natural order inherent to everything in the universe. They help us understand the natural order of life: how it works in a way that enables all living systems to function optimally in harmony with each other. When we understand these universal laws and bring our lives into alignment with them, a pathway to freedom opens. Please note: whatever you think of these laws, they're intended to be used. You do not need to believe in them. Just use them, your experience will speak for itself!

Peter Russell, scientist, and philosopher concluded after thirty years of research, both scientific and mystical, that *consciousness is at the heart of all matter.* Consciousness is everything. The wisdom traditions view our human existence in service of becoming more conscious. You could call this evolution or our spiritual path.

---

58 Ancient mystical, esoteric and secret teachings dating back over 5,000 years from ancient Egypt to ancient Greece and to the Vedic tradition of ancient India, all have as their common thread these Laws of the Universe.

Let's take a look at the main universal laws that we find in all wisdom traditions, such as the hermetic principles, Buddhism, and Vedism. Several sources provide information on this, ranging from Deepak Chopra to the Hermetics, the Vedas and more. There is a relatively recent work of Willem Glaudemans [59] who reclassified the laws, using existing sources and inspiration derived from Ken Wilber among others. His approach creates a very natural order that we find valuable.

Below we follow his order in exploring the main laws and their relevance to us. The aim is to provide you with awareness of the laws, as well as make you aware of the possibilities for practical application.

1 The Law of Creation

> "This universe is not outside of you.
> Look inside yourself: all that you want you already are."
>
> — RUMI

This law gives us insight into the process of creation. *Creating needs a number of elements that together form the roadmap from idea to manifestation.* These are universal aspects, at play in the world at large, in nature, as well as in us individuals creating something. It works on all levels, molecular, quantum physical, physical, mental, organisational, cultural, sociological, etc.. He who creates works in accordance with this law.

We live in a creative universe, a living, conscious organism, where it all starts with a field of pure *potential*. This is a field of free-floating energy at different frequencies. Every creation starts with imagination, with a vision. Then an *intention* is added to this. This intention creates direction and attracts to it those particles that resonate in frequency. This process is called *coherence*. When directed action is added to this coherence, manifestation follows.

Every creation comes about like this. Whether it is building a house or an organisation or creating a painting. The intention (and Essence) of the maker are reflected in the creation. Think of painters like Van Gogh, Rembrandt, and Picasso: you recognise their work by their energy. The same applies to what you create: you create as you are.

The law of Creation is: Potential x Intention = Coherence + Action = Manifestation

---

59 *'Boek van de Universele Wetten; een leidraad voor bewust leven'* by Willem Glaudemans.

Glaudemans views this as the central law that all others form a logical part of.

Applying the law of Creation
When you are creating something, check:
- Is there enough creative space,
- Is your intention clear, and
- Is your action aligned with your intention?

2 The Law of Unity or Pure Potential

> "At the quantum level, reality resembles unset Jell-O.
> It's ripe and ready for any programming you want to give it.
> Living consciousness turns the possibility of something into something real.
> The only thing dissolving this little cloud of 'potential' into something solid and
> measurable is the involvement of an observer."
>
> – LYNNE MCTAGGART

Science is now validating what Eastern mystics have always known – that *we are all part of a dynamic and inseparable field of energy* [60]. We are all connected to source or the field of pure consciousness. It is made up of energy and light, quantum photons and it feeds creation with this energy and light. Everything and everybody is connected to everything and everybody.

In this field of potential, the manifested form shows great diversity. The unity shows through the *frequency* that everything, including we humans, has. Frequency connects via the principle of resonance: like attracts like. Quantum physicists, like Ervin Laszlo have confirmed this O-point field.

The experience of self (our essential nature) is called self-referral, and it points to our internal reference point, our spirit. Object-referral points to the ego as our reference point. Objects outside ourselves always influence us. We want approval of others; we want control and are sustained by (false) power. It is fear-based. Our Essence is pure consciousness. When we experience our source energy, our pure potential, however, there is an absence of fear. Source energy is very magnetising.

We are connected on many levels, but particularly through consciousness. There is resonance, (brainwave synchronisation), and a transfer of information

---

60 Lynne McTaggart, *The Field*, HarperCollins Publishers, 2008.

via the field of conscious intelligence (think, for example, of biologist's Lyall Watson's the 100th ape findings [61]). We can tap into this so-called collective intelligence. *Science has discovered that the brainwave synchronisation between mothers and babies, also applies to groups of people working towards a shared goal.*

The state of your consciousness can be felt as a subtle frequency. To give you an idea, think of the Dalai Lama for instance, or Barack Obama. Can you feel their different frequencies? Being in the presence of someone with a high consciousness can rub off on you. Not only that, as consciousness connects us all, as you grow in consciousness, so will the collective field.

Applying the Law of Potential
- Get in touch with the field of pure potential by taking time, each day, to be silent and *just be*. Meditate, spend time in nature. It recharges you!
- Align yourself with this field of potential.
- Take time to experience your Essence and realise your nature is pure potential.

3 The Law of Intention

"Our intention creates our reality."

— WAYNE DYER

"Intention appears to be something akin to a tuning fork, causing the tuning forks of other things in the universe to resonate at the same frequency."

— LYNNE MCTAGGART

There are two principles at work here: the *Law of Love* and the *Law of Intention*.

The Law of Love – A Course in Miracles [62] states that there are only ever two human emotions or intentions: love or fear. Therefore, there are only two types of acts; an

---

61 Lyall Watson found that when a critical number of a type of animal shows certain behaviour, their behaviour is taken over by the other animals suddenly and without direct contact. Transfer of information happens via the field of consciousness.

62 *A Course in Miracles*, Foundation for Inner Peace, 2008, is a book on achieving spiritual transformation. The underlying premise of the work is the teaching that the greatest "miracle" that one may achieve in one's life is the act of simply gaining a full "awareness of love's presence" in one's own life.

act of love or an act of fear. Love has a high vibration (500 on the Scale of Hawkins). When we choose love, there is no space for lower frequencies like fear. Higher vibrations have the ability to transform lower vibrations.

Although we're essentially made up of a continuum of harmonious frequencies, most of us have no conscious connection with the higher frequencies. When we grow, we open our abilities to accept higher levels of vibration, of energy and consciousness [63]; life teaches us to become more and more aligned with our Essence. Our soul carries the highest vibration and connects us to universal love and wisdom. It is the Higher Self, the key to truth. When we expand and open up, we create expanding realities, and growth is realised.

Life energy or qi infuses all energy layers via our subtler bodies up to and including our physical body. The more our different layers are in harmony, the easier qi can flow through us, the more we feel aligned inside and outside.

The Law of Intention – Intention is the conscious direction of attention and energy. Research has shown that human consciousness is so powerful, that it can direct matter [64]. Intention directs thoughts so they have a strong magnetic pull. *Intention is the cause, manifestation the consequence of what was created.* That's why the intention is still recognisable in what is manifested, think of the paintings in the earlier example.

When your intention is clear and comes from presence, then, like a stone tossed into a quiet pond of water, its ripple is clear and its effect prominent. We must set our intention as though the intention has already manifested in the present moment and our present bodymind.

Applying the Law of Intention
- Investigate: what is the intention behind your actions?
- Connect your intention to that of others: science has confirmed that the combined pure intention of 2 people is quadrupled: the intensity of waves that are coherent, is equal to the quadrant of the sum of the waves, i.e.: 2 + 2 = 4 x 4 = 16! Just think of revolutions like #MeToo.
- Attune your intention to the greater good. It will give your intentions wings!
- Be committed to voice your intention: commitments are a declaration of intention. This invites the field of potentiality to join in.
- Remember, your intention will always return to you.

63 Barbara Ann Brennan & Thomas J. Schneider, *Light Emerging*, TransWorld Publishers, 1993.
64 Lynne McTaggart's *The intention experiment* – Use your Thoughts to Change the World, Harper Collings Publishers, 2008. See page 22 on the work with Random Event Generators.

4 The Law of Centre

> "At the centre of your being you have the answer:
> you know who you are and you know what you want."
>
> — LAO TZU

This law states that everything and everyone in this universe on all levels of creation has a centre and is organised around that centre. Without centre, there is no coherence. In this universe, *centre is the primary organising principle*. Or, as Walter Russell states: the centring O-point of stillness in all things [65]. All of this takes place in a field of consciousness or morphogenetic field.

This goes for atoms, molecules, solar systems, and galaxies. But also living systems, like organisations or countries. Scientists are researching the connection of energy, mass and consciousness and their exchanges. Sacred geometry shows us everything is organised around a centre. Humans too! *What then is the overall organising principle? Consciousness!*

We humans have a heart and soul as our centre. Carl Jung calls this our individuation point, where we come together with ourselves, subconscious included. In accordance with this law, our responsibility is to take our place, and fulfil our role and mission in life, coming from this centre.

> *It feels as if in this time of transformation, we have collectively lost centre. We've lost our own centre, and we've lost a bigger centre, as Josephine Green stated in her interview. We've lost it in culture and religion, but also, for instance, in the US as 'good housefather' of the world. This makes up for a lot of the anxiety which is so palpable at the moment. It needs to be replaced by something else. So that, whatever happens outside, we are secure in ourselves. **We need to reconnect to our own centre, our foundation.***

Carl Jung defined mastery as the ability to remain centred and act from an inner knowing/centre, no matter what is thrown at you. To be present. This is what Part I is about.

---

65 Walter Russell, *In the Wave lies the Secret of Creation.*

Applying the Law of Centre
- What do you consider to be your centre? Are you able to get there at will, even in tense times? And what is it in the various fields you're active in?
- What is your place in your organisation/team/environment?
- How do you create this place?

5 Action, or The Law of Cause and Effect

"Until you make the unconscious conscious, it will rule your life and you will call it fate."

— CARL G. JUNG

"The Principle of Cause and Effect is the base principle of human intelligence, which, together with the power of logic thinking and acting has been given to humans as tools to develop themselves."

— HIDAYAT INAYAT KHAN, SUFI MYSTIC

Every action is like a ripple in a pond. It affects all other things. Nothing exists without a cause, creating an effect, causing another effect. There is no such thing as chance. It's a never-ending process. This law connects the material effect to the immaterial such as the thoughts, ideas, feelings that created them.

We find this in many traditions with sayings like 'As you sow, so you will reap,' and: 'Do unto others as you would have them do unto you': this is the *Golden Rule*. From the perspective that all is energy, the Law of Cause and Effect translates into the principle of reciprocity, or 'give and take.' In that way, the energy keeps flowing and isn't blocked by us holding on to something we know.

The best way to understand this law, is to become aware that your future is generated by the choices you make in every moment. Very often, our responses to outside stimuli boil down to conditioned reactions. We do not act from a conscious place. Try to make your choices consciously, with integrity, and be clear in your intention, so you create the life you desire. There is only one choice that makes you feel good, and your heart and emotions will let you know what it is. The more you witness your choices, and listen to the feelings in your body, the more your life becomes in sync.

Synchronicity [66] means that at the right moment your desire is fulfilled by someone you meet, something you read, etc. The more in line you are with your soul and intuition, the more you can live like this. You then become a conscious co-creator of your life.

Applying the Law of Cause and Effect
- Step back for a moment and witness the choice, to make it conscious.
- Then ask yourself: what are the consequences of my choice or action, and,
- Will my choice make me and those around me feel good?

Now follow the 7 laws of manifestation.

1 The Law of Vibration

"If you wish to understand the universe, think of frequency, energy, and vibration."
— NIKOLA TESLA

Everything in this universe vibrates and has its frequency. Different planes of reality differentiate due to a difference in frequency (dense-ness of energy). People have their own frequencies too. To be more precise, our different bodies have their own frequencies. Our physical body is the densest, lowest frequency. Then our energy body, our mental body, and our emotional body. Spirit has the highest frequency.

All bodies with lower frequencies will be completely infused by the non-physical bodies through higher frequencies. In other words, our thoughts and emotions infuse our body via different layers. The universal laws describe the dynamics along which these frequencies move (by way of least action).

When we understand the *Law of Vibration*, we realise its far reaching consequences. Many wisdom traditions know principles derived from this Law.

For the last 20 years scientists like David Bohm, Rupert Sheldrake and Bruce Lipton have proven that everything is energy. Where Einstein's $E = mc^2$ describes the quantitative relationship of mass and energy, William Tiller stated in 2005 that we now need to describe the relation between energy and consciousness. Following the new insight that *mass = energy = consciousness*.

---

66 Synchronicity: a meaningful coincidence of two or more things where something other than the probability of chance is involved.

Some of these principles, like the Principle of Harmonic Resonance, have found their way into science: similar frequencies resonate together, Rupert Sheldrake's *Theory of Morphogenetic Resonance* – collective consciousness. Impact of energy fields on our physiology: Bruce Lipton's *Biology of Belief*: we live in an energy-based environment with which we are energetically entangled and which influences all biological regulation. Frequencies influence us as much as substances. Thoughts, therefore, influence our physical bodies too! It all has to do with regulating harmony. There is a major interest in the connection between quantum physics and morphogenetic fields, e.g., Carl Jung: the collective (un)conscious – world of archetypes and Karl Pribram: documenting info in the Akashic Records [67] beyond space and time.

> *We all have our own frequency, called our **signature field**. This is regulated more by our consciousness (higher frequency) than by our body (lower energy). Our heart acts as coordinator of the frequencies of our aura, brainwaves, consciousness, and observations. When this is incoherent, we can compare our power to the power of a lantern, while coherent energy gives us the power of a laser. Thoughts are energy, so more focus means more clarity!*

EMOTIONS, AND FREQUENCY

The innate wisdom of our body divides emotions into two categories: lower emotions such as shame, guilt, apathy, grief, fear, anger and pride (resulting in disharmony) and higher emotions such as neutrality, love, peace, and acceptance resulting in *balance*.

A conscious mind combined with the power of intention has enormous effects: it creates coherent, thus powerful waves. Top performers in sports and business are well-known for using this law to their benefit.

Applying the Law of Vibration
   When we raise the frequency of our body, we invite in more of our soul,
   When we realise our consciousness influences the consciousness of the whole, maybe we can see that we have the ability to aid the so necessary shift in consciousness right now! And that self-mastery is not so much a luxury as well our responsibility. 'Be the Change,' as Gandhi said.

---

67 In theosophy and anthroposophy, the *Akashic records* are a compendium of all human events, thoughts, words, emotions, and intent ever to have occurred in the past, present, or future. They are believed by theosophists to be encoded in a non-physical plane of existence known as the etheric plane.

2 The Law of Dynamic

> "The pendulum of the mind oscillates between sense and nonsense.
> Not between right and wrong."
>
> — CARL G. JUNG

There is a constant movement between opposites. Everything has its opposite, but all opposites are simply different manifestations of the same thing. For example: hot and cold, although opposites are both really the same thing, degrees of temperature. Cold is just less hot and hot is less cold. All opposites can be reconciled. Also, in case of feelings, it's possible to change vibrations from one end of the spectrum to the other through transmutation, for example, love and hate.

When we experience life only through our senses, we perceive duality: the source of a lot of pain and suffering. If we understand that our perception is based on our past experiences or beliefs, we may understand that someone else's perception of the same circumstances can be totally different. This is the *Law of the Divine Paradox*: as all people think from the level of their own consciousness perspective, there is no absolute truth. Think for example of the Sufi story about the blind men and the elephant in the room. Every man perceives just a part of the elephant. Only mystics who have experienced becoming One with All can see the whole elephant or truth.

> *Mystics tell us to overcome duality by learning to look at things from a higher perspective. John Anthony West* [68] *writes:* ***"It's the heart, not the head that understands."*** *The more you understand, the more you can forgive, be in relation and reconcile polarities. This asks you to engage from unconditional love and without judgment. The reconciliation we ultimately long for, as long as we're a soul in a body, is a state of harmony between our mind and body in the form of synthesis on a higher level.*

When we understand that everything in the universe, including our lives, perpetually moves between two seemingly opposites, we get the picture of a pendulum. A pendulum that moves toward the centre, and then moves away again. In centrifugal and centripetal moves, moving towards and away from the centre.

On a purely human level, taking into account the central U figure of Theory U, this implies that the more we let go of our old history, the more we become available to the emerging future!

---

68 John Anthony West is an American psychologist and Egyptologist.

Applying the Law of Dynamics
- Realise that there is a continuous move between expansion and contraction in the universe as well as in yourself.
- Look for the overriding centre, in yourself, in your team, and in your organisation.
- Being in this centre, you are no longer at the mercy of external events, you are at peace, in dynamic harmony.

3 The Law of Cycles

> *"Panta Rhei*, everything flows, nothing stays the same."
>
> — HERACLITUS

Just like nature, ebb and flood, moon tides and seasons, we also have our rhythm. *This Law describes how certain phenomena occur and repeat themselves according to fixed patterns.* There is a sequence from which the principle of periodicity has been deducted. We see this reflected in the seasons, time itself, and certain predictions. Everything from circulation of the earth around the sun, to that of the moon around the earth and the rotation of the earth around her axis, has been used to calculate time. Everything has its rhythm.

Joseph Campbell's 'The Hero's Journey' beautifully captures this on a human scale. He saw repeating patterns in all myths and fairy tales and discovered that the archetypical story of the hero describes a deeper development model of every human.

An issue pops up, urging the hero to go on a journey. He *leaves*. Often *hesitating* if he is doing the right thing. But knowing he has to do this, there is no way back. He meets all sorts of tests and hardships but also encounters helpers on his path. And he moves on, looking for his treasure. When he finds his treasure trove, he is not able to open it directly to get to the treasure. He realises that only he can fulfil his own mission and get to the treasure. This is his *initiation*.

Then the hero needs to *return* and *share* his treasure. Only through sharing this, can it grow in value. He needs to go back home and *celebrate* the treasure with his clan.

Departure, hesitation, initiation, return, and celebration are the phases of this journey. It is the journey that the soul makes to fulfil her mission. It helps to know the various phases when you find yourself thrown into a journey like this.

Applying the Law of Cycles
The best way to apply this law is fulfilling your mission in life!

4 The Law of Radiance and Attraction

"The Law of Attraction is this: you do not attract what you want, you attract what you are."
— WAYNE DYER

This law describes how objects and people react to each other and form relationships via emission and attraction of energy. Radiance and attraction are two powers that work in unison. Radiance is the inner energy moving away from the centre, and attraction is the outer energy moving toward the centre.

If you think of yourself as a magnet, you realise that the frequency you emit is very important as like attracts like, or so-called resonance *(Law of Vibration)*. Also, the frequency of your intention returns to you *(Law of Intention)*, continuously, in all walks of life. As life is continuously evolving, you are continuously invited to purify your radiance to attract people and things on higher frequencies.

Lots of attention has been showered upon the *Law of Attraction.* Think of 'The Secret', for instance. This, however, forms only half of this law: it leaves out your own responsibility to make sure your frequency (radiance) matches what you desire. If your radiance is a match with what you want to attract, then it will flow to you. If, however, it is not in alignment with your desire, it will not. You want to radiate that you already feel what it is like to have what you want. Then it will flow to you.

Warning: focus on what you want, not on 'what is.' The mind tends to want to focus on 'what is,' and it can come up with a lot of resistance to 'act as if.' This, however, cancels out what we want to manifest. But, when you embrace that we attract what we are, you will soon realise that it's all about the higher vibrations of gratitude, joy, and love. They will bring you to the realm from which you can manifest effortlessly.

Applying the Law of Radiance and Attraction
- Life acts like a mirror: start by noticing if your intentions are pure or not.
- This law puts us in the drivers' seat of our life. Our outer world is a reflection of our inner world: we need to accept responsibility for our life.
- Look at your relationships: do they reflect who you want to be, or do they reflect who you were?

5 The Law of Levels

> "As is the universe, so is the human. As is the human, so is the universe."
> — THE VEDAS

This is quite a complex law. After a brief overview, we move on to what it means to us as humans. Everything in the universe is put in order according to levels. There are different planes of reality, which are all connected. Everything in the universe is evolving to higher levels of evolution and frequency. This is not a linear process; it involves periods of growth spurts as well as chaos. Ken Wilber says that the cosmos appears to have no bottom and no top: we keep discovering new particles in the smallest particle again and again (holons) [69].

Levels are arranged in the shape of a spiral, similar to the depiction of the order or evolution of human consciousness by Spiral Dynamics. Every spiral evolves around a centre, in alignment with the *Law of Centre*. Every part of one level forms a whole (holon) together with other parts on the next level above. Holon in Holon. The planes differ in a denseness of energy. The higher the density (material) the more we can perceive it. Every level of consciousness has its vehicle for observation.

We have these different layers too. We mirror the reality around us and have a physical, energy and spirit body, as well as a physical, energetic and spirit consciousness. How should we view this? By and large three levels can be discerned:

1 The *physical* level: everything we can perceive through our senses. Both material and energetic matter, although we mainly perceive the material part,
2 The *spiritual* level: the space beyond time and limitations,
3 *Unity* – or the Big Emptiness.

Physical level
We perceive mainly the ego-dominated, rational world and our physical self, which is separate from the other planes of reality. Our mind makes sense of all this. It's the place where we have learned or think we can withdraw to protect ourselves, for physical safety. The energy aspect of the physical reality connects us to all that exists in physical form.

---

69 Ken Wilber, *A Brief History of Everything*, Boston, Shambhala Publications, 1996.

Energetic reality

It's by connecting to the energetic reality that we communicate with all there is. Connecting to this field enables synchronicity and enlarges our perspective on reality. Think of how a swarm of starlings act in their murmuration: they tap into the collective intelligence of the energy field.

We humans possess this intuitive connection too, from birth. Indigenous cultures still use this skill to live and thrive. In the West, however, we have focused mainly on our minds. We can re-activate this energetic connection to tap into our collective intelligence by consciously using attention and intention to reconnect us to our instincts and our (collective) unconscious. This enables us to communicate on a deeper and more connected level.

Soul

The next layer is that of the spirit that moves through all things. Via our energy-body, we are connected with the physical world and via our soul with what lies beyond space and time. Our physical body and soul merge in our aura. Scientific proof for this is provided by, for instance, David Bohm in his book '*Wholeness and the Implicit Order*'. Where modern science and consciousness research meet, there arises an image of a universe offering unlimited possibilities. For instance, our brains can recognise information that is stored in the Universal Consciousness, as such, our brains function like a hologram [70] Karl Pribram found.
Research with Tibetan monks has pointed out that the state of our brain waves has a major impact on our consciousness. Neuroscientist Richard Davidson has, on the request of the Dalai Lama, found that the best way to activate positive emotion circuits in the brain is through generosity. We can also expand our consciousness by moving from a productive mode, creating Beta waves, into a more creative mode via meditation and mindfulness, for instance, creating Alpha waves (or Gamma).

NB: in relaxed state Alpha waves represent 7.8Hz which is the same as the Schumann frequency (the electromagnetic field around the earth or harmony with all that is).

---

70 Holon in Holon: a term coined by Ken Wilber. It is a part whole that on the first level is a whole, and on the next level part of a whole, that in its turn is part of another whole on the subsequent level. Like electron – atom – molecule.

BRAIN STATES

Measured EEC activity of our Brain	State of Consciousness	Levels of Consciousness according to psychiatrist Carl Jung	Observation Of Levels of Reality
Beta waves (14 – 60 Hz)	Ordinary wake consciousness	Personal Consciousness	World of matter / explicit order (matter)
Alpha waves (7/8 – 14 Hz)	Relaxed state of consciousness state of light meditation	Personal Subconscious	World of force/ explicit order (energy)
Theta waves (4 – 7/8 Hz)	Consciousness state of dream or deep meditative state	World of the archetypes: timeless collective (sub) conscious	World of the Soul/ implicit order
Delta waves (0 – 4 Hz)	Deep dreamless sleep or very deep meditative state lack of self whistleblower	Universal Consciousness connected wisdom	Land of the Shaman / super-implicit order melting chaos

NB: in relaxed state Alpha waves equal the electromagnetic field around the earth, or the Schumann frequency @ 7.8 Hz

Unity: the Big Emptiness

Live at the edge of the physical and spiritual world to allow both aspects to become in balance, some indigenous elders say. Then you experience the world of energy and beyond. In that state, you feel intimately connected to yourself and all around you. This is the bridge between physical and non-physical.

Applying the Law of Levels

When we realise what our brains are and how they operate, we can expand their capacity by regularly using a mental practice such as meditation or mindfulness.

6 The Law of Order – Chaos – Order

"Nothing in the world can change from one reality into another,
unless it first turns into nothing, that is into the reality of the between-stage.
And then it is made into a new creature, from the egg to the chick.
The moment when the egg is no more, and the chick is not yet, is nothingness.
This is the primal state which no one can grasp because it is a force which precedes
creation; it is called chaos."

— MARTIN BUBER, *FROM TALES OF THE HASIDIM*

This law teaches us that development comes in leaps of periods with, and periods without a structure. Organisms, organisations, and societies fall into crisis, think of the recent financial crisis for instance, before finding a new order at a higher level.

*Most wisdom traditions view the evolution of consciousness as the main motive of our human existence on earth. Whereas we can view the evolution of our physical body as part of biological evolution, **the evolution of human consciousness relates to the evolution of people on a soul level**. The overall result of evolution of consciousness is the combined result of all individuals on soul level.*

The traditions tell us that our soul is the force behind our development. The challenges come about in our day-to-day reality. The lessons we learn in our bodies shape our non-physical aspect in the spirit world. This is not a linear process, but a spiral shaped process of various cycles in accordance with this law. Periods of spiritual awakening alternate with periods of spiritual sleep.

This process simultaneously happens at the level of the individual and of the collective. Periods of relative stability alternate with periods of chaos. We can learn to use this principle and go with the flow, in line with the *Law of Least Resistance* and the *Law of Surrender*, and recognise chaos as an opportunity of growth to let go of the old, and be present and aligned with our inner core, instead of fighting it.

The *Law of Order - Chaos - Order* is well understood by modern science and is considered a universal law as applied to material things. Consider, for example, the chaos theory and the spiralling biological evolution, Elizabet Sahtouris' view on the evolution cycle and Rupert Sheldrake's Chaos Creativity and Cosmic Consciousness.

148

In the new era, we will move to a higher level of unity and consciousness named **integral** by Ken Wilber and Jean Gebser. *This demands deep self-knowledge and responsibility.*

Applying the Law of Order - Chaos - Order
- Realise the promise this law offers: every chaos period enables new growth and arriving at a new order.
- Maybe that way you can see chaos as a doorway to the future.
- Maybe then you find yourself prepared to move through, knowing it is temporary.

7 The Law of Development

> "Maybe the journey isn't so much about becoming anything.
> Maybe it's about un-becoming everything that isn't really you,
> so you can be who you were meant to be in the first place."
>
> — PAULO COELHO

We can be brief about this law. It is the culmination of all other laws. *The Law of Creation* ultimately, taking into account all other laws, is about evolution. For the world we live in as well as for ourselves. What kind of human are we becoming? We really don't know.

We do know though, that as we develop ourselves along the axis that we have used to write this book: body, mind, emotions & soul (with a special place for the heart), we grow on an integral level, helping us to develop faster. To illustrate this: Ken Wilber performed a study in which participants were divided into three groups. One practised Zen-meditation, one practised weight-lifting, and the third group practised both. The results showed that the third group benefitted significantly from the combination of strengthening body and mind, and developed faster than the other two groups.

The best way to apply this Law
Following the above, practice on a combination of levels within you.

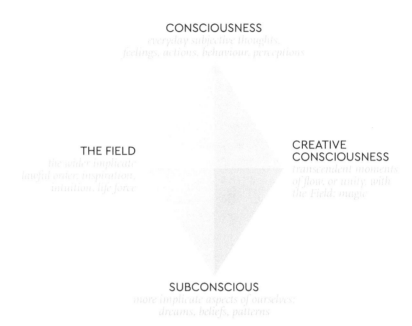

CONSCIOUSNESS

everyday subjective thoughts, feelings, actions, behaviour, perceptions

THE FIELD

the wider implicate lawful order, inspiration, intuition, life force

CREATIVE CONSCIOUSNESS

transcendent moments of flow, or unity, with the Field: magic

SUBCONSCIOUS

more implicate aspects of ourselves: dreams, beliefs, patterns

As we have outlined in this part, we live an interconnected field of unlimited potential. *'The Way of* **nowhere'** [71] beautifully describes and depicts this conscious field in ourselves. The diamond of consciousness they describe has been given to them by RainbowHawk, an earth keeper. We love to share it with you here.

- *The North* of the diamond represents our *everyday consciousness*. Whilst constituting a relatively small part of who and what we are, this aspect of ourselves takes up a hugely disproportionate amount of our awareness.
- *The South* represents our *subconscious*, our emotional Self, which is also a very small, but extremely influential part of who we are, as it drives our needs and desires.
- *The West* represents the largest percentage of who and what we are. It reminds us that we are forever and always from *the Field* [72], part of an interconnected whole.
- *The East* represents that very small and underdeveloped aspect of ourselves which we have called *creative consciousness*. This is our ability to be present and at one with the Field, with our wholeness and the interconnectedness of all things.

71 Udall, Nick & Turner, Nic, *The Way of Nowhere, 8 questions to release my creative potential*, Harper CollinsPublishers, London, UK, 2008.

Practice to flow with energy and create a life in harmony with your desires.

1 What is energy?

Everything is energy. Here in the Western world we're not so used to looking at this subject in this way. But mystics have said all along that there is only energy and everything is connected. Science has confirmed this over the last twenty years. Energy is information. Everything, even our thoughts and beliefs, carries energy. The saying your thoughts create your reality therefore holds truth.

2 Your energy design

Our human energy systems are the connection between the physical and the metaphysical; they connect us to the Field [72]. How do you flow with it? Realise that we are simply like magnets. Creating awareness of your energy design is essential. So too is understanding the vital role the heart plays as the coordinator of your overall energy. As well as the role of our kundalini or chi, or unlimited primal life force. Practicing to connect with this energy, deliberately working with intention, attention and intuition (all contain energy!) and building conscious rituals around these will enable you to flow at a high frequency consciously.

Practising to flow with your energy enables you to create a life in harmony with who you are. It provides you with the fuel to create or manifest what you want.

Practices: Chakra Meditation, page 118, and Kundalini Practice, page 120.

3 High vibrations

David Hawkins has calibrated the frequency of our consciousness. Deliberate rituals as gratitude and loving-kindness (metta), e.g., raise our frequency. In accordance with the Universal Laws, the higher your frequency, the more positive energy you get back in the form of people and experiences.

Practising presence in the heart by practising positive emotions gets us into heart coherence, in a high frequency, feeling connected, creative and energised. This is great for us and our environment!

---

72 Lynne McTaggart, *The Field*, HarperCollins Publishers, 2008.

Practices: The Love Bomb, page 126, Morning Rituals, page 129, and Evening Rituals, page 132.

4 The Universal Energy Design

All wisdom traditions come up with the same 7 (or 12) universal laws governing the way the universe works. The rules of the game so to speak. Here, we addressed:

from the unmanifest:

- the Law of Creation,
- the Law of Unity or Potential,
- the Law of Intention,
- the Law of Centre,
- the Law of Cause & Effect, or Action.

to the manifest:

- the Law of Vibration,
- the Law of Dynamic,
- the Law of Cycles,
- the Law of Radiance and Attraction,
- the Law of Levels,
- the Law of Order,
- the Law of Development.

When we understand the universal laws and align our lives with them, a pathway to freedom opens.

"It all starts with you."

— INTERVIEW WITH MARIKE VAN LIER LELS, MULTIPLE SUPERVISORY BOARD MEMBER

As long as I can remember, I have been interested in consciousness. It's a personal quest. Not in an esoteric new age kind of way, but in a grounded, scientific way. Quantum physics has long shown us that reality is often not what it seems. I'm interested in that bigger field, in discovering there is something like a collective consciousness.

We need to expand our thinking into an inclusive collective: I believe we will only have a better world when we work with, and from that perspective. And I truly believe it's up to us to make a difference!

Radical responsibility to me means being faithful to your values while realising that you are connected to the whole. Acting from a place of responsibility and connection.

It starts with finding your own foundation (consciousness), and operating in accordance with that, staying true to your values. Looking back at my career, this has been a red threat to me.

It started out when I was working at mid-management level at Nedlloyd and had some comments on the way the company was run. Somebody said to me: 'Well, why don't you do it yourself?" This had an enormous impact on me: do not wait for others, rather, take on your own responsibility! So, I created a budget for training my team, and we became highly successful. We had a ripple effect on other teams around us, and they soon followed our example.

At 36 years old, I was appointed as Managing Director of Van Gent & Loos, where I later became Executive Director. I was responsible for 6000 people at a company going through a rough period. Various directors were breathing down my neck, but I told them I could really only do it if I would be allowed to do it my way.

When you sail according to your own compass, it is not only smooth sailing. When I was CFO at Schiphol and came to realise the direction the company was heading towards did not agree with me, staying true to my values meant leaving the organisation. It meant being without a job and having no idea where this would lead me to in the next 5-10 years. But I simply felt I had no choice.

What drives me in my current positions as a supervisory board member is to be of service to the whole. I fully realise that the tone at the top can mean a lot for the feeling of space co-workers have to do things in their own way. But I also feel that people usually have much more space than they think. You do not need to play along! Everybody is a leader, you can step up! Because when you believe in yourself, and your projects, others will feel it!

Radical responsibility is very much needed!

To me, it means waking up and realising you simply cannot permit not to do it! You just need to find a way and timing that work for you. And don't make it too complicated.

It means realising it's all about consciousness, connectedness, and responsibility. It starts with you!

You must (re)create a personal conscious foundation. From there you can consciously connect, and create a foundation for your team and organisation. I believe we will have a better world when we get cracking with that. We are confronted with fundamental issues. We simply need to expand our thinking into an inclusive collective.

Personally, I feel that I have been connecting my heart to my hands for a long time. The past three years, I am experiencing a deeper connection with my body too. This gives me a sense of expansion and a great sense of coming home.

My message would be:

- Consciously (re) invent your foundation,
- Realise you are connected to the whole planet,
- Take your responsibility from there, and,
- Trust the universe.

We need you!

release your personality blocks

by Yvette Hooites Meursing

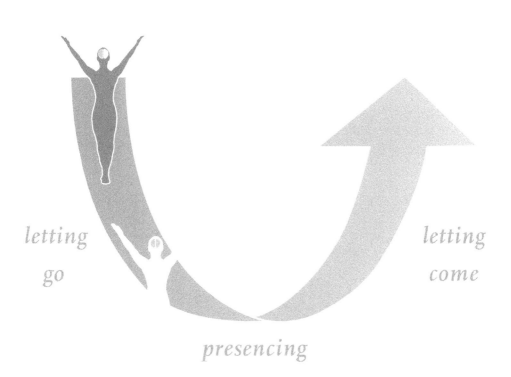

*letting
go*

*letting
come*

presencing

moving from unavailable to available

Letting Go

To access our greatness and see beauty and possibilities, we need to clean the windows of our perception. We all look at the world through our own lenses. And as such, do not always see reality clearly.

When our lenses are very muddled up, for instance when we're under stress and triggered, we are unavailable to ourselves. We are in survival mode and act from a fragmented place where we are (usually) trapped in our mind, and cannot tap into our full inner wisdom. This is caused by the character armour that comes into being at such a moment, as you will read in this part.

*You need awareness of your **personality design**, and the ability able to pause and reflect: do I really choose this, or am I falling into the same old emotional patterns? And then, with this awareness, you can choose a different behavior and deliberately move from being unavailable to being available, by letting go of patterns that no longer reflect who you want to be.*

This leads to freedom!

"We do not see things as they are, we see things as we are."

— ANAÏS NIN

Now that you have an idea of your *human* and *energy design*, as well as that of the universe, and of what flow is, do you know what is blocking you from being in flow? From creating a life in harmony with your desires? Do you know your *personality design* with its qualities and flaws? Do you know what and how to truly let go and how to relax and be open in every situation? In other words, do you know:

- Your defense mechanisms, character styles, or personality?
- That they show up in behaviour, but are located in your body?
- That they can therefore only be addressed through the body?
- How character intelligence improves your personal and business efficiency?
- How it enables freeing others by better communication and less conflict?
- How unlocking the character armour is truly letting go on all levels, and,
- What to do to enable this letting go?

The aim of this part is to provide you with awareness on the consequences of unconscious and limiting beliefs and feelings, so you may let go of your patterns and become more free.

> *Wherever you are, freedom is possible. It is the biggest gift you can give yourself and those around you. Release yourself from what has been holding you back to live your potential to the fullest. Choose freedom, choose life and allow awareness to take you where you are supposed to go. Dare to be you!*

Please note: we have placed this part at the end of this book on purpose. If you have the helicopter view of your overall human design and know how to tap into the energy of flow, it can be so much easier to do the hard work of letting go. You have more motivation and energy.

Please note also: Our goal is to give you the consciousness and awareness of what a character armour is, a feel for how this works in real life (using four character styles to illustrate), as well as a complete overview of all seven main characters so you may assess your own emotional design and that of the people important in your life. This represents quite a bit of theory! In order to make this information easily accessible, the characters have been put in a grid for an overview, and all outlined using the same format. The 4 styles that we used in the story, starting page 164, you'll find in Part III, the remaining 3 styles in the Appendix.

For your own journey, you may want to read the overview, the story and then read in-depth those character styles that you find you might embody. To help you find your design you could click on the link provided for on the *Reinventing Ourselves* website (paid test). It's also very helpful to read up on the styles that the important people around you embody, or read through all styles in one go.

Before we start, I would like to acknowledge my predecessors and colleagues in the field of character analysis, trauma or bodywork: Wilhelm Reich, Alexander Lowen, John Pierrakos, Peter Levine, Stephen Johnson, Rashma Schaeffer-Buss, Jack Painter, Willem Populiers, the team of Bodymind Opleidingen, Wibe Veenbaas, Marianne Bentzen and Susan Hart, Larry Heller, and Raja Selvam.

The body always speaks its mind
We saw that already in Part 1 Embodied Presence. But how does bodymind integration work when the going gets tough?

Think back to your most embarrassing moment. How did that feel? Probably not too great. Just thinking of the memory may cause you to feel the pain again, because its memory will cause a series of physical sensations. You may start to sweat or want to make yourself small and disappear for example. Also, you may start to avoid situations in the future that could cause similar anxiety. Did you know you can only move beyond this anxiety by engaging with these physical sensations, or so-called somatic markers? Only then can you generate different behaviour with a different result.

This is an example of what neurologist and author Antonio Damasio refers to as *the somatic marker hypothesis* [73]. According to Damasio, each event we store in our memory is connected to a series of bodily sensations we felt when we went through it the first time. These markers, or emotional memories, stored in the musculature of the body, are called character structures or character styles. Your personal-

---

73 Damasio, A., *Looking for Spinoza – Joy, sorrow, and the feeling brain*, Harcourt, Orlando, 2003.

ity is the pattern of emotional, attitudinal and behaviour responses that you typically portray. In other words: *you develop your personality through your body.*

The nervous system is the recording system of the body. It is the connecting link between body and mind, a vast network of communication circuits that coordinate the brain with all other body systems. It governs our body chemistry, and also thoughts, intentions, and emotions. It establishes the perceptual base from which we view and interact with our internal and external worlds. It underlies alertness, thought, and precision of coordination. The nervous system, previous experiences (somatic markers) and the mind continuously interact. All experience starts from the nervous system and the somatic markers, we call this the *body-mind.*

Through bodywork we can learn to modify the functioning of our nervous system, by freeing the somatic markers in the body of the dominant character styles.

What is a character?
We use the following definition: "a character is an identity based on physical and brain development. It's a combination of qualities, physical and psychological survival strategies, a set of beliefs, physical characteristics and feelings a person has developed in response to everything she has experienced in her life."

Every character follows certain codes of conduct that ensure anything experienced as a threat is nipped in the bud. As a result of threats (such as: "I am not welcome" or "The world is an unsafe place"), a character structure is developed. This character structure manifests in your worldviews and the pressure you encounter in life. This pressure becomes fixed in your body and ensures any initial impulse is blocked or restrained. The energy flow throughout the body is constrained. Initial needs have been suppressed because energy is focused on what is perceived as a threat. This ultimately leads to stress. *Stress then, is nothing more or less than unfulfilled needs.* [74]

A character is your personal defense system protecting your inner core. In essence, an armour. As we will see later on, this defense system also has its qualities when you can move through it freely. By being aware of how your character works, you can create the space from which to choose how to deal with challenging situations. We call this awareness and freedom of acting 'character intelligence.'

---

74 David Simon, Chopra Center, Carlsbad.

Seven character styles dominate your behaviour, depending on your predisposition or history. Each has a number of fixed patterns of behaviour and patterns of beliefs: feelings, physique, posture, and movement. The bodymind connection determines these patterns.

Although we have all styles, in case of stress the preferred style manifests itself. Two other 'wing' styles help to reduce the stress. The four others are hardly used. People differ, partly due to the different preferences of these character styles. The characters have been specified by their dynamics and the names given to them by Yvette based on the qualities and pitfalls they have. The original Reichian names are added in brackets.

The seven character styles are:
1 Absent / Present – the Analytic (Schizoid), a pattern of leaving
2 Unfulfilled / Fulfilled – the Social One (Oral), a pattern of attuning
3 Self-loss / Individuality – the Saviour (Symbiotic), a pattern of merging
4 Genuine / Image – At the Top (Narcissist), a pattern of presenting
5 Trusting / Controlling – the Leader (Psychopath), a pattern of aggression
6 Autonomous / Sacrificial – the Loyalist (Masochist), a pattern of enduring
7 Accessible / Inaccessible – the Perfectionist (Rigid), a pattern of rigidity

Below we will analyse these styles to become aware of their challenges and gifts. We will also discuss what is necessary to break free from them. First some background.

A number of leading psychologists have made discoveries with regard to the character field. From Sigmund Freud to Erich Fromm, to Wilhelm Reich to Alfred Adler, Alexander Lowen, and Nina Bull. Reich developed the concept and explored the character structure as it applies to bodymind structure and development. In Reich's view, character structures are based upon energy blocks – chronic, unconsciously held muscular contractions – against awareness of feelings [75]. These blocks result from deprivation or frustration of needs at a young age: the child learns to limit its awareness of strong feelings. Reich coined five basic character styles, each with its own body type and belief system developed as a result of the particular blocks. Nina Bull's research proves that the body's muscular-neural patterns of organisation are directly related to their emotional organisation and their behaviour [76].

---

75 Wilhelm Reich, *Character Analysis*, Wilhelm Reich Infant Trust Fund, 1949.
76 Bull, N., *The body and its mind – An introduction to attitude psychology*, New York, Las Americas Pub. Co., 1962 Bull, N., *The attitude theory of emotion*, Johnson Reprint, New York, 1968.

To make it concrete: the *Analytic*, which most of us share, causes fragmentation of both body and mind. How then do we organise ourselves physically and emotionally so that we can remain integrated at all times?

How a character takes shape

A character expresses a life story, and reflects how specific experiences in the early years of life have been dealt with. It shows to what extent you have succeeded in fulfilling basic needs and whether the original vitality and naturalness on all fronts in life and work are retained.

Everyone is restrained in their natural development by influences in early childhood. People often respond inappropriately to a child's natural reaction. This makes it necessary for a child to shut itself off from the outside world. The muscles tighten, so no unpleasant emotions are felt. The mental and physical defenses develop, and respiration proceeds less freely and naturally. This whole bodily process, which forms between birth and the age of seven, and then becomes chronic, is called character [77]. *A character is characterised by limitations in thought and behaviour at the expense of the natural vitality.*

Conscious and unconscious conduct

Most people follow their character unconsciously. This often leads to clashes in relationships. As an example: a *Loyalist* values freedom and being able to finish things in his own time. He does not like deadlines or authorities telling him what and when to do it. A *Perfectionist's* drive and value, however, are to meet deadlines and tell people what to do. All of this is unconscious to both, thus not communicated. When they do not meet each other's needs and values, both are annoyed and frustrated. The result is opposition or sabotage. When it is communicated it often leads to arguments, and further discord, rather than connection, as they do not realise the totally different underlying worldview they have.

Choice of character style

Everyone has a unique combination of favourite styles. One strategy can be used in a certain context, others elsewhere, for instance, one at home, another at work. Just like you have an energy signature, you also have a *character signature*. If you know yours, it's as though you know your own blueprint. If you know that of the important others in your life, you can understand and relate so much better.

---

[77] Lowen, Alexander, *The Language of the Body*, originally published in 1958 as *Physical Dynamics of Character Structure*.

Each style has different drivers, motives, values, and basic patterns as well as different qualities and pitfalls. And each character style has certain dynamics in which it moves.

Drivers: Character drivers are life themes, such as safety, autonomy, attunement, trust, and love, with which one should make ends meet. Drivers are survival strategies designed to protect the core. The root of all characters is fear of life, of feelings, and of scarcity. Fear of life is evident in the way we are always busy and on the run. We have all kinds of fears: rejection, neglect, abandonment, loneliness, betrayal, being truly loved. We also have (hidden) needs: to belong, to be cared for and supported, to be free and to love. When these needs are not met, there is a feeling of scarcity or neglect. People who face their character styles, and work through them, can move more freely.

Qualities: each character has its qualities. Things they are very good at and love doing; their talents. Both influence what people do, where, and with whom.

Values: each character style has its preference in values, as e.g. safety, stability, care, independence, progress, freedom, respect and appreciation.

Behaviour: we are caught up in inner conflict continuously. Usually, this is an unconscious process. The mind tries to control the body and emotions. The will tries to overcome fears and concerns. Characters come in many forms. Forms have to do with: who is the real you and who do you think you should be? This conflict exhausts and disturbs your peace of mind.

It's been said that you learn through experience. However, in the area of character you do not, as long as you are unaware of how your brain and character work. The destructive behaviour is repeated until then, due to forces beyond your control.

For example: suppose you have a natural tendency to help others (character 3, the Saviour). The deep underlying conviction is, for instance, 'If I don't help they will not be able to manage.' When you find yourself in a situation in which someone appears helpless, you may offer help, solicited or unsolicited. If your effort is not appreciated sufficiently, or returned, you may feel used or offended. You may decide to consider if your help is necessary next time. However, when a new situation involving helplessness occurs, this decision is nullified. Your deep underlying conviction automatically kicks in. You don't learn, as you help compulsively: your character and brain working (seemingly) unconsciously, compel you to help.

Resistance through character blocks

Often, resistance is the result of character blocks. Defensive setups limit the possibilities in life. Opportunities remain untapped and unexplored. This is the reason for many failures in collaborations for instance. People follow an ingrained character block, often unconsciously. Consequently, there is little happiness and joy. Anxiety, dissatisfaction, stress, agitation, and depression are felt. Understanding and freeing your character can help you break out of the constraint of frozen, unresolved resistance and conflict.

A OUR BODY AND CHARACTER

Every unresolved conflict in life leaves a trail of armour: hardening in attitude and body. It shows for example in posture, conclusions, and assumptions formed about life. So how does that work?

Take the *Loyalist*, for example. Loyal and faithful in life and work, he has a great sense of responsibility for people and tasks. This may be coupled with a difficulty saying no (not being loyal) and standing up for himself. It's as if this person is more faithful to the task or to someone else than to herself. Body and thinking are compressed. There will often be tension in neck and shoulders and stomach, as a result of this compression. This leads to more difficulty in saying no, as the shoulders and neck can take on more work physically. Mentally the thought that accompanies this is: "I can endure it." The *Loyalist* overrules himself with a chronic overload. If this continues for too long, it will lead to physical complaints such as burn-out and inflammation symptoms.

In the case of character blocks, there seems to be a lack of energy because this is invested in protective and defensive postures, it ensures resistance and opposition. This all leads to poor cooperation.

We assume, however, that vitality is available and can be freed. You can practice to liberate your character armour and attitudes. Behaviour and feelings are freed from fixations. Vitality and flexibility increase when more flow can be admitted and experienced in the body and in the brain. Awareness and physical exercises help to achieve this.

Beyond a character reflex

Take *Leaders*, for example. Usually very driven and passionate, working overtime is a structural habit, even a need. They are relied on to resolve issues, 24/7, particularly in uncertain times. Loyalty to the success of the company, and fear of repercussions on career or income keep this pattern in place. When this continues for too long, it usually comes at the price of burn-out or extreme fatigue. The character style has now become second nature. It acts as a buffer between the inner and outer world. Contact with the outside world is maintained via the character. But it's an emergency measure. The actual problem is a conflict of not being able to take care of oneself and give a little less. Physical needs are suppressed by fear of letting go. Overworking may prevent conflicts or problems that have to do with true relaxation. By ignoring the inner discomfort someone settles for activation, rather than the real need: relaxation.

The true or natural self needs to step forward by setting healthy boundaries. For instance, by indicating that it's time for a break. The need has been felt, expressed and followed up with action: stop working to recharge the battery. This requires courage but will be a big relief. The inner world is now reconnected to the outer world. It makes a person more authentic and balanced, and ultimately benefits their health and general mood. This is a *Leader* in balance.

Transformation results in flexible behaviour

When you transform your character fixation, you move beyond a boundary, and everything changes into something new. New characteristics emerge. There will be a new look at the world and a new posture. Heart and mind get more connected. You are more free. It leads to transformational presence: you act from your whole being, instead of your pain.

Transformation is noticing new behaviour is difficult, yet boldly deciding to show up anyway, and move beyond the social fear of rejection. By applying this consistently, behaviour changes in such a way that it is no longer an issue, as the fear of rejection diminishes. You have progressed.

This new, transformative behaviour is what all progessive leaders are looking for. It means moving beyond resistance and realising your highest potential. Transforming a character needs conscious awareness of your limitations, and changing things in work and life to be more free. It leads to optimal flexibility. Ingrained patterns can be left behind, it just takes eagerness to learn, a genuine interest in how people function and applying the insights of the following chapters to life and work.

When you succeed, a lasting relationship with yourself and others is the result. An optimal synergy between people is possible if character resistances are expertly transformed into character optimisation.

A SUMMARY OF TRAITS OF ALL SEVEN CHARACTERS

	vision / worldview	mission	behaviour	qualities	pitfalls	dilemmas	growth	intelligence to develop
1 THE ANALYTIC	not welcome	be present	absent	clever	all ratio	ambivalence	feeling	*physical*
			analysing	curious	arousal	boundaries	participate	
			fragmented	creative	anxiety	avoiding	connection	
			associative	sensitive	dissocation	denying	boundaries	
			rational	inventive	volatile	pressure	relaxation	
2 THE SOCIAL ONE	shortage	fulfilment	needy	sensitive	dependence	dependency	focus	*creative*
			passive	friendly	depression	little self confidence	abundance	
			frustrated	social	claiming	comparing	independence	
			dependent	collaborative	giving up	no energy	discipline	
			sociable	adaptable	lack of vitality	lack of attention	tolerate energy	
3 THE SAVIOUR	merging	individualise	fusion	sensitive	panic	separation	sense of self	*individual*
			feeling	system view	feeling	individuality	boundaries	
			no boundaries	empathy	lack of reality	structure	distinguish	
			lack of self	connected	melting	organisation	individuality	
			whistleblower	wisdom	chaos	feeling vs reality	structure & organise self	
4 AT THE TOP	presence	authenticity	perform	ambitious	unreal	self	authenticity	*collective*
			image	excellence	cyniscism	no feeling	feeling	
			grandeur	discipline	contempt	self-hatred	love for self	
			performance	energetic	no empathy	insecurity	empathy	
			rational	task oriented	criticism	people	connect with people	
5 THE LEADER	control	trust	will-power	excellence	almighty	support	trust people	*emotional*
			intellect	independent	aggressive	delegation	interdependence	
			topdog	initiative	manipulative	cooperation	support	
			direct	passionate	exhausted	manipulation	relax	
			in charge	overview	controlling	competition	letting go	
6 THE LOYALIST	no autonomy	freedom	pleasing	responsible	low self-esteem	inner critic	autonomy	*social*
			working hard	reliable	discontent	no freedom	boundaries	
			complaining	harmonious	pressure	lack of time	directness	
			sabotage	warm	indirect	lack of space	saying no	
			postponing	loyal	resentment	self-sabotage	true to self	
7 THE PERFECTIONIST	perfection	connect inner & outer world	keeping distance & appearances	precision	self-control	seclusion	openness	*inner*
			critical	disciplined	critical	fear of being hurt	imperfection	
			control	efficient	self-assured	fear of failing	flexibility	
			looking and being perfect	sense of beauty	rigid	empathy	vulnerabilty	

> "I must have a dark side if I am to be whole; and inasmuch as I become conscious of my shadow, I also remember then I am a human being like any other."
>
> — CARL G. JUNG

Below we will go into detail on the main traits of the characters. To illustrate this, we will start with a story in which four character styles are involved. It gives you a feel for how interactions can work when blocked by character, and what the effects are of letting go of the armour. The four character styles in the story are the *Analytic*, the *Loyalist*, the *Leader* and the *Perfectionist*.

How moving beyond your character can set you free

Suzan was a director in a boutique consultancy. While she had always been ambitious and wanted to get to the top, she was worried that others did not see and appreciate her efforts and hard work. Although she was precise and sharp, she was also very insecure. She did, however, not show her vulnerability, instead she acted tough and in control.

She had been promoted one year earlier. But she still felt she had to prove herself. The results of the firm had dropped and the CEO was very demanding. She felt strong pressure. The promotion had involved more responsibilities than she had bargained for. One of the two teams was not operating that well. Now was the time to correct this.

She met with huge resistance when she tried to gain more control through pushing for more meetings, reports, and deadlines. She also pushed herself, compiling reports, constantly checking mail, and arguing with staff. She couldn't let go, she had to finish everything before going home. Prior to this promotion, Suzan had visions of being in control and successful. Instead, she felt pressurised and insecure. Her work-life balance had gone and her husband pushed her to work less and be home more.

Suzan realised that deep down she was very insecure. Always had been. She was comfortable at work, excelling due to discipline and hard work. She felt great when processes and people were under control. Now that this was not going well, her self-confidence dropped. She was worried and stressed. She needed to get a grip! She made a reorganisation plan proposing a huge cost reduction to the CEO. He was fully on board.

It entailed freezing the budget of the two teams for two years. The staff had been with the company for a long time. Now that the company was close to bankruptcy, she decided they should feel privileged to work there. In order for the company to survive, they needed to work more efficiently. This enabled her also to get rid of certain personnel issues in the teams: staff not up for change would probably leave and could be replaced by cheaper and younger hires, more efficient, and more obedient and appreciative of her. She'd get her confidence back, as well as the success and appreciation she wanted. Especially from the CEO, a man she liked very much.

There were two people who clearly didn't like Suzan's plan: the managers of the two teams, Ellen and Mike. Fortunately, Ellen never spoke up in team meetings, and Mike, although emotional, was very loyal to Suzan. She fully expected his support. With the support of the CEO, nothing could stand in her way. She felt confident about the meeting.

The meeting

Suzan walked into the room feeling strong. She greeted her colleagues. She did notice something different in Ellen's presence, and saw that Mike was in time, for a change, but paid no attention to it.

After the minutes and agenda, the CEO gave Suzan the floor to introduce her plan. Suzan was nervous but well prepared, and felt her presentation went well. She emphasised this reorganisation was needed to get the company lean again. Only control could save the company. As she spoke, people as disciplined as her, all seemed to agree. She avoided looking at Ellen and Mike, but felt confident her plan would be supported.

Wrong! Mike turned to Suzan directly and stated he was not prepared to agree. He understood her motives, but from his perspective, this plan was causing more problems. He felt there were other ways to deal with the cost reduction. He said he felt this was moving the problem rather than fixing it. Then Ellen spoke up too, strong, clear and coherent. She said that, before deciding on the plan, the staff needed to be consulted. She warned that it might breed resentment when not discussed properly. Particularly as the plan would possibly involve colleagues leaving, which may weaken teams and expertise necessary to continue to operate at this level. The CEO agreed with Ellen's observation.

Suzan was floored and only managed to get a few words out on how this was not her intention, and that it was about efficiency and in the best interest of all. She fell silent, wondering what had gone wrong. She felt angry with Ellen for speaking up, and with Mike and her CEO for not supporting her. She felt, as always, not appreciated for her hard work and effort. She left quickly after the meeting. Staring at her computer, she saw mails streaming in. She felt upset and stuck.

Ellen, however, felt very confident and satisfied after the meeting. Normally she would never have stood up and now she had! She felt proud; it had gone well! She had been very angry with Suzan, noticing Suzan's nervousness, and deducting that her strategy was to pass the problem to her. But she did not invest in her anger. Instead, she was clear and direct, relaxed and centred, focusing on the issue at hand. She had done her exercises for centring and expansion, just before the meeting started. As a result, she felt free and completely open.

She thought of the leadership program that had taught her these practices. At first working with the body had felt very unusual to her. It had turned out to be however, without a doubt, one of the most powerful experiences in her life. She still did not understand fully how to explain the program, but felt, the experience had helped her tremendously just now. It taught how to act from calm and choice, even when stressed.

It was Mike in fact who had recommended this program, having followed it himself, just a year ago. He was very impressed with the results too. In his case, being the *Loyalist*, he had learned to start being loyal to himself and say *No* to others, rather than opt for harmony. He also felt that centring was key to different behaviour. He felt that it led to being able to be in a situation in a relaxed way, and to choose expansion both in his body and behaviour. Mike was also pleased with his conduct at the meeting. He finally had been able to say no to Suzan, whom he both liked and disliked. He had felt enormous freedom in his body by saying what was truly on his mind, rather than being diplomatic and giving in. He decided to continue the practice. It had a nice side effect: as he became more loyal to himself, people had more respect and did not see him as a pleaser anymore. He also gained more self-respect.

How Mike and Ellen overcame their usual character blocks

Ellen could not easily speak up for herself. It seemed she approved of everything. In order not to get into a discussion with people, she usually gave way. This was very frustrating for her team members as she did not defend them the way they wanted to. Instead, she disappeared in situations when confrontation was needed. Why? She had a lifetime of being ignored, and not having real contact with people around her. She had been forced to behave and adapt to the environment and be silent and wise, rather than speak up. Speaking up was just selfish.

When stressed, Ellen would respond on the base of her *Analytical Character*. It basically meant she was under the influence of her reptilian brain and autonomic nervous system. She often had an increased heart rate, would start to breathe superficially and start to sweat. Her body would contract and freeze. Her fight-flight-freeze system would kick in quickly. Ellen loved learning and had become a true expert, a wise one indeed. However, she could not speak up for herself. She could not stay centred and focused. She had no choice, she responded by withdrawing, a defense mechanism she had picked up as a little girl.

The most important insight she gained from the program was that she was limited in choice when things really mattered to her. She saw that awareness alone didn't help. It required practicing expanding, and as a result of this, obtain holding: the ability to be in your body, regulate your feelings and emotions, and act freely in the world from this safe place.

She had practiced how to relax her nervous system five minutes before she entered the meeting. The result was that she felt warm and comfortable in her body. By relaxing, she was able to use the energy for expressing herself the way she wanted. She could finally speak up, as she kept access to her core and cortex, the language and thinking part of the brain.

The first exercise, or practice, as they called it, in the program was *centring* (see the practice on page 59). Ellen thought it had to do with more space and reducing stress. As it turned out, centring is really the route to more choice internally.

Internally, she did not have a lot of choice in how she would respond in meetings or teams. She normally could not speak up, as she felt so anxious that it seemed that her whole being contracted. This often happened when she was in a group or in a team. She just could not relax very well with too many people around her, or with people that felt strict and rigid. It felt unsafe.

The moment she did not feel relaxed, she was not able to act or say things in the way she wanted to. She could not use her knowledge, as she was literally blocked. She could not speak coherently anymore. The moment she felt anything unpleasant, her body would contract, and she would lose contact with her core. This left her frozen, in her own world, and isolated from the rest of the team. And she was saying things that were not coming from the core, but from emotional patterns.

Unfortunately, most of us respond along these patterns causing automatic ways of behaviour. Most of us, just like Ellen, are either not aware that this happens, and even when we are aware, we just do not know how to change and influence this. This result of unawareness of how old patterns affect our behaviour shows up continuously causing a lot of confusion and dysfunction.

Expansion leads to holding

What is expanding? Expanding (page 61) is about moving the body beyond con-traction. It's about relaxing both the nervous system and making yourself longer, wider and deeper, both literally in your body and as a result, as a person in the way you behave. It's about moving beyond the blocked character armour.

What actually happened when Ellen expanded herself? First, she put herself into the present moment by bringing her attention to her body. Rather than worrying about the outcome, or what could go wrong, she is just present and aware of her sensations. Secondly, she's then able to choose as she has holding, rather than being fixed by her somatic markers. Expansion leads to holding.

Holding is having access to your body, and being able to regulate your feelings, emotions, and actions in an adult way. Your body is the container of all emotions and feelings. It directly gives you freedom of choice.

Mike was a typical *Loyalist*. He loved harmony and disliked arguments. A loyal family man, he was also very loyal to the company. He had been with the company for more than 20 years. He had worked his way to the top. He was very proud of the position he had as a senior manager.

His family history had always told him that he should work hard. That he was not very bright, and that he should obey and be a good boy. Because of this, he held a lot of tension in his body. He made himself small. At meetings, he would always support everybody and harmonise the atmosphere.

Everybody loved him. He was friends with everybody in the team, as he always listened to everybody and made them feel at ease. He was a pleaser. During the program, Mike had learned to stretch himself, to make himself taller. He had felt so much space in his body, doing that. This came as a surprise: he always felt so pressured both in – and outside his body, particularly at work.

He always worked hard for Suzan, who usually gave him the work she could or did not want to do herself. She would pressure him to do things, which he really resented. However, he had never dared to disappoint her, as he wanted to keep the relationship harmonious.

Mike was given exercises in setting boundaries and saying *No*. He had always felt weak and angry with himself for not being able to stand up. As a result, he was often overloaded. The program had taught him to open his throat and express what he did and did not want anymore. It gave him space and air inside. At the meeting, he had remembered to stretch his arms and legs, and his neck and throat.

As a result, he felt sufficiently comfortable to take the risk to clearly state his disagreement with Suzan. He was so pleased with the result.

Finally, he felt free to say yes or no and to be loyal to himself. The disharmony he expected was OK, he could handle it. He realised that the memory tapes of disharmony in his family did not start to run. He experienced an immense freedom instead.

C THE MAIN TRAITS OF THE FOLLOWING FOUR CHARACTERS:

The Analytic (1), the Leader (5), the Loyalist (6), and *the Perfectionist (7).*

CHARACTER 1 – THE ANALYTIC: ARE YOU PRESENT OR NOT?

1 **Worldview, driver, vision, mission, and values**

Worldview – the world is an unsafe place. Your driver is safety, and the perspective is not belonging. There is a sense of insecurity and not feeling welcome from the start of life. This is terrifying: it constitutes a deep fear of rejection of who you are. You flee in fantasy and withdraw from connection with your body and its feelings and emotions. You develop a super strong mind to constitute control in an unsafe world. It helps to analyse and cope with life and work. In a situation where there is little or no sense of security, you become anxious and disconnected. Your vision obstructs and ensures that your behaviour is at odds with the actual needs. *You need to build inner safety.*

Mission – learn to be present in your body. Being present means being more in touch with self and others. This will lead to more joy and belonging. You will feel more free in contact, and you will show up.

Values – safety, security, stability, quality, innovation, creativity, expertise.

2 **Behaviour: anxiety, absence, and fragmentation**

Anxiety – others notice the lack of contact. But they are unaware of the underlying reason, the experience that people do not tune in to you or resonate at your energy. Although they may value your knowledge, they seem to lack a true interest in you as a person. You conclude you are not important, and so this triggers your sense of not belonging. You can feel anxiety or anger. It confirms your perspective and creates a vicious circle. You become more absent.

Absence – withdrawal and seclusion are ways to deal with difficult situations. Contact can feel anxious and may cause you to withdraw. You are highly sensitive to energy from others, and have difficulty to contain or restrict this. Forms of mental migration help to avoid and escape stress, like thinking about work or wandering off in a conversation. Remembering a conversation may also be difficult because of the tension and volatility. Especially when it comes to emotional issues. You may respond reactionary and inadequate. You may dissociate: you are not present but in the future or the past. Others may think you are absent-minded, or do not remember well. As a result, you grow uncertain and angry. The reality is that you are much faster than others and simultaneously do and think, and therefore remember less accurately what was said.

Fragmentation – you are very curious. Diversity is fun; it ensures creativity, sharpness, and happiness. You tend to do many things at once, often losing the overview. Others are often unable to follow. You enjoy this, as you find it hard to stay and feel real contact: this is too nerve-racking. Instead, you play an act of staying and going constantly. You want to be able to go at all times. This enhances the feeling of safety and creativity. Due to a lack of oversight and energy needed for the various projects, however, you long for more structure and fewer projects. How do you find enough peace in yourself to stay somewhere and focus on one thing? There is a fear that slowing down and focus are boring. This makes true relaxation and slowing down also hard.

3 Qualities, pitfalls, dilemmas, and effects

Qualities – due to a vivid imagination, you are creative and good at associating. You could be a leader, scientist, artist, researcher, teacher, business owner or entrepreneur. You prefer to work on content and creativity as it inspires. A quick and abstract thinker, you can analyse and solve complex problems clearly, you are very good at multi-tasking, and comfortable with variations. You also have great sensitivity to the 'spiritual;' your intuition is highly developed.

Pitfalls – these are caused by identification with the intellect and spirit. This leads to a certain speed causing you to become volatile and engage in a way that is too scattered. You tend to rationalise and miss out on feeling. What you conceive is not connected to your body, feelings, or to other people. You keep people at a distance and can become over rational. There is also a tendency to associate too much; ensuring that what is conceived can no longer be used in reality. It becomes a fantasy due to too much imagination; subsequently, others cannot follow it anymore. Business can no longer get manifested: it remains a creative process, concept or idea. Another pitfall is going out of contact or leaving in case of tension. Your memory is poor, especially for interpersonal events and conflicts, due to a quick mind, too much association, and volatility in contact. As a result, you miss information and have to go by your own experience. This then becomes 'the truth', which comes across as uninvolved, absent and limited to others.

Dilemmas – the choice to leave or stay, both literally and figuratively. "Should I keep this job?" "Will I stay in this relationship?" These discussions take place in your mind; you do not feel them in your body. This complicates choice: you try to solve things rationally instead of emotionally. Ambivalence is a constant given. You may flee literally, not be accessible, and avoid or withdraw from contact. You do not invest in relationships. The real reason for this is that you find it difficult to draw the line. It may cause denying difficult situations and avoiding constructive confrontation. You may say "You did a good job," while you really think "You did not at all." You will not tell this unless very angry. Alternatively, you will tackle each problem with content. Once alone, you will reflect and come back with a 'solution' statement in time. There is no access to your world until then; your are shut off. The internal dilemmas are there to prevent rejection. The more fear there is, the more extreme seclusion and absence. Eventually, you discover that avoiding, intellectualising or denying does not always work, and that you should work on contact with yourself and others.

Effects – you are greatly appreciated for your expertise and knowledge. On a personal level, however, you are perceived as introvert and more of a soloist than a team player. People confront you with your absence. Generally, people want clarity on reliability, commitment, and connection from you. You don't understand this, because you feel committed. You fail to see why this is not perceived as such.

4 *Transformation: feeling, connection, participation, and boundaries*
See yourself as someone who is learning, just like everyone else. Accept your character with its need for security and warmth: there may be a desire for connection and contact. The following is designed to give you ideas for further development, should you feel like it.

From thinking to feeling – you are incoherent. Thinking, feeling and doing are not aligned. You think one thing, do something else and may feel something opposite. Feeling your body is the only way to feel who you are and where you belong. It enables making contact in the world, and enjoying work and life more.

Connection – often, you are disconnected from your body, feelings, and intimacy with people and nature. Once you have decided to participate, you will find that connection makes you feel alive and helps you to say yes or no. You become visible. You become present. This will invite others to become more present with you as well.

Participation – you can choose to withdraw from, or participate in life. You have been rejected frequently. This has made you decide not to react spontaneously anymore; it's dangerous. You contract. Fortunately, sometimes you do act spontaneously and it turns out not to be so bad. The point is to come alive, and learn to tolerate that life entails feelings and tensions. It means taking risks, and following your feelings above all. All you have to do is to learn to tolerate stress and relax in contact. This makes you more visible to others.

Setting boundaries – If you feel more, chances are you feel your boundaries sooner, and will have to draw a line. Rather than stepping out of contact, the challenge is to learn to define and speak up on what you don't like. You have to learn to relate this in contact, instead of fleeing, avoiding, or intellectualising. By drawing the line, you will be able to stay in touch.

Physical intelligence – the first step of consciousness

You live the archetype of connecting and being, or of the roamer who cannot stay and disconnects [78]. Instead of being disconnected from yourself and others, link your identity to being present. Embrace your body and connect with others. You do not have to roam. You have a home in yourself. Generate more places where you can stay and feel safe. The higher value you follow is connecting. The qualities you can use are your curiosity and ability to understand.

If you recognise this character style, you know your mission is to focus on increasing being present. You realise that increasing your *physical intelligence* leads to feeling safe, at home, and connected in life. It provides you with a solid foundation.

A SUMMARY OF TRAITS OF CHARACTER I, THE ANALYTIC

vision / worldview	mission	behaviour	qualities	pitfalls	dilemmas	growth	intelligence to develop
not welcome	be present	absent	clever	all ratio	ambivalence	feeling	*physical*
		analysing	curious	arousal	boundaries	participate	
		fragmented	creative	anxiety	avoiding	connection	
		associative	sensitive	dissocation	denying	boundaries	
		rational	inventive	volatile	pressure	relaxation	

78 *'De Maskermaker'*, Wibe Veenbaas, Joke Goudswaard en Henne Arnolt Verschuren, Utrecht, 2006.

1 *Worldview, vision, drivers, values, and mission*

Worldview – the world cannot be trusted. Your driver is your passion for being the best. You ensure you remain independent and in charge at all times. You are suspicious, continuously on the lookout for danger ensuring vigilance and alertness around you. The environment is monitored at all times to avoid unexpected attacks. Naturally strong-willed, you think you can do anything you set your mind to. You are focused on asserting power. You conceal weaknesses and insecurities. You influence situations, even using manipulation.

Mission – learning to trust and daring to be vulnerable. You need to delegate and dare to receive support. Burn-out looms otherwise.

Values – respect, honesty, strength, success, and high-level performance.

2 *Behaviour: distrust, control, top dog or underdog*

Distrust – you shun vulnerability as you believe no one will catch you when you fall. So you increasingly rely on yourself. Through your courage and leadership, you often end up in situations where you need to brace yourself, and lack the necessary backing. You give up hoping for help. You cannot trust people. Deep down, you're disappointed and feel betrayed by the lack of support. You also find it hard to trust the unknown. Although the unexpected and new may offer excitement and adventure, you will be vigilant and ensure you can rely on yourself at any time. Nothing is left to chance. Power and control should keep danger at a distance.

Control – as a decision maker, you thrive on willpower; thinking will achieve anything. You pretend to be stronger than you are. By keeping control at all times and focusing on action and presentation, you avoid vulnerability. Being vulnerable is seen as showing incompetence; this you disrespect greatly. You show strength and pretend to be in control. You don't notice that you neglect your own needs. Nor does the outside world. Because you radiate a sense of not needing anything, you stand alone. You avoid opening up in relationships. As dependency is avoided, quality is excluded. What remains hidden is that when you badly needed support, you did not get it. Being rejected again is just too painful. So, you control your context and yourself.

Top dog or underdog – in your world, it's all or nothing. You feel you can do anything and live up to your own expectations, as well as those of the world. Progress is important. You live in the future, driven by goals. Always on edge: failure is not an option and must be avoided at all cost. You can be arrogant and feel like you can do and influence anything. No one messes with you. You use seduction or threat as needed. Winning is all. When you're on a roll, all is fine. When things go a-wall, you're a poor loser: you simply don't do underdog.

3 *Qualities, pitfalls, dilemmas, and effects*

Qualities – your strength is your ability to excel. Purposefully and decisively, you achieve pretty much what you want. You're a person of action, initiative, and success, and you are capable of good leadership. You take responsibility, and have great communication skills. You inspire others with your charisma and passion. High in energy, you realise a high productivity. Courage and a strong sense of justice stand out, and confrontations are not avoided. You have a good overview and a well-developed sense of what works, spotting opportunities and connecting people and projects. You have a great intellect and excel at managing complex projects.

Pitfalls – you think you always know best. Although often true, this is not always the case. Losing, or losing face, is avoided at all cost, as it is considered too vulnerable. Your 'being right' often comes at the expense of happiness. The other is overruled by a tendency to check to ensure things go as you want them to. Support will not be asked or permitted. It's hard to delegate because you want to impress. And you think you're always better and quicker. This eventually causes exhaustion.

Dilemmas – it's about power and control versus asking and accepting support. Do you dare to confide in someone? Although you often feel uncertain, you will never admit this. By denying support and assistance, you avoid giving power away. Tending to keep control, you keep up appearances of power and independence. You ensure an absence of failure as you cannot afford losing face. As a result, you ask way too much of yourself and others. You burn yourself out.

Effects – with huge charisma, power, and intellect, you can accomplish much. You exude overview and a large span of control. This is appreciated. In relationships, there's a focus on power. Taking the lead is appreciated. But your demanding nature and impatience scare people. They sense a lack of trust. Cause of failure is always placed outside; you blame others. You are sensitive to power struggles, and are very competitive.

4 *Transformation: support, surrender, trust*

The starting point is to see yourself as someone who does not need to do it all alone. If you accept your need for support and equality, you might take a chance to trust yourself and others.

Support – to accept more support, you need to give up your superiority and acknowledge your vulnerability and weakness. Accept that you have a huge need for support, and let it in. Develop a healthy dependence on others, and trust there is help for you. There is good will in the world. It's possible to get it. If you discover this, you can meet the kindness in yourself, and you will be less hard on yourself and others.

Surrender – you show you're in charge. It's vital to admit having hidden dependencies: needing someone is OK. It means realising you cannot control life and people by using your will. That sometimes you should surrender. And admit mistakes and defeat when necessary, this shows character. You no longer live on false power. Most importantly: recognising you have needs too, gives in to your deeper being, which in turn leads to true surrender.

Trust – you desire recognition from your peers. It requires you to have the courage to open up and rely on others. It also challenges your idea that you can only trust yourself. It takes courage for you to let go of your distrust, to learn to ask for help when you would like it, instead of doing everything yourself. In a wider context, you learn to trust that life has something good in store for you, that it follows a natural flow and does not have to be controlled or staged.

Emotional intelligence – the fifth step of consciousness

You live the archetype of lover and healer, or the heartless or weakling. Instead of being hard and cruel on yourself and others, link your identity to *emotional intelligence*. Embrace vulnerability and gentleness. You no longer have to bear up. You will generate more support for yourself. The higher value you follow is love.

If you recognise this character, you are aware you must increase your emotional intelligence to achieve equality, support, and relaxation in your life. You have to face the question of control or surrender of passion and of sharing this with peers.

A SUMMARY OF TRAITS OF CHARACTER 5, THE LEADER

vision / worldview	mission	behaviour	qualities	pitfalls	dilemmas	growth	intelligence to develop
control	trust	will-power	excellence	almighty	support	trust people	*emotional*
		intellect	independent	aggressive	delegate	interdependence	
		topdog	initiative	manipulative	cooperation	support	
		direct	passionate	exhausted	manipulation	relax	
		in charge	overview	controlling	competition	letting go	

1   *Worldview, vision, motives, values, and mission*

- <u>Worldview</u> – life is a sum of hard work and obligations. Your driver and vision are freedom, but you think you have to fulfil everyone's wishes. You're warm, friendly, helpful and loyal, because you think that is what's needed. As you usually make others the centre of attention, you lose sight of your own needs. You sacrifice yourself. You work hard and experience continuous pressure. Pressure comes from the outside as you find it difficult to say no, as well as from the inside as you impose tasks on yourself. You often suffer in silence and resent your sacrifices. You allow yourself little fun.
- <u>Mission</u> – to be free. To feel what you want and to be clear to others about that. To learn to say no, and to be loyal to yourself. To quit your tendency to sacrifice.
- <u>Values</u> – freedom, loyalty, service, respect, reliability, dedication, humour and appreciation.

2   *Behaviour: a sense of guilt, carelessness, and procrastination, the bill*

- <u>A sense of guilt</u> – fun is linked to guilt: everything should be completed before you take the time to enjoy. You take on more than you should. When you do something for yourself, you instantly feel guilty. You are a strong empath. It's never enough, whatever you do. This is because you think you need to carry and solve everything around you. Doing something for yourself feels unfair, as if this means someone is left in the lurch.
- <u>Carelessness, and procrastination</u> – the defense of having to comply and being put under pressure. This carelessness may come out in different ways. Agenda-wise, deadlines are not met, appointments cancelled, or you may show up late. It has to do with a hidden passive resentment coming from anger. This has to do with the fact that you often say yes, but mean no. This leads to a chronic overload, and a frequent feeling of being used. Consequently, you often fail to meet obligations. This is all hidden under a layer of kindness.
- <u>The bill</u> – the hard work and dedication stem from the thought you will get something. You will be rewarded. It's expected everything will be straightened out some day. This keeps you going, even though it's hard. If you do not get enough, you're left with the feeling of an unpaid bill. Emotionally, you feel the other owes you. This may last a long time until the imbalance is too big and snaps. At that moment, you tell the other what is bothering you, even though it's hard. The contact will never be the same; you will continue to look for what you get in return.

3 Qualities, pitfalls, and dilemmas

Qualities – a hard worker, you pull it all together and are reliable. You have a strong responsibility and endurance. You are stable and friendly, making people feel at ease quickly. You have compassion and help happily because you love people. This is felt. You are loyal and faithful to those who need you. You are patient, you take time, and you like to work in harmony.

Pitfalls – you find it hard to say anything possibly aggravating. You are afraid to lose people's sympathy. You do things you do not want for the sake of harmony, thereby sacrificing yourself and your freedom. You impose limits and pressure on yourself. You remain friendly under all circumstances. People around you may feel that something is brewing: discontent, resistance, withheld comments. Restrained discontent only comes out in case of severe anger. You do not ask for appreciation, but resent the lack thereof at the same time.

Dilemmas – themes are about wanting to be close to people and maintaining freedom at the same time. To experience closeness, you make people as comfortable as possible, doing them favours continuously. Consequently, you adapt too much, and cross your borders. When you do so, you want your freedom back. This is first done strategically: 'If I do this, I will not step on anyone's toes.' On the outside, it looks cooperative, but on the inside, there is sabotage. Occasionally, you are obstinate or passively resistant by postponing tasks and decisions. You enjoy stalling. Insecure, you are afraid to choose and stand up for yourself. You believe everyone has a plan for you. The question you ask yourself is 'How do I avoid this, and get away with it?'

4 Transformation: wanting versus having to, relaxation, and fun, autonomy

The main starting point is that you view yourself as valuable, as someone who is worth the effort. If you can accept your character with its need for love and respect for who you are, if it does not have to be different, it's likely there will be a desire for development.

Wanting to versus having to – learn that you are already free to be who you are and to do what you want. This means allowing what you enjoy, and saying 'no' to what you do not want. By focusing on what you want, independent of the wishes of others, you learn to develop discernment. This makes you come out stronger as you indicate what you think and no longer hold back. You have learned to deal with yes and no. This makes you feel free from the inside and outside.

Relaxation and fun – let go of the pressure and stress you experience, and put on yourself. Relax! Learning to enjoy is not easy for a hard worker like you. If you manage to let go of your toiling and enjoy life more, your happiness will increase. You will get more access to deeper moments of happiness. You will get access to a lighter way of life, by playing more.

Autonomy, choosing for yourself – autonomy ensures fewer tendencies to ask others for advice. You pronounce your preferences. You also show more of yourself. This leads to authenticity in relationships, and creates a balance in giving and taking. You impose boundaries on your availability. By asking yourself how it feels, you go out more easily. You've learned that the journey to joy is associated with really enjoying doing something, instead of doing it half-heartedly. This will give your life the peace and simplicity you desire.

Social intelligence – the sixth step of consciousness

You live the archetype of the helper or the victim. You understand that you help the world. In a negative sense, you are the victim, because you focus on helping others rather than yourself. Embrace yourself and set yourself free. You no longer have to put up with people or things. You will generate more freedom for yourself. The higher value you follow is freedom. You are aware that you must practice *social intelligence*, the balance in giving and receiving, to integrate freedom in all areas of your life.

Your life lesson is about self-expression, giving space to yourself in all areas of life. Your mission is autonomy. You will be more socially intelligent, by taking the risk of expressing yourself and imposing boundaries. You will consequently be more true to who you are.

A SUMMARY OF TRAITS OF CHARACTER 6, THE LOYALIST

vision / worldview	mission	behaviour	qualities	pitfalls	dilemmas	growth	intelligence to develop
no autonomy	freedom	pleasing	responsible	low self-esteem	inner critic	autonomy	*social*
		working hard	reliable	discontent	no freedom	boundaries	
		complaining	harmonious	pressure	lack of time	directness	
		sabotage	warm	indirect	lack of space	saying no	
		postponing	loyal	resentment	self-sabotage	true to self	

1 Worldview, vision, drivers, values, and mission

Worldview – from the start of life you have experienced you can be hurt unexpectedly. To avoid this, you are reserved and always need to control yourself. You have decided to control your feelings at all times, and to prevent letting yourself go. This self-control leads to tightness of both mind and body. You use words moderately. Through self-control, a part of the authentic self is lost. This is reflected in the fact that you play a role. You meet the expectations of others. This makes this character irresistible, and ensures others cannot reject you. Your driver is being and looking perfect.

Vision – being rejected is too painful. This is prevented by looking well-groomed and by taking care of business properly. The authentic self, or how you really feel, is often not known to you. Instinctively, you cannot express yourself or have difficulty with it. You put your heart and soul in the presentation. You cannot surrender to fun, as you feel it's dangerous. Desires must be restrained; otherwise, they become uncontrollable. Feelings are monitored and controlled. This will prevent loss of face, or the possibility of being ridiculed. This distant attitude comes across as cold and proud, or unapproachable.

Mission – to be more accessible. It requires you to let your inner world out occasionally. Also, to learn to be less perfectionist. Errors make us human, and thus more accessible. To be more flexible makes one warm instead of cold and distant.

Main values – discipline, beauty, clarity, efficiency, results, success, obedience.

2 Behaviour: hurt, distance, perfection

Hurt – you have resolved never to open your heart again. The world is perceived as offensive. People can hurt, so you are always on guard. You are verbally strong, but you live based on intellect and will. Unexpected events are avoided to prevent feelings. Once you are likely to end up in a 'feeling zone,' you manage to keep your cool and control yourself. In contact with people, you are alert and cautious. You have strong ideas about what is appropriate. When people do not play according to your rules of the game, they can deeply hurt you. Although you are aware of your desire for intimacy and tenderness, you deprive the other of this, and sell yourself short too. For fear of rejection, you do not give yourself completely; you are always reserved. The chance of getting hurt is big when affection is shown, so you stay in control. You focus on the task and the plan. No one can surprise you because of a reserved attitude. You think people who surrender and cannot control their feelings are losers. They are too emotional. If you can control yourself, you are a winner.

Distance – you are always alert. Closeness and intimacy are considered scary, yet desirable. You are vigilant and hold back. Impulses to be spontaneous are held back. You have a rigid attitude, and you are often tense, there is only real connection with the people close to you. Your view is, that if you open your heart, you will be hurt, so therefore you shut yourself off. The fear of surrendering delivers a fear of being carried to the depth of love and gentleness. You also keep your personal and business matters separate; you think this is none of anyone's business.

The effect on others is that they remain at a distance due to your proud attitude. The other is also on guard, because you exude contempt for vulnerability. The biggest fear lies in vulnerability towards losses and being adrift. Because you nevertheless long for adventure, you attempt this in manageable chunks.

Perfectionist – you are disciplined and controlling. You feel that you should make no mistakes. You cannot stand imperfection. You excel to earn love. An excellent work ethic with a strong emphasis on performance is the result. You are very down-to-earth, and always stick to agreements. Order and rules are very important; they are executed to perfection. Importance is given to presentation and detail. You are very critical toward yourself and others.

3 Qualities, pitfalls, and dilemmas

Qualities – you are good at making and sticking to agreements, and are orderly and precise. You are efficient and manage things well. Through order and discipline, you ensure that what is started is fully completed. You are a good organiser and regulator. You are task-oriented, less process-oriented. The task is always done due to iron inner discipline. You operate well in a corporate environment in which roles and rules are well established. You reliably follow the rules and protocol, behaving correctly and properly. You have a high vitality and fuel others with your energy. Perseverance and self-assurance come naturally. You are a clear thinker, and purposefully works towards a specific performance.

Overall, you are world-oriented and ambitious. If you want to achieve something, you are dedicated. Anyone in your way will have to face your fighting spirit. You have a lively energy and an attractive appearance. You have style, an eye for detail and perfection, and a highly-developed sense of beauty. This can be seen in the way you dress and live. You invest in a good atmosphere and beauty. You work very hard. You are good with all types of communication, presentations and other things of that nature.

Pitfalls – you tend towards perfectionism. It's never good enough. You structure and control everything, are often rigid and rarely spontaneous or creative. You do not want to be surprised unexpectedly, because you don't know how to deal with feelings. Everything should be manageable. This makes you come across as distant. Your sensitive side is shielded; others will not get to see that. The attitude towards the outside world is that everything is always going well. But you are afraid of people who feel. Because you seclude your feelings, you sometimes don't even know how you feel. The ability to love and enjoy is greatly reduced. **The heart is suppressed, often unconsciously.** You hold back and come across as unapproachable and proud. You are critical of yourself and others. Criticism is poorly tolerated. Due to your correct behaviour, you come across as unnatural and inauthentic. You are always competitive.

Dilemmas – it's about seclusion and accessibility. You seclude your inner world. The game that you play (un)consciously is the game of attracting and repelling. You are focused on correctness instead of authenticity. Because you follow the rules closely, you are highly critical of people who do not. You demand the best of yourself and others. You want to show your competence. You are focused on your own interests, and do not really empathise with others. The relational aspect is missing. You prefer people who have their affairs in order and prevent issues.

Effects – you set high standards. Because you love order and structure, you sometimes put yourself and others in a straitjacket. You want to follow protocol, and think others should too. You don't hide this opinion. You adhere to rules and regulations, which make you reliable. Your work looks flawless; it's just like you, groomed to perfection. People like this.

However, warmth and flexibility lack in contact. People find you detached, secretive, proud and competitive. Such a perfectionist and so critical. They're afraid of your sharp tongue and gaze: the other is not perfect and so can feel inadequate. Criticism is tolerated poorly. Because of this, people feel insecure and keep distance; it's impossible for others to know what is really going on, as you do not show yourself as a person of flesh and blood. The core of connecting and being together is absent.

4 *Transformation: openness, perfect imperfection, surrender*
The starting point for you is to become confirmed in your inner beauty, not only in your exterior or performance. Know that you are loved, and that you do not need to excel to earn love. This may soften the lack of warmth and love in and around you. If you can accept your character with its desire for love and surrender, there is a good chance that you develop a desire to become more soft and less reserved.

Openness – open up and allow your feelings to come out. You have held back energy for years by keeping control over your feelings, attitude, and language. It takes courage to feel free on the inside, to let someone in your hidden inner world, beyond the facade. By making your emotional life more flexible, you increase your ability to surrender to yourself and others. This invites you to move beyond nervousness and caution. Yes, it involves taking the risk of rejection. But, although you pretend something else, surrendering heart and soul and living passionately is what you desire most.

- *A perfect imperfection* – you are allowed to learn that you do not need to be perfect. You are allowed to make mistakes; the world will not end if you do. That does not mean that you excel less, or are loved less. While striving for perfection is important to you, you must learn to find peace in your sense of imperfection. Rather than trying harder and feeling guilty about what is not going well, you can learn to be more playful. This ensures that there can be more relaxation and authenticity in your body and life. You will no longer have to cover up any imperfections of yourself.

- *Surrender* – by practising spontaneity and surrender, you will move beyond your inner tightness. By working on your fear to open up to others, you get more deeply in touch with others and yourself. Instead of exuding 'come' and 'go away' at the same time, you let people in. This is because the frozen love inside you melts. Your challenge is to become softer, to melt and to learn to accept imperfection and vulnerability. You have to learn to surrender to life, to not control things, but to let them happen and enjoy that.

Inner intelligence – the seventh step of consciousness

You live the archetype of the seer. You understand you create the external world from the inside. In a negative sense, you are the blind one, blind because you focus on the outside, your attractiveness, and perfection.

Your mission is to connect your outer with your inner world. To move from the outside view, to your inside view, your intuition. You are aware you must practice *inner intelligence* and learn to tune into your inner world, so you are accessible to yourself and others.

A SUMMARY OF TRAITS OF CHARACTER 7, THE PERFECTIONIST

vision / worldview	mission	behaviour	qualities	pitfalls	dilemmas	growth	intelligence to develop
perfection	connect inner & outer world	keeping distance & keeping up appearances	precision	self-control	seclusion	openness	*inner*
		critical	disciplined	critical	fear of being hurt	imperfection	
		control	efficient	self-assured	fear of failing	flexibility	
		looking and being perfect	sense of beauty	rigid	empathy	vulnerabilty	

SUMMARY LETTING GO

Awareness of your personality design and releasing your negative patterns will allow you to be more open and perceive the world how it is, rather than how you are.

1 *What is a character armour?* A character is your personal defense system protecting your inner core. In essence, it is a physical armour causing mental construct and constraints. As we saw earlier on, this defense system also has certain qualities when you can move through it freely. By being aware of how your character works, you can create the space to choose how to deal with challenging situations. We call this awareness and freedom of acting 'character intelligence.'

2 *Your personality design and how to create awareness and transformation.* Your personality design can block you severely when you are under stress. Awareness of your design and being able to work with and through it enables you to grow and become more free.

3 *The various characters and their qualities, pitfalls and transformation opportunities revealed.* Knowing your personality design is having the blueprint of how you operate on a physical, mental and emotional level. It allows you to connect with yourself and others from reality and open space, rather than from a personality block.

"Look inside yourself...
You are more than what you have become.
Remember who you are. Remember...
You must take your place in the Circle of Life."
— THE LION KING

"As for the future, your task is not to foresee it, but to enable it."
— ANTOINE DE SAINT-EXUPÉRY

So, here you are.

You know that the way we're working isn't working. You know that we're burning ourselves and our planet out, fast. We simply must reinvent our organisations and our society to survive as a species. We must move to a new human ecology and reinvent what it means to be human. *All of this starts with Reinventing Ourselves.*

- What if... you've been living out of a contracted version, fuelled by your mind?
- What if... all of this is really about choice?
- What if... in doing so, you can step into your full, natural power?
- What if... it is up to us to remember who we are and become whole?

Would you think that to be very radical?

By now, if you're reading this, we hope you've experienced a first glimpse of:
- What it means to grow up, to become aware of and embrace the richness and dynamic of your human design and all it enables you to do. To align with your heart's passion, your body's centre, and your soul's guidance, while at the same time tapping your mind's rational wisdom. Fully realising you can reboot and reset your operating system.

- What it means to wake up and realise that we are all on this evolutionary journey. Remembering that we all have our unique purpose to fulfil and that we are in this together. This evolution invites you to show up and take your part in the orchestra of life. You are needed!

- What it means to show up and come from a place of intention and commitment. Realising that we all live in the centre of our own reality. It all boils down to our focus and perspective. Every day, we can choose to align our behaviour with who we really are and focus on our purpose.

- What flow is and that you can experience it by sensing and following the energy response. Realising that being in flow as an individual is great, but that being in flow as a group is the holy grail: it is tapping into the collective wisdom. It is what everyone is looking for.

- What it means to **free yourself** of beliefs, behaviour, and habits no longer serving you, and adopt those that do!

We invite you to release your old story and grow wings to fly. There comes a moment in everyone's life where you recognise the old ideas, beliefs and stories you carry no longer match the truth or vision of who you can or need to be. This is the moment you enter the chrysalis, preparing for a momentous metamorphosis that unfolds your greatest gifts and allows you to fly. That moment is now!

You see, we believe that in the midst of this time of great change and chaos, we need our human capacities of consciousness, connection, creativity, and imagination more than ever. But we can only access these qualities when we are open and expansive. Not when we're contracted or defensive.

We are being guided in the right direction. We are currently experiencing a shift from the pure physical, or *gross body*, to the next level, the *subtle body*. This means we are more sensitive to our own energy, and the energy around us. We are forced to realise that there is more to the universe than we know and see. We may be able to feel an energetic experience, but often lack the language to express it. Nor are we able to understand it properly or access this field deliberately. Nobody has been there before. There is no roadmap yet!

But what if...

It starts with us, and we are destined to take radical responsibility?

We are creatures of habit. Virtually 99% of what we do is done according to old engrained patterns picked up in the early formative years of our personality. On top of that, our central operating system has not been rebooted since our days on the Savannah. So far, we have lived without too much awareness of these facts.

The bad news: these old patterns don't serve us anymore. The good news: we now know, habits and patterns can be rewritten. We can rewire! Neuroscience has now given us evidence of what works, like many ancient wisdom techniques, for instance.

Naturally, when learning anything new, true transformation only occurs with dedication and repetition. The ancient wisdom traditions have always known (think of Jesus' 40 days in the desert and Buddha's 40 days to enlightenment), and now neuro research has shown, that after repeating a new pattern for roughly 40 days, you can change the neural pathways in your brain to create lasting change. It is possible to rewire or reset!

Every day, all day you can reset yourself:
- connect with your mind, heart, body, and soul to become centred, clear, and present,
- connect with your purpose and be intentional,
- connect with and open up to the energy of the universe, to be in flow.

The key is realising it starts with an open and receptive heart, and conscious intention.

Will you join us on this journey of Radical Responsibility?
Our Reinventing Toolbox can be used as a basis to enable your new foundation. Energy flows where attention goes! When you're tuned in, tapped in, turned on, you can step into your greatness.

Greatness is the highest expression of our human potential. We have depicted it in the diamond of human potential that we introduced on page 100.
At the same time, we are part of an interconnected field as we saw in Part II, a field of consciousness. The Nowhere Group has depicted this in the diamond of consciousness, see page 150.

As we move in the world, we find ourselves both dealing with/moving in our ways of knowing: physical, mental, emotional and spiritual, as well as moving through various states of consciousness. It is in fact, a constant interaction.

CONSCIOUSNESS

THE
FIELD

CREATIVE
CONSCIOUS-
NESS

SUBCONSCIOUS

To enter into the art of stepping into creative consciousness, practicing and mastering our potential is key. The most vital source of innovation is our consciousness.

How, then, do we enable the flourishing of those around us?

Where our subtle body holds all our intelligence and power, the subtle body of a group holds the intelligence of the group, in other words, the *collective intelligence*. In collective intelligence, wholes are more than the sums of their parts, and people tap into a larger pool of knowledge. There's a sense of openness and awareness of something bigger than only you. The group reaches its own level of coherence. Some higher level of order comes to play. Group intuition develops. Consciousness and skills of communication, coordination, and creation are heightened. This could be called collective awakening.

The group is conjuring forth the new, or, to put it in Theory U terms, allowing the emerging future in. Until recently, this was experienced mostly in communion, now it is entering the work floor as well. This may sound rather new, but people who face huge challenges together, like soldiers for instance, or rescue crews, or even sports teams, have a clear sense of this, and have been using this intelligence for a long time already.

There is a vast body of research on this topic, by eminent physicists such as David Bohm, and universities such as Princeton. They research this process in both humans and nature, and have proven that it's the updraft of this energetic field that enables, for instance, swarms of starlings to cross the ocean as a group. They could never do so on their own. This is the same force that allows ants to build living bridges and cross gaps that they run into. *They simply focus on the greatest and most essential power of all taking part, thereby connecting each individual to their highest potential.*

The results for humans are the same: collective intelligence generates implicit trust and synchronicity. Because of this, innovation, creation, and collaboration are amplified.

What then, if it's not only our responsibility to become whole ourselves, but also our task to create conducive environments for others to become whole?

It is only in these conducive environments that humanity and the planet can flourish. Sir Ken Robinson, creativity and education expert, TED speaker and author states:

> "I believe our only hope for the future is to adopt a new concept of human ecology, one in which we start to reconstitute our conception for the richness of human capacity. Our education system has mined our minds in the way that we strip-mined the earth: for a particular commodity.
> For the future, this won't serve us. The only way we'll do it is by seeing our creative capacities for the richness that they are and our children for the hope they are. And our task is to educate their whole being, so that they can face this future."

This means we have to step up to the plate and there is no time to lose.
If we want to bequeath a world worth living in to our children, we have to enable it. We have to upgrade our consciousness to the next phase and move through the world from there. We are in charge of our future. It is our challenge, even responsibility, to lead the way to radiance and to do so with loving intent.

In short: we invite you to reinvent yourself and take your place in the circle of life!

PART IV

Reinventing Toolbox

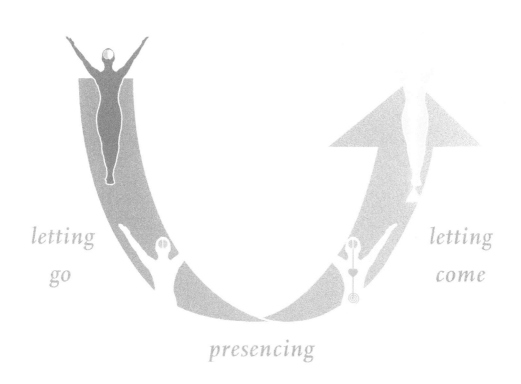

letting
go

presencing

letting
come

moving from unavailable to online

Start close in,
don't take the second step or the third,
start with the first thing close in,
the step you don't want to take.
Start with the ground you know,
the pale ground beneath your feet,
your own way to begin the conversation.
Start with your own question,
give up on other people's questions,
don't let them smother something simple.
To hear another's voice, follow your own voice,
wait until that voice becomes an intimate private ear
that can really listen to another.
Start right now
take a small step you can call your own
don't follow someone else's heroics,
be humble and focused,
Start close in,
don't mistake that other for your own.
Start close in,
don't take the second step or the third,
start with the first thing close in,
the step you don't want to take.

— DAVID WHYTE

It all starts with being curious and choosing and committing to re-connect. Start close in. Just take the time to, and make space for, connecting with all of you. Pay attention to where you direct your attention and energy. Doing so will encourage more consciousness of yourself and your behaviour, facilitating Personal Mastery. It's easy to speed up and do. Now you need to learn to slow down and be.

Come home to yourself!

The idea is to integrate practices that enable integrating all your resources and powers. And so move from unavailable to available, from available to aligned and eventually from aligned to online. How do we achieve this? By building rituals!

Choose to insert practices that allow you to be at your best, all day, every day! Connect and check in with your heart, body, emotions, mind, and soul. Let go of dysfunctional patterns and energy. With commitment, after roughly 6 weeks, the brain will have formed new neural pathways. The new practices will have become hardwired and automated, just like brushing your teeth, and they will override old patterns. It's that simple. But, like any mastery, it does take commitment and practice!

You will find the following practices below, for your:

- **Body** – *Centring,* page 197, *Standing like a Tree,* page 198, and *Coming to your Senses,* page 199.
- **Mind** – *Inner Smile Meditation,* page 200, *Mountain Meditation,* page 201, and *Visualisation,* page 202.
- **Soul** – *Soul Knowledge,* page 203, *Values,* page 204 and *Transformational Presence,* page 205.
- **Heart** – *Heart-brain coherence,* page 206, and *Heart Meditation,* page 207.
- **High energy** – *The Love Bomb,* page 209, and *The Kundalini Practice,* page 211.
- **Stress release** – *Bubble Gum,* page 214, *Breathing Practices,* page 214, *Stress Posture,* page 215, *Blending,* page 216, and *Breath of Fire,* page 216.

Of course, integrating your powers to jump-start your day, or end it peacefully is a great way to begin. That's why, at the end of this Toolbox, page 215, we give you our morning and evening rituals consisting of a combination of practices. Of course, tons of variations are possible. Try it out and see what works for you!

Tip:
Record yourself reading below instructions so you can replay, and relax into the experience.

Starting in the order of the above.

THE BODY

Your body is your foundation. You want to be fully embodied, as through your body you experience life in the present, through feelings and sensations. Being embodied enables you to tap into your innate wisdom.

We see three things as essential: **centring, grounding and coming to your senses**. The practices here teach you how to build the capacity to work with energy. As you do this, notice the aliveness in your body. The sensations will enable you to bring more of yourself to life and the task at hand, even when you're stressed.

Centring
It all starts with centring. Your hara (just below the belly button) is your centre. It's the calmness, true nature, which lies beneath the chatter of the mind.

1 Centring Practice [79]
This practice brings you instantly to your physical centre, allowing you to experience your body fully, and giving access to your body's innate wisdom.
1 Focus on your *breath* – inhale up and out of the top of your head, lengthening your spine as you straighten and uplift your posture. Slowly take twice as long to exhale down your front all the way into the earth, softening your jaw and shoulders as you go.
2 Relate to *gravity* – gravity is your natural way to relax. Feel the width of your body and the weight of your arms pulling your shoulders away from your ears, and relax the tension in your jaw. Allow gravity to settle you into your personal space and onto the earth.

---

79 From *Leadership Embodiment* – How the Way we Sit and Stand Can Change the Way we Think and Speak, by Wendy Palmer and Janet Crawford, CreateSpace, 2013.

3 Balance *personal space* – ask yourself: 'is the back of my personal space, balanced and even with the front? Is the left equal to the right? And is above equal to below?' Expand your personal space out to fill the room.

4 Evoke a *quality* – your quality represents something you want to cultivate in yourself. Working with a quality is a practice of inquiry [80]. Ask: if there were a little more... (ease, confidence, compassion, for example) in my body, what would that feel like? Where do I notice that quality?

Grounding

If centre is the application of your personal energy source, grounding is your connection to the qualities and capacities of that energy. *Grounding connects you to the earth and to gravity and enables you to let go and relax. Grounding through your legs gives a sense of security.*

This practice uses the metaphor of a tree: your legs and torso form the trunk of the tree, your head, and limbs the branches. Your feet, sinking and extending down beneath the ground, establish the roots.

2 Standing like a Tree [81]

The goal of this practice is to open the flow of energy by holding your body in an as relaxed, extended and open position (reducing spine's curvature) as possible. Your mind will be empty, active, and alert.

1 Stand with your feet parallel and firmly on the ground at shoulder width. Grasp the ground with your feet, while keeping the tip of the toes extended.

2 Imagine a golden string extending from the crown of your head into the sky. You want your head to feel like it's floating above your neck, effortlessly suspended above your spine.

3 Roll your hips slightly forward as if you were sitting at the edge of a high barstool. This will straighten the spine in your lower back.

4 Keep your knees slightly bent.

5 Relax your shoulders, round your upper back.

6 Let your arms rest comfortably at your side.

7 Let the palms of your hands face your hips.

8 Tuck your chin in and keep your eyes slightly open with a soft gaze ahead.

---

80 Self-Inquiry is a method for self-observation. It has many meanings in spiritual traditions: it's the quest for your true self, like Percival's quest for the Holy Grail.

81 Ancient Taoist Zhan Zhuang practice.

Sink all of your body's weight and tension into your feet (without collapsing your posture), allowing it to be absorbed into the ground. To support this grounding process, imagine roots growing out the bottom of your feet, extending deep into the ground beneath you.

3 Coming to your Senses
Connect with all 5 senses to give you an intense presence.

1 Begin by bringing your attention to your *sense of hearing*. What is the most prevalent sound you can detect right now? It might simply be your breath, or the birds chirping. Do not judge, or push anything away, but pull the lens of your awareness back, and include all the sounds in your awareness right now, listening for the pronounced and the subtle.

2 On your next breath, gently bring your awareness to the *sense of touch*. So, what is the most prevalent tactile sensation happening for you right now? It may be your bum in a chair, your feet on the ground or maybe you have a headache. Again, no judgment, no trying to change it, just gently waking up your sense of touch. Maybe even imagining that all the hairs on your arm are like little antennae, becoming very attuned to subtle, tactile sensations. Can you even feel the breath coming in and out of your nose?

3 Keeping your eyes closed, gently bring your awareness to your *sense of sight*. Even with the eyes closed, there is still some sort of a sight happening. It might simply be blackness, or maybe you see beyond the blackness, and see colours in your minds' eye, or light streaming through your eyelids. Really give yourself permission to see whatever it is that you see.

4 On your next breath bring your awareness to your *sense of taste*. What's the most prevalent taste happening for you right now? Is your mouth juicy or dry? Do you still taste what you ate just before this practice?

5 And on the next breath, take a big inhale, and bring your awareness to your *sense of smell*. Really smell what you smell. What's the most prevalent smell you can detect right now? Is it the room for instance, or do you smell your perfume?

Now that you have woken up all of your senses, let's start to stack them on top of each other and play with the simultaneity of consciousness. Notice if you hear what you're hearing, feel what you're feeling, see what you're seeing, taste what you're tasting and smell what you're smelling, all at the same time. Give yourself permission to be fully present in your body.

Coming to your senses gives you a direct feel of expanded awareness, and intense presence.

*Essential here are the **clear focus and expansion** of the mind. Meditation is a great tool to achieve this. It expands your personal space. It's a great way to start the day and may be used as a pick-me-up anytime.*

4 Inner Smile Meditation [82]

This meditation takes you to the place inside of you where it is calm, clear and feels great. Where it feels expansive!

1 Sit comfortably, with your whole body relaxed, close your eyes, and let your breath come to its natural rhythm.

2 Connect with something of great beauty in nature. Travel to your favourite spot, the sea, the mountains, a forest for example. This may bring you a deep sense of unity with all there is. You can use the memory of this experience to evoke your core values. Make sure you are alone there. Feel the beauty and abundance of this spot around you, also in your body. Feel, see, hear, smell, taste the quality of this spot. Very often a sense of space and rest will appear, sometimes a colour. Often a golden yellow, but any other or no colour is just fine as well.

3 Let the light of this spot come together in a cloud or spiral in front of your face and let it enter your skin. You can hold your hands there, and use them to let the light flow through your body. Hold your hands in front of or at the spot where the smile is directed. Focus particularly at a point between and above your eyebrows (third eye [83]).

4 Feel how the light enters your skin and permeate deeper into your tissues. Let it flow from your face through your throat to your heart. Feel how your heart reacts when the light, together with your loving smile, enters there. Take your time and let your entire chest area fill itself with this light. Enjoy the space and the abundance of energy. Then, let the energy, together with your smile, flow to your stomach area. From there to your belly area and finally your entire pelvis. Make sure you remain in connection with the abundance of nature.

5 At the end of this meditation, let the light and energy come together in one spot deep in your belly, behind your belly button, in a concentrated ball of energy.

---

82 In the Taoist tradition, each person assumes responsibility for their emotions, regardless of what triggered them. Mantak Chia's Inner Smile exercise helps balance and integrate our sympathetic and parasympathetic nervous systems, promoting health, resilience, and vitality. It transforms emotions by transforming the associated physiological systems.

83 The third eye is your ability to see what might be, to see potential. Everyone has access to this for example, when you have a hunch and act on it, you've used your third eye. It is a sense you can develop to be more refined and accurate than just a hunch.

Because you bring this energy together, you can use it later for things you really value. Such as your work, your leadership, your loved ones.

5 Mountain Meditation [84]
This mindfulness practice reminds you of your unwavering core stability and strength. It is very grounding!

1 Sit comfortably, with your whole body relaxed, and let your breath come to its natural rhythm.
2 Imagine yourself sitting in a field or on a hill across from a beautiful mountain. In your mind, allow the image to form of the most magnificent mountain you have ever seen or can imagine, letting it gradually come into greater focus... and even if it doesn't come as a visual image, allowing the sense of this mountain and feeling its overall shape, its lofty peak or peaks high in the sky, the large base rooted in the earth, its steep or gently sloping sides. Notice how massive it is, how solid, how unmoving, how beautiful, whether from afar or up close... (pause). Perhaps your mountain has snow blanketing its top and trees reaching down to the base, or rugged granite sides. There may be streams and waterfalls cascading down the slopes, or there may be one peak or a series of peaks, or meadows and high lakes.
3 Now, imagine that your body becomes one with the energy of the mountain; like it's taking that on. Your hips and legs become the solid, grounded foundation; the base of the mountain, deeply rooted in the floor or your seat. Your torso becomes the slopes and the body of the mountain, being lifted through the spine so that your head and neck become like tall peaks, supported by the rest of the body. With every breath, becoming a little more like a mountain; steady and stable, grounded yet tall, still and magnificent.
4 And when we think of a mountain, the mountain in the image that you created in your mind, you will notice that as the days, months and year go by, 'life' happens around the mountain. Seasons change: in spring, it might be covered with trees and flowers; in summer, sunshine, and grass, and in winter it might be completely covered in snow. There may be violent storms on the mountain, blizzards, glaring sunshine, people and animals coming to visit it, but see how the mountain itself, its core and foundation, doesn't change. None of the outside circumstances matter to the mountain, which always remains its essential self. All of the outside changes come, and they go. They are not permanent. The only thing that is permanent is the mountain itself.

---

84 Based on Jon Kabat-Zinn's Mountain Meditation.

5 In the same way, in our lives and meditations, we can learn to experience the same things in our self. We can connect to the part of us that is grounded and does not change, regardless of what life throws at us. We can connect to the stillness that is always inside, through both stormy days and sunshine.

6 As you sit here, take a moment to feel your sense of groundedness and stability, keeping this feeling as your anchor.

7 Then gently bring your attention back to your breath and your surroundings. Move your fingers and toes a little bit, maybe stretch out your arms overhead and make take a big stretch. When you're ready, you can open your eyes.

By attuning to the mountain in our practice, we can connect with its strength and stability and adopt them as our own. It can help us to see that our thoughts, feelings, and worries, are a bit like the weather on the mountain. They too come and go while the essence of who we are, always stays the same.

6 Visualisation [85]

A wonderful tool to set yourself up for creating the best version of you is a visualisation. It is powerful as it creates new neural pathways, and so expands your mind.

1 Sit comfortably, with your whole body relaxed, close your eyes, and let your breath come to its natural rhythm.

2 Now imagine you're on holiday, you don't have a care in the world.

3 You're in a mountain meadow, surrounded by snow-capped peaks.

4 You're barefoot; you feel the wet grass, the crisp mountain air and the sun on your face.

5 You feel peaceful and powerful and so relaxed.

6 You walk along a little stream and enter a forest. You smell the pine trees – so lovely!

7 At the end of the forest, you hear the sound of water. You follow the sound and see a very special little waterfall.

8 You know that this waterfall can clean you of all your negative beliefs, fears, doubts, insecurities and anything else that has been holding you back from being the best you.

9 You step under the waterfall and feel the water take away all the negativity.

10 When you're done, you step away to a spot in the grass and let yourself dry up in the sun.

---

85 Inspired by Robin Sharma.

11 You feel so great; you feel like you have activated your full potential!

12 You start to walk back to the forest, on a winding path.

13 At the end of the path, you see a golden door.

14 As you approach it, you start running faster and faster; you're so excited to open the door.

15 When you open the door, you see the life you've always wanted.

16 Take a very good look and notice what your life looks like in terms of:

- You: how do you look and feel, inside and out?
- Your relationships: who is around you, how is the interaction with family, friends, colleagues?
- Your work: what do you do? Does it fulfil you? Does it bring you joy?
- Your impact: what are you bringing to the world?

17 Take some time to take in the greatness of all you are and all you can be.

18 Then go out and build what you just saw!

THE SOUL

Your soul is the aspect of you that resides in the physical and in the spiritual world. Its main interest is fulfilling its purpose and growth in service of the evolution of consciousness. Its deepest desire is to know and experience your greatest potential.

7 Soul Knowledge [86]

To get to know your soul, a good start may be to begin creating your 'Soul Profile'.
Answer the following, be candid and intuitive and let first responses guide you:

1 What is my contribution in life?

2 What's the purpose in what I do?

3 How do I feel when I have a peak experience?

4 Who are my heroes and heroines?

5 What are the qualities I look for in a best friend?

6 What are my unique skills and talents?

7 What are the best qualities I express in a relationship?

---

86 Deepak Chopra, *The Soul of Leadership*, Random House, 2011.

Using keywords, write a brief profile of your soul as if you were describing another person. Keeping your Soul Profile at hand, move on the next step: defining your personal vision. Answer the following, questions according to your truths:

1 I want to live in a world in which...
2 I would be inspired to work in an organisation that...
3 I would be proud to lead a team that...
4 A transformed world would be...

To match your present work with your vision, answer the following:

1 How does your work in the world reflect the vision you outlined above?
2 What do you need to get closer to your ideals?
3 What can you offer to move it closer to your ideals?

Define your vision as specifically as possible to start bridging the gap. Clarify the world you envision and how you see yourself in it. Lastly, create your mission statement. Merge your values and vision into a statement of your overall life mission. Using the following template: "My mission behind everything I do is...." Keep it simple and concise so that a child would be able to understand it.

8 Values
Deeply held values define who you aspire to be. This is both true as an individual and as a team or organisation. They provide an inner compass helping you to make the right choices and navigate calm and stormy waters.

What if you could fully create your own story to navigate life from a blank canvas, rather than from the beliefs instilled in you by your parents or culture? Then, who do you want to be? What is meaningful to you? How do you want to contribute? How do you want to show up?

Your core values connect you to your soul. They enable you to create the future the way you want to create it. If you value love, let love inspire your actions and decisions. If you value integrity, let integrity inspire your actions and decisions. Values enable you to remain true to your Essence!

If this is new to you, here are some ideas what possible values could be: accountability, balance, commitment, compassion, courage, discipline, enthusiasm, efficiency, ethics, excellence, fairness, friendship, honesty, humour, integrity, intuition, love, openness, respect, responsibility, trust, wisdom.

To connect to your values, think of your role model(s), who might be anyone from Mandela to Gandhi to your grandma, and think of why they seem like a role model to you. Pick three to five core values. What are the beliefs behind these values? And what behaviour do you show because of these values? Then, practice this, go out, and connect with everyone and everything you come across, with those values in mind. If you find yourself in a difficult situation and one of your values is trust, for instance, ask yourself: what would trust do here?

9 Transformational Presence: coming online

Body and soul need to work in tandem to manifest the soul's purpose. The following exercise will help you get a feel for this.

To align yourself with your being bring your attention to your breath. Feel your central column by making contact with the earth (grounding your body) and connecting with the crown of your head (making contact with your soul). Now imagine a column of energy (or light) spiralling from your feet to your crown. Stay in this visualisation until you feel a solid column of vibrating energy from top to toe.

This vertical alignment brings you in contact with your innate power. It aligns your inspiration with your head, heart, and intuition. It brings all aspects of your being; your thoughts, beliefs, intentions, and perspectives in alignment with your

Essence. It puts you in contact with your soul's mission. When you are aligned vertically, you will feel centred and grounded in your being, full of trust, full of energy and full of inspiration. You have come online!

When you have found your vertical connection, you then move into the horizontal for action, the doing. Taking your innate power and aligning all aspects of your being into the action that needs to be taken. This vertical axis and horizontal axis overlap at the heart, there soul and ego come together and align. Remember:

The deeper your consciousness on the vertical, the more alignment between all aspects of yourself, the emerging potential and consciousness, the bigger your success and influence on the horizontal plain. The more magnetic.

THE HEART

The heart functions as coordinator of the frequencies of our brains, our consciousness, our perception and our energy field (aura). Heart coherence is key; it makes us feel good and safe.

10 Heart–brain Coherence [87]

This is the hotline to our subconscious. When we harmonise the brains in our heart and head, we get access to our extended neural network. This sets us apart from all other forms of life. It gives access to fast information recall, deep intuition, and empathy.

This simple quick exercise allows us to enter this state. Which gives you access to your extended neural network, and improves your physical well-being and access to your intuition. It triggers 1300 biochemical reactions and its effects last up to 6 hours.

1 *Shift your awareness from your mind to your heart.* Place your hand on your heart centre. Your awareness will follow this touch. This signals your body that you are turning your attention inwards.
2 *Slow down your breathing.* As a guideline, think 5 seconds on the inhale and 5 on the exhale. This sends a signal to your body that you are safe, and it allows your body to let go of stress. It awakens the healing chemistry.
3 *Focus on feeling.* Feel one or a combination of the following: care, appreciation, gratitude or compassion. These four keywords will trigger the experience between your heart and brain that creates coherence. This simple ancient act takes you to this deep place inside of you where all is calm, is key to who you are in this world.

---

87 The HeartMath Institute.

11 *Heart Meditation*
An open heart is crucial to harmonise all bodily functions, to make us feel safe, reduce our stress levels and open us up.

As a metaphor, we give you the Sufis' view of how heart, soul, and mind cooperate. Here is a meditation to enable you to experience this for yourself:

Consider this...

The Sufis view the soul as the queen or king of your heart. In their view, your soul is meant to make the decisions in your life. Your heart is the throne room of your soul, it's your ability to feel. The mind is the servant, whose job it is to guard the door to the heart. But for most of us, painful things happened in our lives and have caused us to become afraid. So our mind locked the door to our heart bit by bit, trying to protect us. Sadly, however, when your heart is closed, it's as if your spirit is asleep.

What we need to learn is give our mind permission to open the door to the heart, to feel again. That way you can wake up your soul and regain that deeper intimate connection. This leads to being free from fears and avoidance of the negative patterns of childhood no longer serving you.

The next meditation may help you feel that living in connection and love, instead of trapped in fear is the way to be open to receive what is. This practice creates neuroplasticity. In other words, letting in the new creates new neural pathways that replace fear (old pattern) with pleasure.

Settle down. Close your eyes. Put your hands on your heart. Take a deep breath. Inhale: feel you're opening that door to your heart, and tell your mind that it is OK, it's safe. On the exhale: let go of expectations or fears.
   Take another deep breath. Inhale, receive the present moment and this feeling of being connected with everything around you. Feel the beauty of it. On the exhale: let go of expectations or fears. One more time, take that deep inhale and see if your heart can open a little more to this present connection and intimacy. And exhale: letting go.

Practice this for as long as feels good and sit with it. Take a moment and feel how much more open your heart feels. Feel how good it is and allow yourself the feeling of being vulnerable, to let go even though you can't control everything. Feel how it feels to be more creative, more expansive. To be in touch with the right side of the brain and open to new experiences. To truly connect.

To experience presence and deep connection in your heart, you have to let go of control and allow yourself to be released from fear and into experience and love, and the beauty that surrounds you.

Take a moment and ask yourself: is there a place or a relationship (in your private or professional life) where there is a blockage? A blockage preventing you from opening your heart? Where did it come from? Was there some moment that you shut down your heart and your mind locked the door to your heart to protect you?

Perhaps you feel that you're now ready to wake up because your soul wants more. That waking up process is waking up to your heart, your senses and the now. It's about starting to live life in technicolor where you now maybe live in black and white, trapped in fear, afraid of experiencing openness and your power as a human.

THE ENERGY

It's all about raising your frequency. When you elevate the frequency of your physical body, more of your spirit can come in. What will it bring you?

- You'll be able to tap into energy, vitality, harmony and inner balance 24/7,
- You'll learn to expand your intuition to experience a life of synchronicity,
- You'll take charge and be able to enjoy a life of love, abundance, joy, and fun,
- You'll be able to manifest what your heart desires, and, above all:
- You'll feel your **true Essence**.

Raising your frequency can be done by anything that makes you feel better. This could be as simple and quick as putting on some music, dancing, being with people you love, spending time in nature or practising gratitude. In fact, most of the practices that you will find in our morning and evening rituals raise your frequency.

One of our favourites has to be this one.

Tip:
Record yourself reading below instructions so you can replay, and relax into the experience.

12 The Love Bomb [88]
Fully opening up to love transforms all issues to a level of understanding, a broader perspective and, ultimately, peace. Your Essence is love; it's a state you 'love' to be in!

Make yourself comfortable and close your eyes. Imagine someone you love sitting about two feet in front of you. Really see their face, their hair and what they're wearing. Are they happy? Ideally, this is someone you love very much. Alternatively, imagine something that inspires the feeling of love inside of you.

On your next inhale breathe that sensation of love into your body and supercharge every single cell of your body with it. As you exhale, imagine that you're sending this out to this person you love. Almost blasting them with love, so that you're supercharging every cell in their body with this feeling of love.

On your next breath, breathe into the sensation of love, charging every cell of your body with it. And as you exhale, imagine sending that out to the entire room. Just filling the room you're in with this beautiful current of love. Some people like to imagine this as white or golden light. Whatever feels good to you is perfect.

On your next inhale, breathe in the sensation, supercharging your body with love, and as you exhale imagine sending this out to the entire city. To every person, place, and thing in the city where you live. To all your friends, colleagues and your boss. Just blasting them with love.

If you feel like you're losing that sensation, simply come back to the person you love and just see them across from you, notice how that changes you, notice how that softens your face, and changes your heart.

Let your next breath be a delicious inhale, supercharging every single cell in your body, and as you exhale, imagine sending this love out to the entire universe. Blast the whole universe with as much love as you can possibly create. And know that as you're sending this sensation out, it's absolutely coming back to you.

Imagine sending this love out as far as your mind can conceive. Beyond the solar system, beyond the galaxy, the clusters of galaxies, and out in the entire universe.

---

88 By Emily Fletcher.

Just for a moment, as you send this love out to the whole universe, remind your-self that you are part of a greater whole. Remind yourself that you are part of the universe and that the universe is part of you. Allow yourself to surrender into this sense of connectedness, and support. Almost imagining that you are one wave in a giant ocean of consciousness. You are one wave in this giant ocean of energy. And you allow yourself to receive all of the love that's coming back to you from the universe. Let that fill you up from the source. Let it supercharge your body. You can take that with you into your life. Into your job, into your family.

Translating it from practice into real life
From this place of connectedness and having supercharged your body with the sensation of love, imagine that you're going into a situation that's important to you. Imagine that you're just about to give an important presentation to your board for instance. You really want to show up at the top of your game. See yourself right there, about to open the door.

Here's a little pep talk.

Notice what feelings come up for you. Maybe it's a little nervousness, or anxiety, or what-if, or... Simply come back to the sensation of love or the breath, and allow yourself to feel the following as true:

You are meant for greatness. This situation is important to you, and you might be feeling some nervousness or anxiety, because you care a lot about what you do. You want to show up as the most amazing version of you. Give yourself full permission to feel everything that you're feeling. If you're nervous, be nervous. If your heart is racing, let it race. Don't push against the feelings; they'll only push back harder. So take a moment to accept what is. Let it talk to you. Usually if you simply listen to the body, it will say whatever it needs to say and the sensation will dissipate.

Now this opportunity you care about wouldn't even show up if you hadn't been through a lifetime of work and dedication and creativity. So take a moment here to acknowledge all of your successes and celebrate them. Celebrate every win that brought you here. You can't build on top of success that you don't acknowledge. Celebrate the success that has led to this big opportunity.

Imagine that you could have a magic wand and this situation could go any way that you would want. The board says yes. You're confident, you're easy, you're funny, and you're charming. Play this movie in your mind best-case scenario. You get the deal! Let whatever comes up in your imagination come up. There is no right or wrong way to do this. Just play with it. Imagine you're leaving the room, and just notice the feeling inside you. Proud and excited about what you brought to the table.

Now from that place, step through the door. Deliver what you just imagined. And when you feel that you've done your best, you've done everything you can, let it go and give yourself a big high five.

Take a big inhale, breathe some life into your hands, into your feet, and exhale let go of what isn't serving you. One more big inhale, breathe some life into your body, bring your awareness back into the room. And in your own time, whenever you're ready, you can start to slowly, gently open your eyes.

Where your heart chakra is the coordinator of all energy; kundalini is the fuel for all energy in the body. Consciously filling yourself with your life energy, or kundalini makes you feel radiant and alive.

Tip:
Record yourself reading below instructions so you can replay, and relax into the experience.

13 Kundalini practice – *for the brave ones!*
Something that causes us much suffering is getting into rigid brain patterns. This is when you get stuck on things and repeat them over and over again. The first part of this exercise is about *shaking*: it allows you to experience more free-dom, and to let go of emotional baggage. The shaking frees your vagus nerve and brain. As you do this shaking, you want every bit of your body to move. As you shake and exhale, make sounds. This is important. It can be any kind, what mat-ters is that it's real to you!

The second part is a meditative *visualisation* in which you begin by activating your kundalini energy in the root centre, bringing awareness to your pelvis. Try to visualise a ball of light, and feel your kundalini energy inside that ball. The alive-ness that is part of you as a human being. Acknowledge it, and start from a place of total self-love, and acceptance. As soon as you feel grounded in love, bring the ball up your spine to bring this energy and vibrancy to all other parts of your body. After this practice, you'll feel a change in your aliveness and awareness, and how you go about your day.

Phase 1 – shaking
Start with your feet a little bit wider than hip distance apart, and let a shake come through your entire body like a rumbling. It will relax all your muscles, your inner organs, and release pent up energy. As you continue this full body shake, inhale deep, full and slow. On every exhale make a sound. Continue shaking like this for a few minutes, inhaling deeply and sounding with every exhale.

Phase 2 – awakening kundalini energy, and let it feed the chakras
Visualise a ball of light at the height of your first chakra, and make contact with your primordial kundalini energy. Feel this radiance that is part of your being. Start from a place of total self-love and acceptance.

Phase 3 – circulating the kundalini through all your chakras
1 *Root chakra* – come to a seated position, and visualise a pearly ball of light at your pelvis. Allow this ball of light to grow, and expand until it's as big as your hips and your pelvis. Feel this pearly ball of light as your primordial kundalini energy. The beauty, innocence, and pleasure you came here with. Shrink that pearly ball back down feeling it at your pelvis.
2 *Sacral chakra* – inhale, and move the ball from your pelvis to your tailbone. Feeling a luscious energy awakening your whole sacral area. Exhaling that pearly ball bringing it back down via the front of your body to your pelvis. Inhale the pearly ball up to your tailbone, feeling luscious energy, and exhaling back down to the pelvis.
3 *Solar plexus* – inhale from the pelvis up to the back of the spine to the level of the solar plexus. Feel your power, fire and will increase. Exhaling, bring it back down via the front of your body feeling it melt down back into the pelvis. Inhale that pearly ball up along the back of your spine all the way up to the level of the solar plexus, feeling heat, fire, willpower, exhaling all the way back down to the pelvis.
4 *Heart chakra* – inhale all the way up the spine to the back of the heart. Feel this ball of light enhance love, air, and compassion through your entire chest area. Exhale letting that pearly ball drop all the way back down, bringing it back down via the front of your body to your pelvis. Inhale all the way up the back of the spine to the heart. Feeling love and compassion, exhaling all the way back down to the pelvis.
5 *Throat chakra* – inhale all the way up the spine to the back of the neck, feeling the ball increase the amount of space, a connection to the metaphysical, openness, the highest genius. Let it expand the power of your voice. Exhale, and bring it all the way back down via the front, to the pelvis. Inhale all the way up, to the back

of the throat at the level of the spine, feeling genius, high creativity, the spaciousness of the universe. Let it melt all the way back down into the pelvis.

6 *Third eye chakra* – inhale all the way up the spine to the centre of the brain. Visualising an increase in meditative awareness, expansion, and ability to move beyond duality into greater and greater truth. Exhale, bringing it back down via the front of your body to the pelvis. Inhale all the way up the spine to the centre of the brain. Feeling deep meditation and peace. Exhale, feeling that pearly ball of energy come all the way back down to the pelvis.

7 *Crown chakra* – inhale now all the way up to the very top of the head. Feeling an increase in spirituality, and heightened awareness, and the activation of your deepest and truest Self. And bring it all the way back down via the front of your body to the pelvis. Inhale all the way up to the very top, the crown of your head. Feel the expansion, deep truth, and your true nature. Exhale all the way back down to the spine to the pelvis.

One more time inhale all the way up to the top of your head. This time, touch the roof of your mouth with the tip of your tongue to facilitate movement of this energy up and down your body, and exhale that energy down using your hands. Step by step, melting that pearly ball of energy down from your crown to the centre of your brain, down your throat, your heart, through your solar plexus, your belly, your sacral chakra, and all the way back down to your pelvis. Feel it solidify at the base of your body. And exhale growing roots from the pelvis all the way deep, deep, deep into in the centre of the earth. Feel those roots going all the way down, as deep as they can go, rooting and grounding you.

Feel your body alive with kundalini, radiant, while deeply grounded and centred.

The key to managing your state of mind and stress level lies in your ability to activate the calming parasympathetic pathways of your nervous system on command.

Typically, this cannot be controlled at will, but can be regulated via the body: via **centre, breath, and grounding (gravity)**. Through the body, we can learn to create a solid foundation from which to operate and deal with stress and transition in everyday life.

14 Bubble Gum

The easiest and fastest exercise when you're in sudden total overwhelm: take a minute (when in the office, maybe in the bathroom) and simply very slowly move your jaws as if you were chewing bubble gum. Deliberate, repetitive slow movements of the jaw will release your vagus nerve.

15 Breathing Practices

It's possible to consciously influence your nervous system by managing your breath and making deep, relaxed breathing a regular practice. That way, the nervous system takes cues from your deliberate action, and you can begin to reverse any negative spiral or any damage that stress has created.

Deep belly breathing: A very easy way to begin to deliberately deepen and slow down your breath, is by trying to expand the belly on the inhale, then feeling it relax naturally on the exhale. Continue with this for a few full breath cycles, or, if you have the time, take 5 or 10 minutes to breathe this way. Preferably, this would be made into daily practice. Doing this a couple of times a day will create a shift in making this way the new norm for your body and mind, counterbalancing the effects of stress and shallow breathing.

Another way to relax is by expanding the exhale to last longer than the inhale: A simple exercise is to breathe in for 5 seconds, and then exhale for 7. The point is to have the exhale last at least 2 seconds longer than the inhale. While exhaling, focus on completely and fully emptying the lungs. What this does, is send a signal to the nervous system that you are safe, and that it is time to relax. For this reason, it's a perfect exercise to do in the evening, after work, or even right before bed while already lying down. Follow this breath for 5 to 10 cycles or set a timer for 5 to 10 minutes. As with the first exercise, this can be done for a very short period at any point during the day as well, when you feel the need for instant calming down.

Stress usually plays out in relationships. Do you know what your natural stress tendency is? Knowing this enables you to make a change should you desire so. Choose more space for instance, or choose to stay in your centre, choose to stay in connection, etc. It's an insightful and fun exercise you can use in any situation, at work, but also with your family!

16 Stress Posture – *discover your pattern* [89]
1 Stand so you and your partner are facing each other,
2 Extend your arms forward,
3 Ask your partner to take hold of your forearms slightly above your wrist,
4 Ask your partner to quickly apply light pressure (push you), and sustain it,
5 Notice where and how your body constricts or puts up a boundary in an attempt to keep the pressure from entering into your personal space,
6 Survey three areas of your body:
   Head and neck,
   Chest and arms,
   Abdomen, hips, and legs.

Notice and reflect on the position of your head, heart, and centre core opposite a partner. Discover: what moved forward and back? What did I withdraw?

---

89 From *Leadership Embodiment* – How the Way we Sit and Stand Can Change the Way we Think and Speak, by Wendy Palmer and Janet Crawford, CreateSpace, 2013.

Many variations are possible. You may step aside (flight), you may focus on the head to try and control things with the mind, you may push back (fight). Or you may freeze.

When we work with this exercise, people are always amazed at how accurately the body shows what their stress tendency is! Knowing your natural stress signature enables you to know what's needed for change. For instance, you may need more space, or need to stay closer to your centre core or stay in connection.

A fundamental Aikido practice that empowers us during a crisis is *blending*. In case of an attack, blending ensures that the attacked works with the motion and force of the aggressor's attack, thus redirecting the energy. We ensure we see the viewpoint from the attacker's point of view.

17 Blending [90]

1 Stand about 10 metres away from your partner, and have him begin walking directly toward you.
2 When he is about one metre away, step to the side, allowing him to continue his walk.
3 As he passes, begin walking next to him.
4 As you walk next to your partner, see if you can enter into, and blend with his rhythm, speed, and length of stride.
5 Blend as deeply as possible with your partner, breathe like him, swing your arms the same way, take on the attitude of the walk. Is it aggressive, timid, relaxed?
6 Try to blend with your partner so thoroughly that you begin to feel what it is to be this person. So deeply, that you can feel yourself in their skin.

Recharging

When you need to recharge after stress: try one of the practices we mentioned to raise your energy. Like dancing or jumping up and down, or the following breathing exercise:

18 Breath of Fire [91]

This breath sounds like the rhythm of a panting dog. An active exhalation, as if you're blowing your nose, almost like a vacuum followed by a passive inhalation. Imagine there's a balloon in your belly, squish the air out of the balloon on the

---

90 Richard Strozzi-Heckler, *The Anatomy of Change* – A Way to Move Through Life's Transitions, North Atlantic Books, California, 1984.
91 Kundalini yoga exercise.

exhale. Stop, and on the inhale let the air right in. Begin with one breath per second if you are a beginner, move up to two per second. This is a very powerful energiser and toxic cleanser!

As with all meditation and yoga practices, posture is key: your spine should be straight, and your rib case lifted slightly. So you could, for instance, sit up or lie down.

Finally, our favourite morning and evening rituals.

19 Morning Ritual – 15 minutes

Here we go! In the morning it's great to feel in flow: loving, centred, intentionally focused and free! So, start your day with consciously connecting to your heart, your body, your soul, and mind. In that order:

- *Metta* – tuning in, and connecting to your heart,
- *Move* – the body by grounding, and centring,
- *Méditate* – to empty and focus your mind,
- *Meta* – raise your intuition, and set a soulful intention for the day.

A *Metta* – loving kindness

Step into a short but beautiful Buddhist loving-kindness practice. Being kind to yourself can prepare you to relax your mind, and open your heart. Get settled in a comfortable position to meditate. Close your eyes, and say the mantra: "May I be in my heart, may I be happy, may I be healthy, may I be safe." It all starts with self-love! Feel this. Then repeat this for your loved ones. See them vividly, see their faces, feel their presence, insert their name. Then for your circle of friends, again, making it a heartfelt experience. Then extend it to strangers, and finally the world. This practice should leave you with the charge of love built in your heart.

B *Move* – centring [92]

1 Focus on *breath* – inhale up and out of the top of your head, lengthening your spine as you straighten, and uplift your posture. Slowly take twice as long to exhale down your front all the way into the earth, softening your jaw and shoulders as you go.

---

92 From *Leadership Embodiment* – How the Way we Sit and Stand Can Change the Way we Think and Speak, by Wendy Palmer and Janet Crawford, CreateSpace, 2013.

2 Relate to *gravity* – gravity is your natural way to relax. Feel the width of your body and the weight of your arms pulling your shoulders away from your ears, and relax the tension in your jaw. Allow gravity to settle you into your personal space and onto the earth.

3 Balance *personal space* – ask yourself: is the back of my personal space balanced and even with the front? Is the left equal to the right? And is above equal to below? Expand your personal space out to fill the room.

4 Evoke a *quality* – your quality represents something you want to cultivate in yourself. Working with quality is a practice of inquiry [93]. Ask: if there were a little more… (ease, confidence, compassion, et cetera) in my body, what would that feel like? Where do I notice that quality?

C Meditation – **Inner Smile**

1 Sit comfortably, with your whole body relaxed, close your eyes, and let your breath come to its natural rhythm.

2 Connect with something of great beauty in nature, the sun, a tree, the sea… This may bring you a deep sense of unity with all there is. You can use the memory of this experience to evoke your core values. Make sure you are alone there. Feel the beauty and abundance of this spot around you, but also in your body. Feel, see, hear, smell, and taste the quality of this spot. Often a sense of space and rest arises. The colour people often see is a golden yellow, but any other or no colour at all is just fine as well.

3 Let the light of this spot come together in a cloud or spiral in front of your face, and let it enter your skin. You can hold your hands there, and use these to let the light flow through your body. Hold your hands in front of or at the spot where the smile is directed. Focus particularly at a point between and above your eyebrows (third eye).

4 Feel how the light enters your skin, and deeper into your tissues. Let it flow from your face through your throat to your heart. Feel how your heart reacts when the light, together with your loving smile, enters there. Take your time and let your entire chest area fill itself with this light. Enjoy the space and the abundance of energy. Let then the energy, together with your smile, flow to your stomach area. From there into your belly area, and finally your entire pelvis. Make sure you remain in connection with the abundance of nature.

5 At the end of this meditation, let the light and energy come together in one spot deep in your belly, behind your belly button, in a concentrated ball of

---

93 Inspired by the Inquiry method (see footnote 21).

energy. Because you bring this energy together you can use it later for things you really value. Your health, loved ones, work, or your leadership.

D Meta **– raise intuition, and tune into energy** [94]
Ask yourself the following questions:
1 What are 3 things I know to be true right now
2 Which of these holds the power?
3 What wants to shift there?
4 Who's that asking me to be?
5 What is one step I can take today?

24 Evening Rituals

To close off the day, we want to move into calm, peaceful energy where we are grateful for the things that were good, and leave behind the things that were not. We could simply keep a gratitude practice, where we journal on the five things we were grateful for that day for instance. Then imagine standing under a shower, cleaning us from all that we want to leave behind. Or, actually, take one! Or we could enter into the following practice:

Cleaning the Temple [95]
1 Sit with your legs lightly bent before you.
2 Circle with your hands around your belly button, with a soft touch. Take care to melt your attention and your eyes with the places of your touch. Spiral until you feel yourself sinking from your head deeper into your belly.
3 Then bring both hands to your lower back and move them via the sides and back of your legs to your feet. Stroke the soles of your feet in circles and follow the insides of your legs back up to your belly. Repeat this 3-10 times until you feel that you are calmer and the reactions subside.
4 Then spiral again with your hand palms around your belly button, and move up via your stomach to your chest area. Stay spiralling until you can make contact with your heart. Then, using one hand, follow the inside of your arm to your palm. Stroke via the back of your hand and the outside of your arm over your shoulder and via heart and stomach back again to your belly. Re-

---

94 *The Deep Simple*, Alan Seale.
95 A Taoist practice to clean our three energy centres: head, heart, and belly.

peat with both arms, again until calm.

5 Finally start, by using one hand, to spiral via your navel, stomach, heart, your shoulder, over your neck and skull, face, to the inside and outside of your arms, and back again to your navel.

Your body may react in different ways to the cleansing of your three energy centres. The reactions will tell you what kind of tension you hold in your body.

PHYSICAL REACTIONS TO CLEANING THE TEMPLE

Reaction	Organ	Element	Points to
yawning, damp or sticky feeling, dry mouth	stomach, spleen, pancreas	earth	worries, anxiety, lack of confidence, low self esteem
teary eyes	liver, gall bladder	wood	frustraton, anger, irritation, impatience. Trying to see things as they are not
heat (in head, hands or feet)	heart, small intestine	fire	hurt, overactivity, anxiety
cold, wet feeling (often in hands and/or feet)	kidneys, bladder	water	fear, blocked life force
shivering in the body (often rising)	lungs, big intestine, gall bladder	metal	sorrow, guilt, sorry, melancholy, depression, difficulty in processing experiences and disbalance between inner - and outer world

APPENDICES

1 **Worldview, vision, motives, values, and mission**

Worldview – Your worldview is one of shortage. Your motive is nourishment. From the start of life (and career), a shortage of essentials is experienced. This is solved by settling for less, and by pretending to be satisfied and fulfilled. The feeling remains, however, often unspoken but palpable, and is taken out on the person inflicting this. The shortage is covered by all kinds of detours, by leaving the office earlier for example.

You like to take care of others, are considerate and generous. You hope people return the favour. The reality is different. You are often disappointed or frustrated by an uncaring context. By caring for others, credit is built up, which can be collected occasionally. One assumes "It is my turn now" and "It is about me now."

Responsibilities of work, children, and home are often too much. There is a hidden reluctance to take these. Often a collapse follows big efforts. Physiologically caused, as the soft, slender body is not filled with inexhaustible energy. It lacks construction and musculature. Deep down, you believe that you cannot do or get things. This leads to playing a waiting game in life. The _Social One_, without hindrance, in this case, takes a view of being fulfilled; one is satisfied.

Values – attention, care, customer-friendly, openness, kindness and desire to feel comfortable.

Mission – The mission of the _Social One_ is to be clear about goals and fulfil these: and to be satisfied through good self-care. It requires initiative and perseverance to care for yourself and stand on your own feet. Tapping into creativity helps. Ask yourself: what are my mission and goals? How can I learn to deal with adversity? How can I learn to persevere? More satisfaction is derived by clearly knowing your mission and taking good care of oneself.

2 **Behaviour: desire, passivity, disappointment**

Desire – There is a craving for food and attention. Because it isn't given, a sense of emptiness and dissatisfaction remains. Feelings of anger and sadness arise at the lack of attention and abandonment. The dilemma is to express what is missed or to remain avoiding escalation; consequently, you end up all alone, your worst fear! There are two solutions here: either you give up on the desire 'there is no point', or you become independent and deny desires and needs. It may also mean 'compulsive' caring for others secretly hoping others will take care of you too.

223

Passivity – This character becomes passive as a result of not getting what is needed: attention, time, interest and support. You cease to stand up for yourself, because you think it will not help. The belief that something can be obtained by asking also ceases. You go on strike hoping loved ones or colleagues will see how unfairly you are treated. Commitment is lessened by not giving your 100%. In case of severe dissatisfaction, others who have given you the feeling that they have mistreated you, will frequently hear that they owe you something. A nagging, aching emptiness remains. You do not take care of yourself too well anymore.

Disappointment – The lack of attention and reward makes you feel tremendously short-changed and disappointed. To provide your own fulfilment is difficult. Once it is felt others do not give enough, you give up fighting and quit. There is little perseverance and low frustration tolerance. By quitting, it seems as if you settle for less. Dissatisfaction festers on. You tend to look for fairness in all things. Often, a seemingly unfair distribution will leave you dissatisfied. You cannot enjoy what is there, because of disappointment about what is lacking.

3 Qualities, pitfalls, dilemmas, and effects

Qualities – Its sensitivity and empathy make this character a pleasant person with a very good eye for people's needs. You are friendly, adapt well and have a strong sense of group solidarity. A great collaborator and partner, you're unlikely to take the lead. You are spontaneous and a good networker because you are nice. You are good at helping others start new things, and excited about new tasks. If truly free, you believe in the power of the here and now.

Pitfalls – You adopt too much an attitude of dependence. Only a few responsibilities are taken and a few decisions made. You depend on the approval and support of others. This can make you cling to others and claim them. Because of the denial of your inner potential, weakness and dependence come into play. At times, powerlessness and inner weakness are shown. There is a tendency to give up quickly; there is low tolerance for adversity, and you cannot pay attention for too long. There is a tendency to underestimate problems. Being overoptimistic and taking on more responsibility and independent action than you can handle may result in a collapse. You are demanding, even indirectly. Seemingly never enough, your wish list has no end.

Internal dilemmas – It's about the choice between what you need, and denying you need something. About dependence and independence: either too dependent, leaning on others and being too passive, or too independent, underestimating matters resulting in exhaustion. The result is that a project can't be finished fully.

In addition, you think you do a good job but get too little reward. This is expressed by criticising the supervisor. There is no sympathy for their position, because you only see the shortage. There is a lack of success in work. It makes you rebel against work's demands. You complain about payment and reward. You continue to compare yourself with others, and hold a grudge about seeming unfairness. You are jealous of others' success, yet you do not truly strive to achieve what you want. There's a lack of aggression and hiding behind disappointments suffered. You hope to get something without having to put out.

External effects – You are perceived as kind, gentle and interested. People feel at ease because you're friendly and show no aggression. You focus on feeling in life. Eager to start something, you have low productivity and difficulty finishing off. You make promises that you don't realise. This leads to conflicts.

You take little responsibility. Problems are identified, but you hope others will solve them. You may feel like an energy drain due to your seeking attention by, e.g., talking about yourself a lot. You invite people to mother you. As you tend to talk a lot, without tuning in, some people are allergic to you. Because of little discipline and low production, people may feel they are being taken advantage of. They perceive you as powerless. Because your need for affection and acceptance is big, you come across as dependent. In unfavourable conditions, you get irritated. You cannot handle stress well.

4 *Transformation: focus on abundance, action, standing on your own two feet, creation*

Focusing on abundance and satisfaction – This requires that you notice when you receive, accept it, and appreciate what you get. In addition, it also requires you to commit to yourself, so that you can succeed in what you desire.

Action – Realise that you have to take action consistently. You have to learn to make a stand for your needs in an open and mature way. To accept your grief about what you did not get, and actively focus on your desire: how can you shape this as clearly as possible? This requires you to let go of the idea that someone or something is going to do it for you, and to stop playing the waiting game. You can strengthen your vitality by getting into action, breaking the passivity. An example is sports because it helps you gain physical strength, making you feel stronger mentally and creating more self-esteem. You can also work on self-care: this contributes to your joy and gives you more energy. Examples include active cooking (cooking exciting things) and healthy eating (to give you more power and nutrition). Finally, yet importantly, it is imperative that you actively learn to increase your willpower by simply deciding to do it. If you do not fight and stand up for yourself, who will?

- *On your own two feet* – With more energy, it's easier to stand on your own two feet more. Greater independence ensures overcoming feelings of powerlessness. It requires you to stop seeing the other as a source of support, and take yourself as such. To take responsibility, and motivate yourself for things that you do not like and for which you normally have no energy. Developing discipline by, for example, doing the permanent tasks that you do not like or have difficulties with at first. This ensures that you are less tired, because you are no longer lagging behind. It also ensures that people notice you doing things on your own. This commands respect. It changes your collaboration. As a result, you have energy left for moments of game and fun in your life. By becoming more independent, you get more fun in your life. It is important to set achievable goals, without under- or overestimating yourself. Achievable objectives lead to a sense that you succeed.
- *Creation* – Realise you want something in every situation. Then take care of fulfilling this wish yourself, and be satisfied with it. Because you have found the wish in yourself, you are capable of recharging your own battery. You will find that you have many more resources than you thought possible. More so, you will notice that you are the source of the realisation of your needs. The greatest gift you can give yourself is that you can take care of yourself. You will feel fulfilled.

Creative intelligence: the second step of consciousness

Your life lesson is about creation. About being who you want to be. Uncertain as you are, you create too little of what you need or want. Your lesson is to learn how to write your own story. You live the archetype of the creator or the martyr. In a negative sense, you are a martyr, as you give up your own dreams and creations for the dreams and creations of others. You can replenish yourself as you focus on your mission to create fulfilment. The qualities that you use are your sensitivity and your ability to take care of yourself.

You will no longer struggle with something that fails. You are aware that you need to raise the *creative intelligence* of yourself to be who you want to be and to be satisfied.

A SUMMARY OF TRAITS OF CHARACTER 2, THE SOCIAL ONE

vision / worldview	mission	behaviour	qualities	pitfalls	dilemmas	growth	intelligence to develop
shortage	fulfilment	needy	sensitive	dependence	dependency	focus	*creative*
		passive	friendly	depression	little self confidence	abundance	
		frustrated	social	claiming	comparing	independence-	
		dependent	collaborative	giving up	no energy	discipline	
		sociable	adaptable	lack of vitality	lack of attention	tolerate energy	

CHARACTER 3 — THE SAVIOUR: ARE YOU YOURSELF OR THE OTHER?

1 *Worldview, vision, drivers, values, and mission*

Worldview – Without the other, you have no place; your driver is to merge. You have surrendered the contact with yourself and with who you are. In contact, you continuously focus on the other. You find a sense of safety in looking how others go about their life. Your own feelings are underdeveloped.

Vision – Symbiosis merges. Being alone and standing on your own two feet evokes fear. You have difficulty structuring yourself when you're alone, becoming chaotic. Opposition, aggression, and abandonment are perceived as dangerous. Your restricted vision as the Saviour causes you to take someone else's view. A free individual takes one's own view from one's deeper need to be a separate, fully individuated self.

Values – Connection, patience, peace, tolerance, solidarity, collegiality, equality, social involvement.

Mission – To be individual, to develop an identity in your work, so that you operate more independently, and feel individuality. You take responsibility for yourself and for what you observe. It makes you clear and concrete.

2 *Behaviour: struggling with together and separation, blurring of boundaries, who am I*

Struggling with together and separation – Distance and closeness are difficult. In case of distance, the panic of being abandoned occurs. Intuitively, the benchmark of you is shifted to the other, causing you to lose your own identity, because you are not able to cope with being alone. A desire to merge makes you dependent. You live in the illusion of being together, while you are not there yourself.

- *Blurring of boundaries* – Occurs where you disappear and focus more on the other than on yourself. This is confusing. Practicing setting boundaries and learning to keep distance is needed to get out of this and to become more autonomous.
- *Who am I?* – This type of character lacks the sense of a self, of an own identity. There is an interrelationship with the other. This makes it difficult to take responsibility for your choices. 'We' language covers up feelings of unsafety and fear of being alone. Important questions are 'Who am I apart from the other' and 'Who am I really.'

3 Qualities, pitfalls, dilemmas, and effects

- *Qualities* – This character is sensitive: feeling people, the energy and mood in their surroundings, and how things work. There is a tremendous sense of the whole and the connection to it, that is entered into, instead of small pieces of something. You can put yourself in someone else's position. You seamlessly connect to the world and the experience of people. You are also heavily involved with people. Your strength is the ability to attune to these people and situations, allowing deep connections. You're the link, spider in the web, networker pur sang. You are selfless and loyal, sometimes even at your own cost.
- *Pitfalls* – The merging may lead to fusion. In doing so, you lose yourself but usually find this out too late. You have disappeared in the relationship, focusing on the other instead of yourself. You always look for what is wrong or missing, which may lead to dismissal. The relationship must be confirmed continuously: are we still OK? You focus on feelings and check if it still feels 'right.' Claiming may occur in case of issues. In such cases, you cannot work properly or use your ratio, you 'suffer' from feeling. You prefer collaboration, instead of operating solo.
- *Dilemmas* – It's about the inner struggle between the wish for autonomy and the fear of being in charge. It's about learning to deal with being together and alone. It takes courage to go your own way. You would like to leave your adaptive behaviour behind and feel what you really want. You wonder if you dare to break this merging. What remains, if you succeed, is the person you are, as well as what you want. The challenge is to shape independence in all facets of life. This provides a new perspective: a sense of individuality and autonomy, the right to make independent choices and decisions. The details of your life are paramount once you move beyond your internal dilemmas. Life consists of paradoxes: as soon as you become more of an individual, you can develop more together in a relationship, simply because you are now present instead of merged with the other.

Effects – You are very friendly to people, and genuinely interested in them. Your warmth and hospitality are highly appreciated, as is your adaptability.

Dependency, clinging or chameleon type behaviour are ill liked: you are not present, people find this annoying. Sacrifice in case of conflict leads to either irritation, or people taking care of you. This character is an outsider, a whistle-blower focused on finding out what is right; and sensing when not. Someone that gets lost in a fight, wanting to be heard, reconsidering often issues already agreed upon. Your postponing, undermining, sabotaging or suggesting reconsideration, stirs up ill feelings.

4 *Transformation – what do I want, practice boundaries, autonomy*
The starting point is knowing where to find your orientation on who you are, focusing on yourself, your feelings, what is important to you, your desire and your deepest want.

What do I want? With everything you do, you can ask yourself: what do I want? Take your time to explore how this feels for you. What is your point of view? Discuss this. It ensures that you become more present, and get a better sense of your own identity. Learn to observe your processes. Who am I and what do I like? Explore your inner world. Attune less to the outer world. Once you become aware that you have taken over another person's view, focus on yourself again. Note the pleasure you get from making your own choices. Enjoying your choices is an indicator of who you really are and what you really want.

Practice boundaries – It is important that you learn to distinguish between the energy of the environment and your own energy. It helps greatly if you practice boundaries and keeping distance. Get in touch with your core and learn to feel yourself deeply.

A big leap is learning to say no without breaking contact or delaying or sabotaging. This makes you present and strong. You distinguish yourself instead of merging and dissolving. If you lose yourself in your story, or if you are overwhelmed by emotions, it is important to limit yourself, before chaos arises.

Autonomy – Make sure you cultivate a stronger sense of self. Act first and then feel. Learn to do things by yourself. Create your own place in your home and work situation. Get a grip on the chaos so that you have a good oversight again. Practice making your own decisions. Buy something for yourself every now and then. Make sure you have a defined set of tasks. Make sure that your orders are clear and concrete, as well as feasible. Learn how to work with a time limit. Learn how to take a stand and stick to it. The greatest gift you can give yourself is that you are you, that you know who you are, that you can be alone and feel comfortable.

Collective intelligence, the third step of consciousness

You live the archetype of 'doing good' and 'doing evil'. Having the quality to merge with others, the collective (what is in the interest of all) and with energy, you tend to lose yourself in others, their projects or issues, and their energy. In the end, you will have to break the bond, as you have lost yourself along the way. You are able to heal in light and dark situations.

Your lesson is to redirect your ability to sense others' energy, into sensing yourself. Your quality to sense people and energy around you is connected to an inner, individual orientation, through which you remain conscious of the difference between you and others. Through connecting with this inner space, you can stay out of fights and situations that are not helpful to you, as you remain true to your *individual intelligence*.

A SUMMARY OF TRAITS OF CHARACTER 3, THE SAVIOUR

vision / worldview	mission	behaviour	qualities	pitfalls	dilemmas	growth	intelligence to develop
merging	individualise	fusion	sensitive	panic	separation	sense of self	*individual*
		feeling	system view	feeling	individuality	boundaries	
		no boundaries	empathy	lack of reality	structure	distinguish	
		lack of self	connected	melting	organisation	individuality	
		whistleblower	wisdom	chaos	feeling vs reality	structure & organise self	

CHARACTER 4 — AT THE TOP: ARE YOU GENUINE OR ARE YOU PROJECTING AN IMAGE?

1 *Worldview, vision, driver, values, and mission*

- *Worldview* – The world is full of opportunities for the smart and willing. If you work hard enough, you will get there. You use your effectiveness and efficiency and see yourself as what you make of yourself. You succeed! You have a tremendous goal and result orientation. Promoting and strengthening your self-image is the basic drive. Using your own truth as starting point, rationality, and individuality. An achievement demands a reward. You ask yourself 'what is in it for me?' You tend to play out every urge. There is no restraint in reaction. You feel free to live in your own way and not bound by the rules of society.
- *Vision* – Take a view of your own self-image without any hindrance, to who you truly are inside.

Main values – Profit, improvement, growth, wealth, rationality, a market leader.

Mission – Writing your own story. Who am I really? Who am I beyond how I present myself? What is my desire? Getting a deeper sense of your true nature. This ensures a deeper contact with yourself and others, making you more authentic.

2 Behaviour: lack of feeling, presentation

Lack of feeling – Results and success are deemed more important than the need to give and receive warmth. Due to not living in your body, you feel little. You live in images and fantasies. You hardly invest in relationships. It makes you less human. Sometimes you feel the real need to change, but pretend not to feel it. Done so in self-defense. You're afraid that when you become aware of this need, you may be dragged along by your emotions, or out of control. You try to suppress your feelings constantly and frantically. Logic, reason, and willpower are deemed more important than feelings. Your life is goal-oriented and logical; feelings are of no use.

Your image requires you to come across successfully. You do this by denying your feelings. Restrictions are not felt, because every feeling is literally not felt. Restrictions are regarded as restrictions on potential. Because this character cannot do anything with the world of feelings, you don't know how to deal with people in an ordinary human way. You can be very confrontational, even scaring people, as you come across as cold and business-like. Due to lack of self-esteem and empathy, you focus on pragmatism and lose the relationship with the other.

Presentation – This personality is fixated on an image. It is identified with the ideal image. This may be accompanied by megalomania. You gather information, make strategic plans, and head towards the best outcome you can imagine. You use technology and science to present yourself even better. You live the good life in abundance and it is crucial that people see this. You invest in being the best and most attractive. You want to be the best and to win; you enjoy competition. Much time is spent on your presentation. There is also a tendency not to tell things, especially when you think they do not fit your image to the outside world. So, you keep up appearances.

You are very successful because you make it in the world of power and money. You think in possibilities, your motto is "You have to believe in yourself." You believe in success and presentation, with your identity outside of you. You have big ambitions and are dependent on admiration and acclaim. You want to be seen as perfect. You don't know any better: you believe in progress and in yourself. In what you have experienced and what you know yourself.

3 Qualities, pitfalls, dilemmas, and effects

Qualities – This character is ambitious, entrepreneurial, productive and result-oriented. Individualistic, energetic, smart, rational, business-like and direct. Daring to take risks and to be in the fire line. In your work, you have a lot of discipline and resolve issues. This creates opportunities. Combined with the fact that you are initiating and focused on achieving results, this ensures success. In adversity or in an argument, you use the power of your excellent debating skills. You also excel at accomplishing tasks. Your benchmark is success. You think in terms of 'the Haves' versus 'the Have Nots.' You are committed to improving yourself and your products. You continuously ask '(what) do I gain from this?' Due to this, you realise a lot for yourself and your clients. You like status and a certain lifestyle, you like belonging to 'the happy few.'

Pitfalls – Authenticity or real contact is hard to find. You often respond to this with cynicism and contempt due to the fear of being overcome by emotions. You try to feel yourself, but at the same time, this is your biggest fear. The other is seen as fake, sometimes you see yourself that way. This angers you: life is fake, everyone is playing a game, and underneath all is empty. Criticism is seen as an attack. Uncertainty is pushed aside; the heart is made cold and you radiate that all is well. Immediate feedback is interpreted as a criticism: "I'm not doing a good job."

You often lose sight of the human aspect and the relationship: you are capable of sympathy but not of empathy. You do not really listen, everything is linked to you. You take over conversations. You want to be the centre of attention and preferably the one talking. Only very short attention for someone else is allowed. You have a short memory for things that relate to others. Success sometimes frightens you, because you are not sure whether this was expected of you. Your successful actions don't stem from your own impulses, but from outside expectations. You have many ideas, but often not concrete or applicable. There is only motivation when something can be gained. The stability in an organisation or a team can be undermined by such individualistic tendency. The internal infrastructure is neglected in favour of flashy projects.

Dilemmas – You follow false notions about yourself. For example, your ideal says you should be at the top. Your real self (un)consciously longs for a different life of rest and relaxation. You live in the illusion you can be anything you want. This is due to the ideal image of who you think you should be. You are not aware of who you truly are.

The real issue is that, (un)consciously you don't think you're OK! You chronically feel insecure and inferior, and sometimes you even experience self-hate. You don't love yourself, it is never enough, it can always be better. Satisfying your ideal image, hiding behind an attitude of grandeur, is, however, not sustainable. The ideal image is also reflected in your relationships. Only people who fit your ideal image are accepted. You're not interested in others; you're only interested in yourself. You don't want to know the other, because you don't know yourself. You have not learned to view relationships as valuable, unless you can use them. You're deemed special within the organisation, but you miss a deeper fulfilment. You do what is expected and, on the way, lose your soul.

Effects – You are successful, good for business and results. You ask the tough questions, identify the blind spots, and avoid things that don't help towards achieving success. You're the life of the party. But you need to be the centre of attention and get applause. You exploit people (un)intentionally. You use, and afterwards, dump them. You may attack or put people in a difficult position. Not everybody appreciates this. You're experienced as selfish and ruthless. People are afraid of you and avoid you. You want to be the best at everything. You suffer from jealousy and envy, and deprive other people of what they need: a sense of warmth, attention, and encouragement. You speak in monologues, can be cynical and contemptuous and turn 180 degrees in an instant. People are afraid of contradicting you, get bored and tune out. They will not tell you. It is lonely at the top.

4 *Transformation: presence instead of presentation, relate to yourself and others, passion*
Presence instead of presentation – You have invested in an image, in being the best. You need to develop and discover who you really are and what is truly important to you. On what you're denying in yourself. Attune more to your subconscious than to the things that have a future purpose. Be more present. Start to live from being instead of doing. You get more access to humour and fun, because you can handle flaws in yourself and others. You're more in touch with your feelings. One step from an ideal image to a proper self-image is the insight "I am not who you think I am." You realise that what people think of you ultimately says nothing about who you are in essence. It's important that you organise all the impulses from within and act from there. You do what you do because you want it, not because others expect you to do it.
You notice different perceptions of presence and presentation when you move more from an internal place, you may even notice yourself becoming shy. It calls for unconditional kindness of yourself and others around you to move beyond your image and go to a place where you can meet and be your true self.
Relate with yourself and others – Learn to know and accept your true self and that

of others. Allow more people and friends to come closer. You don't have to pretend to be better or different anymore. You won't be alone anymore. You're focused more on collaboration than competition.

Passion – You need meaning in your life. You feel lonely and experience a lack of human contact. Your consciousness about feelings increases. You see the consequences of a lack of attention to people and other things that are important in life and work.

Mental intelligence, the fourth step of consciousness

You know you have to deal with ego-realisation or self-realisation. Your life lesson is about identity. The identity lives in the _mental intelligence_: this is I. You live the archetype of the warrior: do you have the courage to be you, or are you your ego? Is matter a substance or a supplement to you? Instead of improving yourself, you will examine whether you are truly rooted in who you are, or whether you are rooted in the identity that you have adopted, linked to external factors such as a car, house, job, income, image or status. You will say to yourself 'I am me' instead of 'I meet your picture of me.' The higher value you are following is authenticity. You are no longer an actor. You work on your presentation on the outside being consistent with who you are on the inside.

As a leader, you make sure to check if the goals you pursue are important to you from the heart. You examine what gives true meaning. Because you no longer get satisfaction from quick success, status or wealth, you have shifted your focus to human contact and awareness of feelings. You see the consequences of a lack of attention to people and the environment. Your conscience is evolving. Meaning you carry out what you find important, linked to authenticity coming from within. Decisions are no longer driven by achieving, but by meaning.

A SUMMARY OF TRAITS OF CHARACTER 4, AT THE TOP

vision / worldview	mission	behaviour	qualities	pitfalls	dilemmas	growth	intelligence to develop
Presence	authenticity	perform	ambitious	unreal	self	authenticity	_collective_
		image	excellence	cyniscism	no feeling	feeling	
		grandeur	discipline	contempt	self-hatred	love for self	
		performance	energetic	no empathy	insecurity	empathy	
		rational	task oriented	criticism	people	connect with people	

234

Please find below the books that inspire us in the various fields that we've brought together. We fully realise that it is a personal and partial choice.

ON EVOLUTION OF HUMAN CONSCIOUSNESS
- Beck, Don Edward & Cowan, Christopher C., *Spiral Dynamics*, Blackwell Publishing, Oxford, 2006
- Barrett, Richard, *The New Leadership Paradigm*, Values Centre, 2010
- Wilber, Ken, *A Brief History of Everything*, Boston, Shambhala Publications, 1996
- Wilber, Ken, *Integral Psychology: Consciousness, Spirit, Psychology, Therapy*, Boston, Shambhala Publications, 2000
- Harari Yuval Noah, *Sapiens*, A brief History of Mankind, Vintage, UK, 2015

ON LEADERSHIP AND CONSCIOUSNESS
- Senge, Peter, & Scharmer, C. Otto, & Jaworski, Joseph, & Flowers, Betty Sue, *Presence; Exploring profound change in people, organizations and society*, Nicholas Brealy Publishing, London, 2005
- Scharmer, C. Otto, *Theory U, Leading from the future as it emerges*, SOL, Cambridge, 2007
- Jaworski, Joseph, *Synchronicity*, Berrett-Koehler Publishers, San Francisco, 2011
- Jaworski, Joseph, *Source, The Inner Path of Knowledge and Creation*, Berrett-Koehler Pubishers, San Francisco, 2012
- Barrett, Richard, *The Values-Driven Organization, Unleashing Human Potential for Performance and Profit*, Taylor & Francis, 2013
- Barrett, Richard, *Liberating the Corporate Soul, Building a Visionary Organization*, Taylor & Francis, 1998
- Laloux, Frederic, *Reinventing Organizations, A Guide to Creating Organizations Inspired by the Next Stage of Human Consciousness*, Nelson Parker, Brussels, 2014
- Udall, Nick & Turner, Nic, *The Way of Nowhere, 8 questions to release my creative potential*, Harper CollinsPublishers, London, UK, 2008
- Oellibrandt, Dirk en Buchholtz, Harm, *De Alchemie van Leiderschap*, Life Projects, Belgium, 2010
- Hoogendijk, Cees, Meemakers, *Krachtbron van een lerende organisatie*, Uitgeverij Quist, 2010
- Hoogendijk, Cees, *Kracht Zonder Macht, Onweerstaanbare Managementrecepten Met De Smaak Van Verticale Dialoog*, Uitgeverij Quist, 2008

- Boyatzkis, Richard & McKee, Annie, *Resonant leadership*, HB Press, Boston, 2007
- Seale, Alan, *Create a World That Works, Tools for Personal and Global Transformation*, Weisser Books, 2011
- Palmer, Wendy with Janet Crawford, *Leadership Embodiment, How the Way We Sit and Stand Can Change the Way We Think and Speak*, CreateSpace, 2013
- Strozzi-Heckler, Richard, *The Anatomy of Change, A Way to Move Through Life's Transitions*, North Atlantic Books, California, 1984
- Hamill, Pete, *Embodied Leadership, The somatic approach to developing your leadership*, Kogan Page, UK & US, 2013
- Brack, Anouk, *De verborgen dimensie van leiderschap, evolutie van macht naar kracht*, Thema, 2017
- Brack, Anouk, *Leiderschap in verandering, samen doen wat ertoe doet*, Thema, 2019

ON THE BODY, EMOTIONS, MIND, AND THE CONNECTIONS BETWEEN THE THREE

- Damasio, A., *Looking for Spinoza: Joy, sorrow, and the feeling brain*, Harcourt, Orlando, 2003
- Dossey, L, *One mind: How our individual mind is part of a larger consciousness and why it matters*, Hay House, Carlsbad, 2013
- Sapolsky, R. M., *Why Zebra's don't get ulcers*, Holt Paperbacks, New York, 2004
- Sills, F., *The Polarity process: Energy as a healing art*, Element, Rockport, 1989
- Pert, C., *Molecules of Emotion: The science behind mind-body medicine*, Simon & Schuster, New York, 1999
- Levine, P.A. & Frederick, A., *Waking the tiger-healing trauma: The innate capacity to transform overwhelming experiences*, North Atlantic Books, Berkeley, 1997
- Levine, P. A., *In an unspoken voice: How the body releases trauma and restores goodness*, North Atlantic Books, Berkeley, 2010
- Van der Kolk, B.A. & McFarlane, A.C. & Weisaeth, L. (Eds.), *Traumatic stress: The effect of overwhelming experience on mind, body, and society*, The Guilford Press, New York, 1996
- Ledoux, J. *The Emotional Brain: The mysterious underpinnings of emotional life*, Touchtone Simon & Schuster, New York, 1996
- Goleman, D., *Emotional intelligence: Why it can matter more than IQ*, Bantam Books, New York, 1995
- Ken Dychtwald, *Bodymind*, Pantheon Books, New York, 1977
- Damasio, A., *The feeling of what happens: Body and Emotion in the making of consciousness*, Harcourt, Orlando, 1999
- Schore, A. N., *Affect regulation and the repair of the self*, W. W. Norton & Company, New York, 2003

- Goswami, A., *The self-aware universe: How consciousness creates the material world*, Penguin Putnam, New York, 1995
- Johnson, S. Ph.D., *Character Styles*, W.W. Norton & Company, New York, 1994
- Johnson, S. Ph.D., *Humanizing the Narcissistic Style*, W.W. Norton & Company, New York, 1987
- Johnson, S. Ph.D., *Characterological Transformation, the hard work miracle*, W.W. Norton & Company, New York, 1985
- Johnson, S. Ph.D., *The Symbiotic Character*, W.W. Norton & Company, New York, 1991
- Heller, Laurence, Ph.D. & LaPierre, Psy.D., *How Early Trauma Affects Self-Regulation, Self-Image, and the Capacity for Relationship*, North Atlantic Books, Berkely, 2012
- Hart, S., *The Impact of Attachment*, W.W. Norton & Company, New York, 2011
- Reich, W., *Character Analysis*, Wilhelm Reich Infant Trust Fund, 1949
- Reich, W., *The invasion of compulsory sex-morality*, Farrar, Strauss, and Giroux, 1971
- Cattier, Michel, *The Life and Work of Wilhelm Reich*, Horizon Press, New York, 1971
- Pierrakos, J., M.D., *Energetica van de Ziel (Core Energetics); Ontwikkel je vermogen tot liefhebben*, Gottmer, Bloemendaal, 1996
- Raja Selvam Ph.D., *Restoration of Body Resources Lost in Trauma based on the Bodynamic Somatic Developmental Psychology Model by Raja Selvam Ph.D. Lori A. Parker Ph.D.*
- Lowen, A., M.D., *Fear of Life*, Macmillan, New York, 1980
- Lowen, A., *The Language of the Body*, Macmillan, New York, 1958
- Lowen, A. & Lowen L., *The Vibrant Way to Health: A Manual of Exercises.* Harper & Row, New York, 1977
- Lowen, A., *Pleasure: A Creative Approach to Life*, Penguin, New York, 1975
- Lowen, A., *Depression and the Body*, Penguin, New York, 1975
- Lowen, A., *Narcissism: Denial of the True Self*, Macmillan, New York, 1991
- Lowen, A., *Love, Sex, and Your Heart*, Macmillan, New York, 1988
- Lowen, A., *The Spirituality of the Body*, Macmillan, New York, 1990
- Lowen, A., *Bioenergetics*, Penguin, New York, 1975
- Josephs, L., *Character and Self-Experience*, Jason Aronson, London, 1995
- Rank, A. & Rank, D., *Je lichaam als spiegel*, Servire, 1996
- Bäurle, R., *Körpertypen*, Servire, Utrecht, 1997
- Veenbaas, W. & Goudswaard, J. & Verschuren, H.A., *De Maskermaker*, Phoenix Opleidingen, Utrecht, 2006

- Keleman, Stanley, *Emotional Anatomy*, Center Press, Berkeley, 1985
- Keleman, Stanley, *Embodying Experience*, Center Press, Berkeley, 1987
- Bentzen, Susan, & Hart, Marian, *Through windows of opportunity*, Taylor & Francis Group, 2015
- Mipham J. Mukpho, *Ruling your world*, Random House, New York, 2005

ON THE SOUL AND SPIRITUALITY
- Barrett, Richard, *What my soul told me*, Fulfilling books, Bath, 2012
- Barrett, Richard, *A New Psychology of Human Well-being: An Exploration of the Influence of Ego-Soul Dynamics on Mental and Physical Health*, Lulu, 2016
- Seale, Alan, *Intuitive Living: a Sacred Path*, Red Wheel/Weiser, San Francisco, 2001
- Chopra, Deepak, *The Soul of Leadership*, Random House, 2011
- Singer, Michael, *What my Soul told me*, New Harbinger Publications, 2007

ON ENERGY AND UNIVERSAL LAWS
- Chopra, Deepak, *The Seven Spiritual Laws of Success*, Bantam Press, 1996
- De Vries, Marja, *De hele olifant in beeld*, Ankh Hermes, Deventer, 2007
- Schwartz, Tony with Gomes, Jean, *Be Excellent at Anything*, Simon & Schuster UK, London, 2011
- Glaudemans, Willem, *Boek van de Universele Wetten; een leidraad voor bewust leven*, Ankh Hermes, 2015
- Andeweg, Hans, *The universe loves a happy ending*, Turner Publishing Company, New York, 2016

ON HUMAN BEHAVIOUR AND FREQUENCY
- Hawkins, David R. M.D., Ph.D., *Power vs. Force* Hay House, Carlsbad, 2012
- Hawkins, David R. M.D., Ph.D., *Letting Go*, Hay House, Carlsbad, 2012

We work and live from the heart, sharing a love for people and a calling to enable access to consciousness. We also share a commitment to pioneering, a love of teaching, a curiosity in transcendental psychology, the unseen, and a wicked sense of humour.

Erica E.C. Harpe

Erica has moved from the outside-in: a trained lawyer and banker, she connected parties globally for large scale deals for 15 years. Living and working in different cultures she developed a curiosity for culture and systems and what makes people tick and flourish.

For the last 10 years she has pioneered in the field of leadership and transformation, synthesising learnings and creating for example *globally used research*, backed by the Dutch Ministry of Economic Affairs, *large-scale social dialogues* with the Dutch Financial Paper and *a learning community* of 1600 female leaders with 16 leading multinationals such as IBM, Shell, Unilever and Philips. Working from an integral perspective with Integral Theory, Theory U, Spiral Dynamics, Constellations, Values, Purpose, Transformational Presence, inquiry, and energy.

The leadership journey she developed with this community has been further deepened culminating in this book. Erica realised it was time to combine the world of leadership (mind) with the world of body, emotions, and spirit. Time to be able to access all of ourselves, to become whole. Time to Reinvent Ourselves! For more information or contact details you can visit her LinkedIn profile, or visit the website at **www.reinventingourselves.eu.**

Yvette Hooites Meursing

Yvette has moved from the inside-out: a trained sociologist, body-oriented psycho-therapist and integral somatic psychologist she worked for over a
decade, in the field of body-oriented psycho-
therapy as teacher/trainer/supervisor and as-
sessor at the Bodymind Opleidingen Institute
in The Netherlands.

For the past 25 years she specialised in the
field of characters and embodiment. She also
trained in the spiritual, with i.e. the Chopra
Center (meditation) and Bart ten Berge (work of
Bob Moore). She is a team member of Bart's Interna-
ional School for Spiritual Psychology (ISSP) and a teacher of this work. Using her
own experience and research in her practice with clients. Yvette is the author of
Character Intelligence, Í am the Leader and *The Happy Client* which was nominated
Coach Book of the Year 2012 in The Netherlands by the NOBCO, the Dutch organization of Professional Coaches.

During the last decade she has extended her work field to the world of business,
coaching senior executives and facilitating management teams. For more information or contact details you can visit her LinkedIn profile, or visit the website at
www.ifci.nl.

A Metaphor for Global Transformation

"I like to use the metaphor of the butterfly.
In metamorphosis, within the body of the caterpillar
little things that biologists call imaginal discs or imaginal
cells begin to crop up in the body of the caterpillar.

They aren't recognized by the immune system so the caterpillar's
immune system wipes them out as they pop up.
It isn't until they begin to link forces and join up with
each other that they get stronger and are able to resist the onslaught of the
immune system, until the immune system itself breaks down and the
imaginal cells form the body of the butterfly.

I think that is a beautiful metaphor for what is happening in our times.
The old body is going into meltdown while the new one develops.
It isn't that you end one thing and then start another.

So everybody engaged in developing healthier systems for themselves and each other
is engaged in building the new world while the old one collapses.

Its collapse is inevitable. There is no way around that."

— ELISABET SAHTOURIS, EVOLUTION BIOLOGIST

෴

Lightning Source UK Ltd.
Milton Keynes UK
UKHW020450130819
347835UK00002B/2/P